Historical Simulation and Wargames

This book is a comprehensive study on analog historical simulation games, exploring both their theoretical concepts and practical solutions. It considers the various ways used by simulation games to depict the different dynamics of historical events and analyzes how commercial analog miniature and board wargames can become valuable tools for historical research and provide a more modern and captivating interpretation of past events.

The nature of "simulation" is discussed, exposing its differences with other forms of ludic activity, both analog and digital, as well as intellectual speculation. Many of the most common game mechanics are analyzed in depth and in their practical use, to answer whether "reconstructive" simulations dedicated to historical episodes can provide valuable, reliable and useful insights for researchers. It critically examines the challenges presented to game designers that look to produce an accurate (even if not necessarily complex) simulation of historical events.

The book will be of great interest to those curious about the potential applications of such a powerful research and experimental tool for historical, sociologic and anthropologic research, as well as wargaming and board gaming enthusiasts looking to gain a deeper understanding of the inner workings of historical simulations.

Historical Simulation and Wargames

The Hexagon and the Sword

Riccardo Masini

CRC Press
Taylor & Francis Group
Boca Raton London New York

CRC Press is an imprint of the
Taylor & Francis Group, an **informa** business

Designed cover image: Shutterstock Images

First edition published 2025
by CRC Press
2385 NW Executive Center Drive, Suite 320, Boca Raton FL 33431

and by CRC Press
4 Park Square, Milton Park, Abingdon, Oxon, OX14 4RN

CRC Press is an imprint of Taylor & Francis Group, LLC

© 2025 Riccardo Masini

ISBN: 978-1-032-55110-4 (hbk)
ISBN: 978-1-032-55120-3 (pbk)
ISBN: 978-1-003-42909-8 (ebk)

DOI: 10.1201/9781003429098

Typeset in Times LT Std
by Apex CoVantage, LLC

Dedicated to all the wonderful people
I met in this journey . . .
especially those that are still travelling with me,
and those that are waiting for me
on the other side of the gaming table.

Contents

Foreword

Riccardo Masini is a maven of the wargaming hobby. He may even qualify as a synonym for Italian wargaming. His knowledge runs deep—there are references to somewhere well over one hundred games in this book stretching across the entire history of wargaming—and his joy in the pastime of playing and contemplating the history these games address is effervescent. Since 2007 Riccardo's WLOG YouTube channel reviewing wargames has clocked up nearly 300,000 views, with episodes in both Italian and English, covering new releases, older games, and games in development. Riccardo's LudoStoria community, established in 2023, boasts over 1,500 members and has already held its inaugural convention in Rome.

Riccardo is also co-author, with his father Sergio Masini, of 2018's *Le Guerre di Carta 2.0. Giocare con la storia nel terzo millennio* (*Paper Wars 2.0. Playing with history in the third millennium*), an introductory-level exploration of the major characteristics of the hobby, sadly not yet available in English. Riccardo is also co-editor, with Fred Serval and Jan Heinemann of the forthcoming *EuroWarGames. The history, state and future of professional and public (war)gaming in Europe.*

In *Historical Simulation and Wargames* you will find Riccardo further ruminating on the qualities of this utterly fascinating hobby and its intersections with the philosophies of design, history, science, play, and education. You will find mention of not just Clausewitz, Hellwig, Charles S. Roberts, James Dunnigan, Redmond Simonsen, Mark Herman, Volko Ruhnke, Ty Bomba, Jason Matthews, Brenda Romero, Cole Wehrle, and David Thompson, but also Plato, Aristotle, Al-Khwarizmi, Ramon Lull, Leonardo, Galileo, Leibniz, Johan Huizinga, John von Neumann, John Nash, Philip Sabin, and even Einstein.

You will hear Riccardo's typology of simulation, which he defines in three levels—what he terms deterministic, probabilistic, and nonlinear. Whereas deterministic simulation has no systemic random inputs to derive outputs (but may have random player inputs—moving in unexpected ways or revealing unexpected but non-stochastic information), probabilistic simulations have uncertain but calculable inputs—for example, with combat results tables with differing odds ratios affording differing probabilities for the results from a cross-referenced die roll. What Riccardo terms nonlinear simulation increases the uncertainty of any outputs by adding more layers of systemic inputs—for example card decks (perhaps with multi-use elements within the deck and/or multiple decks), a range of player actions, and asymmetric capabilities and objectives.

You will also hear from Riccardo on Ty Bomba subverting the "movement then combat" paradigm, to the player deciding the order in which to conduct these phases, and how it disrupts strategic and tactical management of forces on a battlefield.

You will hear Riccardo discussing the nature of simulations, framing them as art, and espousing what he terms a "shutter theory", using the language of the theory of photography to consider depth of field and the specific focus of a design accounting for the range of differing design approaches to the same subject matter.

And you will hear much, much more about this world of historical simulations, the designs, and the designers, and the players. It is rather like spending several hours with an intense wargame enthusiast as he talks you through his vast collection of games curated over a lifetime, taking them off his shelves and unboxing many of them as towers of games stack up in front of you. He has a great deal to say about all of these games, and they all seem to connect in some way to something else he also wants to unbox in front of you, or something else he wants you to understand about how these games are significant and helping to further evolve the hobby into new and exciting forms. This book might be as close as we will get to putting Riccardo's boundless enthusiasm inside a box of its own. And here it is, for you to unbox. Enjoy the ride . . .

Maurice W. Suckling
February 2024

Acknowledgements

It is not always easy to write an exhaustive list of all the people deserving to be thanked for their contribution to what has been an outstanding journey as this book, written in the same foreign language that I learned thanks to my (time and time again) repeated reading as a kid of the rulebooks of those very games I write about now, more than thirty years later.

Actually, it is quite hard not only to cite them all without forgetting anyone (and I am sure I will not be able to accomplish the task, so my apologies in advance to all those who will be unwillingly left out), but also to mention all the many reasons why I should thank them, since so many and so diverse have been the contributions given to my study by all the wonderful persons I met at the gaming table, during a convention, online and in many other situations. I take a great relief in knowing that the nature of all the different kinds of inspiration they have given me is so great that it could not be possible to describe them in full detail, anyway.

However, some names have to be put in those last pages, and so here we go with this forcedly partial, but totally honest list.

First of all, I just need to thank the one person who started my journey in the perilous and fascinating world of simulation, someone whom I know quite well and who knows me even better: my father, Sergio Masini. It is thanks to him, his pioneering essays and articles in the early 1980s (and to the good patience of my mother, Mara Belgrano, whom I have also to thank for her deep love of rational philosophy and Francis Bacon in particular transmitted to me) that I got to know what playing with history really means, and what immense gifts its practice could give to the imagination of a young boy, growing with "childhood friends" like Alexander the Great, Scipio Africanus, Frederick of Prussia, Napoleon Bonaparte and others. Nothing that you have read thus far in this study would have ever been written without them . . . so you know who deserves the credit or the blame, depending on your personal opinion of the aforementioned study.

Speaking of family, I have to express my deepest gratitude also to my wife Benedetta, who not only supported me in all my work, tolerated the presence of game boxes and ziplocks virtually everywhere in our house and essentially accepted my disappearance before a PC screen for a good portion of last year's nights, but also—being a very good journalist and accomplished writer—put the entire thing to profit and got to write a book about her experience of "living with a Geek", that is me. She, and our two beautiful cats, aptly named Faramir and Eowyn: the followers of my videos on YouTube will surely get to know the latter, a worthy successor to the onscreen exploits of the former, who regretfully did not stay with us long enough to see the conclusion of this work. All of our furry companions always remind me that being a wargamer and having cats in the house does not necessarily make your life impossible . . . just more interesting.

Speaking of videos, my next thanks is for the followers of my channel *WLOG*, the listeners of my podcast *Checkpoint Charlie* and the kind readers of the (too) many books and articles I write in Italian and English among various publishers, magazines and websites. I can really say that everything I do in this field is for them, encouraging everyone in finding not what I think the "good path" towards gaming is, but their own personal route in the discovery of this amazing universe composed of infinite worlds enclosed in tiny paper boxes, only waiting to be discovered. They are my best teachers, since every time I speak with a fellow simulation enthusiast, no matter what his or her experience may be, I always learn something new and precious.

I also feel happily obliged to thank the entire Italian wargaming community for the various discussions, interactions, opinion exchanges and even mere chats about our common passion, that got inside those pages. In particular, I'd like to thank the Board and all the members of the *LudoStoria* group, dedicated to all forms of historical gaming who don't really care about any artificial distinction in terms of complexity, any genre or sub-genre label, the presence or absence of open warfare, hexagons or wooden block, cards or miniatures, maps or role-playing master screens or anything else on the gaming table. People who just love playing with history, judging a simulation by the only principles upon which it should be judged: not by the presence or absence of this or that mechanic, but by the capability of the system to produce statistically sound, historically believable and emotionally engaging results in the infinite interactions of a good game. *Grazie a tutte e tutti!*

Also, thanks to the many game designers, developers, publishers and fellow players I had the privilege of meeting in all those exciting years of wargame practice, especially after the digital revolution allowed us to get into contact beyond any divide in terms of geography, language, culture and national borders. Ah, if only I were just a bit better in dealing with timezones when setting up videocalls!

Among them, I want to mention Sebastian Bae, who introduced me to the great Georgetown University Wargaming Society and gave me the privilege of presenting my work on non-linear simulation on their amazing channel; Volko Ruhnke for the incredible support given to me and for those great days spent together at the Modena Play in 2022 (I will reciprocate in the US, that's a promise!); Enrico Acerbi for all the great discussions and the precious sources he sent to me during the preparation of this study; Andrea Angiolino for being Andrea Angiolino and for sharing his incredible knowledge on all forms of gaming with rest of the world; Mario Aceto, aka the only man who manages to make *ASL* look simple while he teaches it!; Lorenzo Nannetti for the endless exchanges on the differences and common features between recreational and professional simulation (I am waiting for you to complete your book on wargaming, Lorenzo!); Luca Fiorentini for having taught me that good friends are often just one *Facebook* group away and for chatting with me all those nights while I was writing the book (including right now!); the amazing Dan Pancaldi for all he has done for the online wargaming community with his aggregating channel *No Enemies Here* . . . and for being one of the funniest and dearest friends I ever had, even with an entire ocean dividing us: *Sei un grande e ti voglio bene, cuggì!*

Together with them I want to remember also those fellow gamers and friends who are now no longer with us, playing on unknown tables: their names are far too many and far too painful to mention them all, one by one.

Furthermore, many thanks to the most patient and competent staff at Taylor & Francis, that followed me in this long journey in the mysterious Realms of Simulation: without them and their constant trust and support for this project, I would have surely lost my way in the vast seas of hexagons or in the dark forests of CRTs!

As the last name I left Maurice Suckling: it is thanks to him that I found the courage of sending the most improbable proposal to an English language publisher, a book on wargaming written by an Italian author (and got it accepted, too!). His knowledge of game design, storytelling through rules writing, historical representation and interactive mediums almost overshadow his amazing qualities as a simply wonderful human being. Almost.

But the very last thanks go to you, my dear reader, for having had the patience of following this dissertation on history, simulation and everything that stands in between up until now.

When dealing with wargames, just stay curious, take care and most importantly . . . have at least as much fun in playing them as I have had in writing these words.

Ciao!

Riccardo Masini, (The Sword and the Hexagon)
February 2024

Author Biography

Riccardo Masini is an experienced wargamer and military history author, a member of the Italian Military History Society, and an active member of several wargames and role-playing games clubs. He is also one of the most prominent wargaming content creators in Italy, thanks to his YouTube channel, *WLOG*, his many contributions to Italian and international gaming magazines and websites, as well as his several essays on wargaming and historical research. He is also on the Coordinating Board of the Italian Facebook group *LudoStoria*, dedicated to all forms of historical gaming.

Introduction

The Greatest Story Ever Told (and Played)

"What is history, but a fable agreed upon?"

Napoleon Bonaparte (attributed)

One of the lesser known (and accepted) aspects of an historian's work is that the actual subject of his investigation is not the chain of causes and consequences binding together the individual facts of the past. Rather, it *should* be, and our poor scholar will undoubtedly try at the utmost to provide "impartial analysis of the true nature of events", or something like that . . . but in the end, this would remain an unattainable goal. The sad truth is that, until some crazy scientist will discover anything even remotely resembling the time machine so dear to sci-fi enthusiasts, no one will really understand what was happening on the small Greek beach of Marathon in the summer of 490 BC, on the muddy Belgian fields near Bruxelles at Waterloo in June of 1815, nor in the SHAEF conference rooms just before the beginning of Operation Overlord in 1944.

Also, not even those that were present in those locations at that time could enjoy a similar privilege, considering how inevitably partial and in many measures flawed their actual knowledge of the general situation in which they were operating was. These errors and biases were so ingrained in the thinking of those decision makers of the past that they became an integral and even fundamental element of their reasoning process, thus attaining the title of historical factor of their own.

What we are dealing with here is thus perception, or rather *perceptions.* On one side we have the image of past events coming to us from generations of previous human beings that have dealt with those events and their consequences, analyzed them, written novels and popular stories on them, composed music inspired by them, dreamt about them, used and even misused them for their personal purposes (and often those "purposes" have become further historical events of their own . . .). On the other, we have the protagonists of those events themselves who have operated and determined the next step of the cause-effect chain without a clear understanding of what the "cause" really was.

Still, those deviations form an integral part of how history first develops and later is interpreted, with those same interpretations becoming part of the process leading up to the next historical developments.

This is where we ought to introduce another common misconception, which is the belief that all our rationalizing about the past is just a neutral activity, without any effect on the historical process itself. And this is the third, possibly the most dangerous, mistake.

DOI: 10.1201/9781003429098-1

1

To fully understand the magnitude of those consequences, just ask a British infantryman lying mortally wounded on the fields of the Somme. How did he get on that ground, stuck in the terrible mud just out of his unhealthy, dirty and woeful trench? Even more, who sent that poor man and all his dreams, life projects, economic potentials and possible descendants to be all squandered by a German machine gun bullet at the very first steps taken into a batch of terrain named "no man's land"? And why?

The general consensus of traditional historiography, after the very first years spent into portraying the great value of the "heroic sacrifice" of that man, is that his existence was destroyed in a strategic and tactical mistake of insane proportions, made by generals totally indifferent to the expense of countless human lives, engaged in the greatest game of rugby ever held, on a continental scale. The "lions led by donkeys" theory, as some would later summarize: a clear, understandable, tragic historical interpretation, teaching us the cruelty of war and how military commanders should be wary of committing those crimes ever again.

And, also, a comfortably self-absolutory vision, in which all the guilt for those tragedies and the immense loss in human development potential of the later generations (as well as many of the seeds of a second Great World War) could be pinned on the shoulders of insanity, inhumanity, incapacity of understanding the reality of the general situation, all determined by preconceptions, stupidity and—why not—also a classist detachment of higher bourgeoisie generals from the sufferings of lower popular working infantrymen.

Now, the problem is that most commanders and decision makers of all sides involved in the great catastrophe of World War One were probably no champions of human sensibility, but were also not sadistic monsters. At least, not so many as to irresistibly influence the course of the events.

In simpler terms, those poor infantrymen could be brave "lions" (or, more realistically, just a great mass of reasonable people trying to survive the horrors of war) . . . but those generals (let's say, *not all* of them) were no stupid "donkeys".

So, our question remains: who sent that poor guy to die on the Somme, and why?

The answer: a (smaller) mass of reasonable people, incidentally professional people that had studied and prepared for war as their life choice, that made their general strategic decisions based on those professional bases and transmitted those choices down on the chain of command to lower-level commanders, themselves reasonable people that had their own professional military preparation or direct first-person experience. Bottom line: since the days of ancient Greece, the tragedy lies not on some eccentric "insanity", but on what people consider "reasonable" in their historical contest.

Yet, our infantryman still is lying on the mud, bleeding to death thanks to an objectively absurd decision to send him marching through an open field at a heavily fortified position, held by enemy soldiers armed with heavy machine guns with pre-registered fields of fire . . . so, how can we accept that definition of "reasonable" for all those who sent him down this dreadful path? We cannot, and in fact we don't accept it, being forced to resort to such powerful, accurate and eminent expressions of historiography such as "lion and donkeys".

Or we should, if we accept the fact that all those decision makers were indeed reasonable people, but *misled by their perceptions* of what war actually could look like in their time, considering the developments of military technology and tactics.

They had all the warning that their ideas were flawed, but they ignored them. The long trenches of the second half of American Civil War, the disease-ridden armies of the Crimean War, the great massacre of Solferino, the long series of inconclusive conflicts in the Balkans—and yet, those generals found all the possible rationalizations to explain how war still could be won thanks to the concerted maneuver of great masses of soldiers on a single battlefield, even when that battlefield included entire nations.

Those previous conflicts were fought in remote regions, or by inexperienced armies, or with unreliable technology that could not be replicated and used on mass scale, or under very special political and cultural conditions . . . and so on, and so on, until all those misconceptions led to an unnamed lieutenant blowing his whistle and sending our poor Somme infantryman to his fate.

Misconception on misconception on misconception: not exactly a crystal-clear chain of events and cause-effect relationship, but a *truly* historical chain of events.

So, if we still accept the wholly revolutionary idea that not every single member of every single military HQ involved in World War One had been taken over by a bunch of moronic and incompetent leaders, we can get a better understanding of all the later attempts made by every side to end what was clearly perceived and even openly defined as something of a military "pathology": an immovable front stretching from the English Channel to Switzerland, from the Alps to the Adriatic.

Strategic decisions like the Gallipoli campaign or the offensives in modern-day Albania and the Middle East, as well as the expense of resources on innovative weapons such as planes and tanks, or even tactical experiments such as advanced assault tactics are all in total contradiction with the usual view of blind top-level commanders accepting countless deaths just to push a coloured pin a few squares forward on a map.

Sure, some resisted those innovations and stayed on course with their personal ideas of big frontal assaults preceded by thunderous artillery bombardments over large portions of the enemy front . . . but so many more believed in, promoted and exploited those ground-breaking developments with the explicit purpose of breaking a deadlock of which everybody was fully aware. Up to the point in which the social and economic exhaustion of one of the involved coalitions forced that side, after the failure of the last attempt at breaking the attritional deadlock, to finally concede defeat.

Those were—roughly in the same measure—the consequences of previous, contemporary and successive false interpretations of the past events, the current situations and the possible future developments. Furthermore, this was the collective image of what a conflict was, a vision that deeply influenced the respective public opinions of all the greater world powers through academic historiography as well as popular accounts of the war in novels, movies, music, art and many other media: in essence, a catastrophe to avoid at all costs.

With all this in mind, however, someone still has some military planning to do for the inevitable future wars. The presence of an unforeseeable and imponderable element in war and in foreign affairs has always been an accepted fact in human reasoning, but in order to still obtain some strategic insight and previsions with the prospect of organizing and executing future military, economic and political initiatives in the context of a rational (if not outright "scientific") decision-making process, even this irrational element had to be in a sense "rationalized".

A good philosophical as well as practical description of all this is one of the basic concepts of a masterpiece in political literature, incidentally useful also for military purposes: Carl von Clausewitz's *Vom Kriege*.

> Everything is very simple in war, but the simplest thing is difficult. These difficulties accumulate and produce a friction which no man can imagine exactly who has not seen war.[1]

With this term—"Friction" or *Friktion*—the well-known nineteenth-century Prussian intellectual indicates the sum of all the uncontrollable events that influence, alter and usually derail rational military thinking and its actual application on the battlefield, however large it can be.[2]

So, the irrational and imponderable factors have to be included in the complex equations and reasonings of military planning, so much that:

> Friction is the only concept that more or less corresponds to the factors that distinguish real war from war on paper.[3]

It is not by coincidence that the very same Prussia from which von Clausewitz hailed, and in which army he was serving as a (not terribly successful) subordinate commander, was at the forefront of a general re-thinking of military theory, especially after the disastrous 1806 campaign culminated in the double Jena and Auerstedt defeats, two catastrophic debacles that temporarily saw Napoleon's emerging vision of the world temporarily dominate over another seemingly unshakable perception of the times: the myth of Prussian invincibility, established by none other than late King Frederick II, called "the Great".

In those same years, a new pastime was becoming increasingly popular: wargames—also known as *Kriegsspiel*. Or, in other words, the main object of this work.

So many different versions of the origin of this game have been written that the casual observer might be sincerely convinced that we are dealing with not just a single system, but an entire family of very different rulesets. And that casual observer might not be too far from the truth, since from the early beginnings we will find the seeds of future subdivisions of the wargaming world.

The first real step into what we can define as "modern wargaming" comes with Johann Christian Ludwig Hellwig and his *Versuch eines aufs Schachspiel gebaueten taktischen Spiels von zwey und mehrern Personen zu spielen* (literally, *An attempt to create a tactical game playable by two or more people, starting from the game of Chess*), published in 1780. Hellwig designed a (very) revised form of chessboard for his game, multiplying the number of boxes and giving peculiar features to each of them according to the dominating terrain. By adopting a modular grid, the players could freely change the composition of the battlefield just by changing the disposition of the tiles, thus creating fantasy maps as well as, with a sufficient documentation, historical confrontations.[4] The 1803 edition of the ruleset was published with a much simpler title: *Das Kriegsspiel*. The new handbook included rules to manage the interaction between attack and defence values of the involved units (the original concept of what would later be known as CRTs, Combat Results Tables, based on force ratios or differentials), new victory conditions based on terrain capture and not just unit elimination, accurate military symbology with different features of specific units, line of communications used for supply and rudimentary limitations for stacking more units in the same tile.

In the meantime, one of the more talented disciples of Hellwig proposed another interpretation of the old master's ruleset. Johann Georg Julius Venturini decided to totally dispense with the remaining relics of a chessboard and adapt Hellwig's intuition to a three-dimensional model of the battlefield, with the units moving freely in proportional speed to the marching distances of actual military units of the time. Venturini also introduced special rules for weather conditions, accurate depictions of the various forms of entrenchments and fortifications, as well as a broader grid to accommodate actual military maps of the involved terrains.

It is evident that those two versions of the same game, the "game of war", were the ideal precursors of the great distinction between board and miniature wargaming, two distinct categories of military simulation that will remain embroiled in a very turbulent but mutually beneficial relationship for the following centuries, up to our days. What is even more important, they both left the abstractions of chess behind them, adopting a scientific approach towards an entirely new process: simulation.

Contrary to what many still today believe, the military were not the first to use these new instruments for their training and planning programs. As we have seen, among the very first modern wargamers we could find two royal pupils in search of entertainment among a troublesome (and boring) court in disgrace: the Crown Princes of Prussia, the future Frederick Friedrich Wilhelm IV and Wilhelm I (which would become in 1870 the very first Kaiser of Germany).[5]

Together they played another version of the original Hellwig's system, modified and demonstrated by a young officer by the name of Georg Leopold von Reisswitz. Significantly, all the main elements of the Prussian military reform movement after Jena, spearheaded by Field Marshal Blücher and Generals Scharnhorst and Gneisenau (the soon-to-be victors at Waterloo), were perfectly embodied by von Reisswitz's new take on such an eccentric pastime. Quickly staff officers gathered around the two young princes playing with their toy soldiers on such elaborate and accurate map renditions of fictitious battlefields; it was not long until some unnamed general decided to copy this game, make it a bit more serious by adding advanced statistics and accurate topography, expert referees adjudicating combat outcomes, advanced renditions of elements such as logistics, intelligence and command, obtaining a new precious tool: professional *Kriegsspiel*.

This would be a true "secret weapon" of German armed forces for almost an entire century with other countries such as Great Britain and France desperately trying to copy this new method, sometimes obtaining successful applications and other times suffering the consequences of superior German military planning.[6]

So much "German-style" wargaming became synonymous with Prussian military prowess, a bit ironic considering what "German-style" boardgames would be known for a century after, that in Great Britain "war gaming" (the literal translation for *Kriegsspiel*) was initially not so favourably considered. So, while Royal Army and

Navy headquarters began adopting the former Prussian methodology, civilian hobbyists had more problems in accepting it.

In this context miniature wargaming, that is the old Venturini approach, became more "accepted" in good families' homes and this attitude would partly explain the ideological premises for what is unanimously considered the first miniature wargaming ruleset for the mass public: H. G. Wells's *Little Wars*. In these pages, the famous sci-fi pioneering writer describes, with his trademark highly evocative style, a game whose purpose is to teach new generations the possible horrors of wars, "a game out of all proportions" that should never be played for real. And the sentence "You have only to play at Little Wars three or four times to realise just what a blundering thing Great War must be" remains today one of the best pacifist slogans of all time, as well as a true cultural manifesto for a good practice of wargaming.

In the next chapters we will see the following of this story of how a game of war became what we now know as a "wargame" or, even better, a "simulation game". What should be considered now is how military enthusiasts before, military officers after and military analysts in the end did their best to go beyond the very first attempts with allegoric "military Chess games", introducing scientific methods such as statistics, topography and logistical calculations to create an objective rational model in which non-linear Friction could be finally determined and accounted for, reducing it to a manageable element of a predictable function.[7] We will also see how, when and in which measure all those military experts utterly failed at the task.

More generally speaking, if we accept the concept that simulation games were born with the declared purpose of making sense of the chaotic reality of military operations by condensing that in a manipulable mathematical model, we can also better understand the nature of one of its many derived applications: historical simulation.

Due to its oscillating nature between simple pastime for bored aristocrats and professional tool for planning hypothetical and future operations, the past remained somewhat an undiscovered country for wargaming, until someone who enjoyed the game turned to the books in his library to transport this game back to its original purpose: intelligent entertainment.

Only this time it was not just a couple of young crown princes, but the general public to be exposed to such a powerful device as a series of arithmetic procedures expressly designed to recreate a specific reference reality. No abstract attack on "Blue land" by "Red units", but the 1812 invasion of Russia, or the battle of Breitenfeld, or the epic confrontation between Scipio and Hannibal at Zama—soon, such became the more frequent objects of "civilian" wargames.

The first steps were made starting from the historical sources available to the general public playing the games. So, once again, the wilful university students that had found enough money to buy their own nice *Kriegsspiel* table, complete with all the different types of troops and all the modular tiles, ran to their libraries in order to find maps, orders of battles, contemporary accounts, analytical essays and any other material needed to obtain a plausible translation of the desired event into a playable scenario. Modern wargamers should be able to easily relate with that experience, considering it an integral part of "the hobby".

The lack of confrontational historical studies, sufficiently diversified sources and simple knowledge of material findings that would happen in later decades just made the first wargames instrumental in reinforcing already accepted visions of the past, very rarely being able to put them into question. Paradoxically, this makes it much easier for us to understand that vision through products of popular culture such as books, music, forms of art and even games: a form of "derived historiography" that could give very valuable results to a discerning researcher.

But, in rather unexpected ways, those preconceptions created a sort of "circular culture" phenomenon, since by exercising their influence over mainstream renditions of past events they also gave their peculiar contribution to the collective conscience of their times. This brings us back to that poor dying infantryman on the Somme battlefield, a victim of how his society had still considered the nature of war being fascinated by visions of varied nature, both in academic as well in popular sources . . . and even in the professional wargames that had led his commanders to the conclusion that a modern conflict could still be won by moving a line of wooden red and blue blocks on a map, not unlike true "role models" like Napoleon Bonaparte or the Duke of Wellington had done a century before.

And, by every passing year, wargames were becoming more and more an active part of that process: the game about history was turning into history itself.

This will be the main object of this work, analyzing the relationship between actual history and historical simulation games, in both directions of this dynamically interconnected process. We will examine how a game designer's personal interpretation of the simulated events permeates the definition and calibration of all the single parameters included in the final model, as well as their complex interactions, but also the first step of the chain, that is how the collective vision of those same events influences the game designers. By reverting that sequence, our analysis will be able to make plausible assumptions on how a specific period considered specific previous battles and conflicts also based on the simulation games created, published and played in that period. One has just to look at the evolution of all the different wargames dedicated to the Vietnam war, dissect their oftentimes-contrasting approaches and methodologies, and even more the very diversified final renditions of that crucial conflict to understand the meaning of "not universally accepted historical interpretations".

In order to obtain such a multifaceted image of a cultural, social and growingly economical phenomenon, we will proceed by clearly defined steps in the logical exposition of the main features of such a complicated interaction.

The first portion of the book will give a conceptual framework of the inner nature of simulation games. Starting with a brief overview of their evolution since the earliest allegoric and symbolic games, often tied to religious and philosophical elements, the study will try to ascertain how, when and most of all why one of the very first applications of an emerging scientific method was to create believable models of reality through games. Models that could be repeated over and over again, modifying their mathematic and combinatorial balances and dynamics, in order to prepare their players for the possible challenges of the future . . . or even gain some insight into what exactly those challenges would be.

To fully understand all the possible applications of simulation games, however, one should first obtain a good knowledge of what really makes them work. This is the object of the second chapter of the book, the one dealing with a comprehensive (but not uselessly detailed) guide to the most frequently used game mechanics and even more of the different reasons on why game authors choose some of them and not others to obtain specific purposes, both from the point of view of their authors as well as that of the final recipients of all this work: the players themselves.

After so much theory and detail, it will be time to finally face the consequences of the previous studies: actual applications of simulation game design and their effects on the interpretation of history by those who practice this very peculiar hobby. The chapter will thus start from specific historical dynamics and highlight the many different ways in which those same processes have been simulated in different games. Once again, with all due prudence, it will be also possible to include historical simulations in the context of an extensive research process, exploiting their value as counterfactual methods about past events and even studying the very same periods in which those titles have been created.

The next segment will deal with a very peculiar, and in many regards an even much more interesting, facet of analog simulation: the real engines of the games, that is the game designers and gamers themselves. This fourth chapter will focus then on the subjective and psychological aspect of the matter, trying to understand how those elusive elements influence the final representations, their internal diversity, including their ambiguities and contradictions over the different time periods. The inner workings of the game design process will be exposed, especially considering how they originate from the analysis of historical sources, their treatment, the inclusion of an "author's message" coming from the designers' personal vision of the simulated facts and how all this translates in the complicated relationship with the final recipients of all this: the individual players, and their community as a whole.

After all those praises of simulation games, their cultural value and the intellectual depths of their practices, the following chapter will be the most critical, with an objective study of all their ambiguities, pitfalls and distortions. This will properly highlight their potential value but with an honest eye on recognizing their shortcomings, in order to avoid them or at least contain them. Material as well as conceptual limitations will be exposed, seeing how production and publishing needs might force the game designers to introduce sometimes notable deviations from their intended original path, but also how personal biases influence the research on the represented events and thus the final model proposed as an "historical simulation game".

Finally, of course, conclusions. The last portion of the text will provide a synthetic but comprehensive conceptual framework to rationalize all the previously illustrated elements, with the purpose of applying all that knowledge in a better awareness of all the potential—as well as the unavoidable risks—of using simulation games as tools for historical research. This will contribute to a more complete and profitable use of simulation games in public history events, teaching environments and diffused individual practice as instruments to gain a better awareness of past historical events, their relationship with our present world and their possible impact on future events.

As a final note, it should be remembered that simulation games are always based on accurate mathematical procedures, and also that those same procedures are based on documental research and historical interpretation by the game designers (and sometimes by the players, too, with the application of impromptu variations and "house rules"—encouraging, by the way, a critical approach to historiography).

No arbitrary elements are included in a proper simulation game, ironically not even chance itself since every form of unpredictability and randomness is managed through statistical instruments (combat results tables, terrain modifiers, scenario rules, etc.) formed upon that very same historical interpretation. You just have to compare a CRT from a wargame set during World War Two to the analog table provided in a simulation about World War One (possibly regarding battles fought in the same locations!) to appreciate the different historical modellings under those two titles. And the same can be said for every other recurring game element.

So, we come back to von Clausewitz's famous assertion regarding how the closest thing to war is not a game of chess with all its symmetries, abstraction and determinism . . . but a game of cards, with the players dealt unequal resources, sometimes asymmetrical victory conditions, imperfect knowledge of their adversaries' assets as well as the nature of future draws from hidden decks, and finally a very chaotic environment in which to make the most out of what they have in their hand.

Because this is war, actually: a constant attempt at managing the unmanageable, harmonizing totally contradictory and incomparable factors, trying to reach an overall objective with limited knowledge about the general situation, the actual enemy strength and weaknesses, gathering tactical victory after tactical victory while proudly marching towards our final strategic defeat (just ask the British generals during the American War for Independence or, on their turn, the American generals during the Vietnam War). This, and statistics.

Lots of statistics. About distances, topography, logistics, material consumption, human resources (aka, soldiers and even civilians), ammunition expenditures, economic impact, resource management, weather conditions and so on and so on . . . so much that one of the very fathers of modern applied mathematics, Georg Wilhelm von Leibniz, argued:

> One could represent with certain game pieces certain battles and skirmishes, also the position of the weapons and the lay of the land, both at one's discretion and from history.[8]

So, by using this mathematical approach, applying it to the multifaceted and ever changing nature of war and using it with the declared purpose of recreating past events (belonging to the military sphere, as well as to the political and economic domain, or a combination of all those three) we get what we can truly call "an historical simulation game": a highly playable, deeply interactive, yet fully rationalized model in which numbers, words and even images and feelings cooperate together in order to create an immersive and historically plausible experience.

A weird intellectual product, an entertainment that strives to be something more than a simple pastime, a time machine getting us back to a past that not necessarily coincides with the actual past but that still gives us precious insights onto those events and the various forces that conjured to create them. If only we keep our eyes open to see, our hears ready to hear, our minds free to imagine what a few cardboard pieces, a big map, a couple of dice and a few tables can create on our own dining table whenever we want.

This is the "magic" of simulation games, a hobby that can, among other things, get history out of the books and make it truly alive, taking us back to those terrible fields of the Somme, look at our poor dying infantryman and maybe, just maybe, give him some more time to breathe, at least in our memories.

NOTES

1   *On War*, bk. 1, ch. 7.
2   In order to have a more general and non-exclusive definition of all these different and sometimes contradictory elements, personally I used the term "non-linear elements", which sounds at the same time sufficiently vague and all-encompassing. This concept is at the basis of Masini, R., *Il gioco di Arianna: Guerra, politica ed economia nel labirinto della simulazione non lineare (Ariadne's game: War, politics and economy into the labyrinth of non-linear simulation)*, Acies (Milan, 2020).
3   Von Clausewitz, C., *Della guerra [On war]*, Book 1 Chapter 7, curated by Cardona, G., BUR (Milan, 2009).
4   The first confirmed use of Hellwig's system to recreate an historical battle is that of the reconstruction of the Battle of Krefeld (1758), made in 1782 by a small group of the very first generation of "hobby wargamers".
5   Interestingly, also Napoleon II had a personal set of miniatures built for him, presumably based on a French version of Venturini's system. The young heir to the First French Empire, though, would not be able to play much with his golden toy soldiers, since he was to be forcedly transferred to Austria when he was just three years old.
6   As a sidenote, reception in recently unified Italy was far less enthusiastic: former Piedmontese (now Royal Italian Army) officers compared the game of *Kriegsspiel* introduced to them by their Prussian colleagues at the onset of the Seven Weeks War against Austria (known in Italy as the Third War of Independence) to "playing with tarot cards", uselessly practiced instead of attending "serious business" on their maps and the actual training grounds. This note was written just a few weeks before the Battle of Custoza (1866), of course.
7   By other authors, wargaming in its essential form (playing at the war) is as much a practical as a psychological necessity for the human being. One such author is van Creveld, M., *Wargames: From gladiators to gigabytes*, Cambridge University Press (Cambridge, 2013).
8   Peterson, J., A game out of all proportions: How a hobby miniaturized war, in Harrigan, P., Kirschenbaum, M. (curated by), *Zones of control: Perspectives on wargaming*, The MIT Press (Cambridge, 2016).

1 What is a Simulation Game?

"Stat rosa pristina nomine,
nomina nuda tenemus."

Bernard of Cluny

It is common knowledge, both from formal studies and collective first-hand experience, that one of the very first occupations a human being indulges in at the beginning of his life is playing games.

This is something so ingrained to the very essence of "being alive" that ludic activity is not at all an exclusive trait of humankind, since animals also enjoy mimicking the act of hunting or fighting among themselves, aware that those free movements are not at all the real situations they are meant to represent. And, while it is debatable whether animals have a definite sense of "fun", for sure they enjoy those pastimes, while also getting more prepared for actual situations of need or danger.[1]

However, leaving cats (big and small as they are) and other pets to their caprioles and funny verses, when we move our attention to human beings, more depth in our analysis is needed. In effect, the word "game" is much vaguer than one would suspect. Countless anthropologists, historians and ludologists have tried to obtain a more comprehensive, and at the same time more accurate, definition of this fundamental activity.

Among its many forms, one of the most fascinating is simulation, that is the use of games whose purpose is the interactive reproduction of real-world dynamics, past and present. A really peculiar category, somehow similar to a dark forest full of strange symbols, apparently senseless mathematical relations and fascinating yet incomprehensible artistic trappings.

All these things form the great "optical illusion" of simulation games, capable of suspending our disbelief and taking our intellective conscience, if not our physical bodies, to other times and places through the human power of mental projection.

In simpler words, this is everything that makes us feel as if we are on the "real" Waterloo battlefield, just using a very approximate map, some pieces of cardboard, a handful of statistical tables and a couple of dice.

1.1 THE GAMES PEOPLE (AND NOT ONLY PEOPLE) PLAY

Let's start from the beginning, by counting the different types of games immediately played by children as soon as they gain a clear conscience of the space around them, also known as "the world".

DOI: 10.1201/9781003429098-2

The very first games are deeply tied to physical activity, mostly to get a first glimpse of feelings and sensations: holding their own feet, hitting small bells so that they produce sounds, making funny noises with their mouth and so on.

Later, these physical games become more connected to two crucial features: dexterity and strength. Our little growing baby will throw small things to hit specific spots of the room, turn over objects out of curiosity for what is hiding underneath or just for the joy of being able to do so. The youngling is beginning to flex his or her muscles, both literally as well as metaphorically, so that they can be ready, trained and useful when the real need arises.

In doing so, the baby will sooner or later be interacting with adults or other babies, introducing another fundamental feature of all animal life: relationship. This will be a particularly important milestone in the understanding of games, since it will bring with itself the need for rules to resolve all the possible conflicts that will arise during the game. Did I really "catch" Susy just by seeing her, or do I need to touch her arm, too? Who defines when my toy rifle actually "hit" Andy, and is he "dead" or just "wounded"? How many times should I pour tea in my plastic cups to have a "proper" picnic with Liza and Robbie?

Rules—formal or informal, conventional or just made up on the spot—then introduce children to the next set of games, that is elaborated activities with fixed behaviours, clearly recognizable decision processes and most of the time easily identifiable purposes, also known as "victory conditions". It is not by chance that these are occupations in which adults (or, if you prefer, "grown babies") are also more willing to participate and that they recognize as closer to their own conception of game, often considered in opposition to the previously described "child's play".

In the realm of regulated games, even more categories spring up.

There could be purely random games, such as throwing coins or dice and seeing who gets a better result (with "better" defined in relation to the ruleset). There could be abstract strategy games, such as *Checkers* and *Reversi*, or allegoric games reminiscent of struggles of different kinds, such as *Go* and *Chess*. There could be combinatorial games, in which you use different assets obtained partly by chance and partly by your decisions to obtain previously established sets of dispositions that give you "points" upon which the victor is defined (a very complicated definition of card games).

There could also be games that combine all these three elements—randomness, allegory and combinations—in order to do something . . . well, radically different.

One of the first activities children indulge into, in effect, is trying to "pretend" to be someone or something else. Apart from (but not excluding) the use of costumes during Carnival or Halloween or the continually recurrent similar festivities of all cultures,[2] children regularly use adults' make-ups, put on their dresses, imitate their voices to impersonate animals and reference figures of all kinds, be they favourite pets, parents, imaginary friends, movie or TV characters.

This activity is commonly known as "emulation", that is trying to do your best to be that very someone or something else you are striving to imitate, copying it to the last detail of your personal image of it. You try to be like your father as you consider him, Princess Leia as you saw her on the screen, your cat as you watched him grow beside you with all his funny behaviours, an imaginary "Timmy" as you would love your best ideal friend to be.

The common factor in all these "plays" is that what you are trying to do is impersonate that object, in other words be as close to it as possible. Your performance is not at all free, except from the general interpretation of the object, because you have clearly defined sets of reference points to uphold. Your father will not be radically different from your perception of him, your Princess Leia will always be the brave leader of the Rebellion against the evil Galactic Empire, your cat will not go on barking as your dog (well, in most cases . . . cats are unpredictable creatures . . .), your dearest Timmy will always be your best friend in the world.

For how enjoyable and satisfying emulation is, its main use is that it is a totally self-enclosed activity. Somehow gaining new points of view and perfecting your acting abilities could reveal itself to be useful in your psychological development, but an average human intellect needs more to reach its main evolutionary objective: refine its vision of the surrounding world and learn how to use the identified resources in order manipulate them and obtain positive results.

This is where the principles regulated games come in, shifting everything from the emulation domain to another and more evolved field of expertise.[3]

We then start with the act of imitating an object but with a much freer attitude, that is not by mechanically copying its features, but using those same features in other ways through a formal decision process. This process is managed through precisely recognizable procedures, as simple or as complex, as fixed or as variable as our intellect could devise them, often using mathematical and combinatorial tools. Those rationalizing assets also include chaotic elements such as randomness or unforeseen events in the general process, which can originate or even evolve into deeply allegoric, even symbolic experiences.

Thus, by combining randomness, allegory and combinations in different order and measures, we push the natural drive towards emulation to another level: simulation.

The purpose of this new activity is not to obtain totally identical *images* of the reference objects we have chosen as they *appear*, but a more complete *knowledge* of what they *are*. This is done through rules coming from all the different types of games, through which all the almost infinite potentials of informal intellectual applications and speculations are bound into a coherent cognitive flow resulting in usable results. All this is done while maintaining the freedom of thinking and decision making that is necessary to conduct a profitable experimentation process, an unavoidable condition to gain better knowledge by exploring unexpected fields with unexpected combinations of unexpected tools and ideas encountered along the way.

Oh, and it is also very fun, with entertainment and personal satisfaction being the natural rewards conceded by our brain chemistry when we do something deeply useful for our physical life and psychological development.

This is not to say that every kind of emulation process has no intrinsic value, either as a teaching and self-teaching tool, or as an intellectual activity per se. The first examples of wall paintings in caves and secluded places are at the very heart of what we now call human culture, and for many anthropologists starting with Johan Huizinga, as we shall see, they enjoy a very close relation with "gaming", even if in a deeply conceptual form. The fact is, however, that depicting hunting or farming scenes as propitiatory means could maybe provide some direct examples but no actual knowledge of hunting tactics or farming techniques. They still need a physical expert to provide education; they are not models with an independent value of their own, re-usable by anybody who sees them.

On the contrary, by simulating the Battle of Waterloo in a wargame, the legislative process in a political game, the negotiation procedures in an economic game, we obtain a better knowledge not just of those single events, but also a better experience of similar, analogous events. This deep awareness and usefulness would never be reached by re-enacting—that is, emulating rather than simulating—the Battle of Waterloo, the writing of the US Constitution or the 2008 debt crisis step-by-step as they happened.

The difference, however, lies much, much deeper than this. While emulation contents itself in just mechanically capturing the more evident exterior parts of a situation to represent it in an interactive environment only vaguely inspired by the reference reality, simulation undergoes a much more elaborate preliminary phase. In this preliminary first step, as we will see, raw data are collected, categorized, and recombined into an interactive system capable of reproducing the inner workings of cause-and-effect formal processes of the reference situation, regardless of their material contingencies, providing for plausible results—even if highly variable and dependent on players' choices—representative of the reference situation. This is what game experts call "historical modelling" and is at the very heart of what a simulation is, at the same time defining its core dynamic as well as the very purpose for which it exists.

In fact, the word itself helps us understand the nature of this evolved activity: simulation, or *simul actio* in Latin, that is creating "similar actions" to the object of our gaming experience through a free analogic process. This is in contrast with emulation, which in Latin contains the prefix *ex*, that is making actions "taken out of" the object, through mechanically limited reproductions. The difference, in conclusion, is that with emulation we are dealing with just one single object and its peculiar perceived identity, whereas with simulation we are dealing with the inner dynamics of that object.

An activity could yield great cognitive results if we are good enough in exploiting all the potential of this powerful tool, with a much stronger understanding of the dynamics of all the similar objects in the world, be they real or just hypothetical . . . and even imaginary, too, since the applications of this tool extend even beyond reality itself.[4]

But that would be—literally—another story.

1.2 THE CONCEPT OF "SIMULATION": FROM ARISTOTELES TO DUNNIGAN . . . AND BEYOND

Even if this could be something of a disappointment for some readers, what will follow is not the usual "history of wargames" paragraph, already exposed by so many excellent works over the last decades.

The next pages will rather deal with the reasons that prompted so many thinkers, intellectuals, mathematicians and artists to devise a way through which one could not only mechanically replicate reality, but also understand its deepest dynamics regarding past events, present situations and possible future happenings. A goal achieved through an unstable, imperfect and sometimes inaccurate, yet at the same time totally free, interactive and highly flexible tool: games. Not all of these noble attempts would be successful, some would be plain wrong or even misleading . . . but some would be steps in the right direction, creating a single line that connects so many different points in so many different centuries—if not millennia.

This line is not at all a continuous trace. It is composed of segments, often interrupted and fragmented, sometimes multiple, parallel or even divergent pieces of a single interconnected tapestry.

The main point is simple: create a free but rational, flexible but regulated, dynamic but rigorous instrument through which one could explore all the different facets of reality in all their possible configurations (something that could adhere to the formal definition of "reference reality"). A game would be needed, then, for its innate freedom, but also for its rules that can maintain stability and fixed points of reference in the entire experience.

As we have already discussed, this peculiar application of human intellect oscillates between the two different poles of *emulation* and *simulation*.

The first one, as often happens, is the more intuitive and quicker to grasp. If I want to understand how something works, I can recreate a smaller version of it by drawing its shape or describing its essence through words and allegorical images.

These contraptions can be summarily called "examples", in the sense of being allusive objects made as similar as possible to the reference reality in order to reproduce it. There is no formal reasoning at work in this stage, since we are just trying to fabricate "working copies" of reality, shift them into another environment detached from the actual "real world", devise some mutually accepted limits to keep everything together and, essentially, see what happens when all the single elements of the "example" get to move.

One of the very first ludic objects of this kind is the Indian game of *Chaturanga*. Literally "The Game of Four", its first testimonies are from sixth or seventh century AD even if it is very probable that earlier forms of it existed much before those times, possibly dating to many centuries, if not millennia before.

The game was about war, which is not at all surprising considering the central role played by conflict in ancient (as well as modern) societies. What is interesting, though, is the relative accuracy permeating its rules in the depiction of the traditional four different branches of contemporary Indian armies: infantry, cavalry, elephantry and chariotry. The players could then confront themselves in a symbolic "battlefield" with their own "armies" in what undoubtedly became a very popular pastime, both in the high noble houses as well as the more popular districts.

What is even more interesting for our purposes, *Chaturanga* had another variant, *Chaturaji*: this game was played by four different players instead of just two, could be the basis also for elaborated negotiations, had a much more complex board with tiles representing different sets of terrain (mountains, forests, rivers, cities . . .) each with its own particular rule: in other words, the ideal precursor of many modern simulation wargames.

To better understand the importance and popularity of this game, it should be noted that *Chaturaji* or at least some version of it had the honour of being mentioned in the Hindu revered text *Mahabharata*, composed in the fourth century BC:

> Presenting myself as Brahmana, Kanka by name, skilled in dice and fond of play, I shall become a courtier of that high-souled King. And moving upon chess-boards beautiful pawns of ivory, of blue and yellow and red and white hue, by throws of black and red dice, I shall entertain the King with his courtiers and friends.

While earlier forms of *Chaturanga* and *Chaturaji* were formalized in the Indian subcontinent, hundreds of miles west, in the Greek peninsula, games like *Petteia* (literally "The Game of Foot Soldiers") were commonly enjoyed, so much that even intellectuals like Socrates and, most of all, Plato were well-known enthusiast practitioners.

Petteia shuns the use of dice, considered to be a random device unworthy of rational human beings,[5] and gives us the traditional image of war in ancient Greek culture: hoplitic formations fighting each other in linear fashion over a clear and featureless battlefield. This configuration would become, when assimilated by Roman culture, the basis for the much more "vulgar" *Ludus Latrunculorum* ("The Game of Thieves") and the higher intellectual version of *Ludus Duodecim Scriptorum* ("The Game of the Twelve Writers"). Interestingly, in Rome dice were not so deprecated and all these games used them in various measures, including the more complex final version of the game called *Tabula* (literally, "The Boardgame"). Emperor Claudius himself was so enamoured of the game that, in a truly monumental feat of geekdom, had a *Tabula* set engraved inside his personal carriage, forcing Imperial dignitaries to join him in endless tournaments or, if this proved to be impossible, engaging in entire days of solitaire play. This game would later provide the basis for the evolution to modern *Backgammon*.

Getting back to Athens and its surroundings, Plato did two great things for the history of games: he included boardgaming among the accepted and even encouraged activities in his ideal "Republic of Philosophers" and in his philosophical *opus Laws*, and played *Petteia* every day with one of his most promising pupils: Aristoteles.

The disciple of Plato always maintained a deep connection with reality. For Aristoteles, "practical" and "theorical" are not at all opposite terms, since both of them are manifestations of the only true thing at the foundation of all the universe: Reason. This great force is expressed through the ways of rationality, which means perfectly understandable relations among objects and their respective natures.

And what could be best to describe those relations but a good game of *Petteia*, which even his old teacher Plato would surely appreciate? What a cruel fate awaits those men far from their own country, their laws and society, subject to all possible tribulations and standing isolated as the lone pawns of *Petteia* that the enemy will so easily capture, Aristoteles would write in his fundamental essay, *Politics*.

As we are seeing, a game vaguely inspired by military feats of arms is once again used as an instrument to give an "example": a recognizable vision of the relation between human beings, their different societies and the laws regulating them. It is an intuitive process, an allegory of elements that is clearly inserted into a rational explanation in order to capture the attention of the reader . . . but not a rational research of the dynamics of reality *per se*: a very elevated form of emulation (and we could not expect anything less from the great theorist of art as *poiesis*, that is "creation" of another reality), but by no means a simulation.

Aristoteles' successor in this line of thinkers would be undoubtedly illustrious, but not a philosopher at all, even if he played many, many "Games of Foot Soldiers" in his life, just on a bigger scale. His name would be Alexander the Great, and he would be a frequent *Petteia* player, too.

Now, the idea of Aristoteles teaching the arts of war to Alexander the Great through an early form of wargame would surely be fascinating to many *grognards*[6] out there, but reality is a bit less obvious than that. *Petteia* would remain a nice game, somehow reminiscent of the Greek and later Hellenistic conception of war, but still based on a highly stylized image of a battle, with no real intention of recreating its inner dynamics.

It is true, however, that the many campaigns fought by Alexander, together with the unending infightings among his successors and their descendants, would bring a much closer contact between Western and Eastern cultures. This would facilitate the circulation and hybridization of their different games, especially those aimed at emulating different elements of the world. Probably Alexander was not aware that, by bringing his *Petteia* boards into his tent he was giving to *Chaturanga* its first opportunities to meet a new friend and to travel west, becoming over many centuries *Shatranji*, then *Shamat* and finally *Chess*.

This constant exchange of games, with their related different depictions of reality, continued for centuries among the many cultures of antiquity, at least until the dark times of the Middle Ages. Or did it?

The first thing to understand here is that those new times were certainly placed in the figurative "middle" of human history, but not "dark" at all. Cataclysmic conflicts such as the Norman conquests both in the north and in the south of Europe, the long succession of Crusades with the related rise and fall of religious knightly orders, the unending struggle between England and France and the epic *Reconquista* of Spain from the Muslim emirates all brought with them constant occasions for cultural confrontation, dialogue and finally regular blending of different traditions and heritages. Far from being an age of continuous fighting among noble houses on one side and against the "Infidels" on the other—as much traditional historiography and popular culture might lead us to think—those were centuries in which exchanges of all kinds between peoples and religions were the norm during the long pauses between one conflict and the next one, and often even during those dreadful events.

In short, this was an age in which so many different traditions came into much more frequent and closer contact than before, both during wars and during peacetime.

This had serious repercussions. First of all, it was also thanks to this mixing and reciprocal contact that both Muslim scholars and Christian monks found ways to preserve as much of the patrimony of ancient Greek and Latin culture as possible. Many texts copied in Benedictine monasteries all over Europe had been previously guarded in the houses of Muslim scientists or nobles, either in their original form or in Arab translations. The trade routes between Syria, Egypt and Palestine on one side and Rome, Paris and Trier on the other were almost inexhaustible sources of cultural treasures, at least as much of exotic spices, fabrics and precious artefacts.

Of the many men and women of culture of this so-called "dark" period to whom we owe much of our current knowledge, methodology and even elements of our way of thinking, few can be as highly regarded as Abu Jafar Muhammad al-Khwarizmi. If the name sounds familiar it is because he was the inventor of the concept of "algorithm" itself, and algorithms are just the kind of mathematical device that allow this book to be written on a computer, printed on a modern press and delivered to you.

In essence, an algorithm is a sequence of ordered operations, all conceived and regulated with the purpose of delivering not just a single result, but also of creating an open-ended process capable of delivering different but still coherent results, based on all the possible inputs given by a human operator.

The creator of an algorithm does not need to know those initial variables, leaving them to an operator that he or she could never get in touch with, since the sequence would be self-maintaining, persistent and adaptable to every possible use of it without the necessity for any further modification. The system was so flexible that most of the algorithms devised by Al-Khwarizmi and brought to us are still perfectly valuable today, more than a millennium after the death of their inventor.

As we have seen, along with mathematics and theorical sciences, applied observation of nature and philosophy (two disciplines that, at least until the end of the Renaissance would be practically undistinguishable) were also taking many steps forward.

Spain, with its constant friction, confrontation, and interchange between the Christian kingdoms and the Taifa emirates, was a particularly fertile land for these studies, reaching amazing heights of sophistication in fields like medicine, architecture, navigation and general speculation about the nature of the universe and of its many relations.

Those relations were precisely the field of action of another great intellectual active in the thirteenth century, Ramon Llull. His main work, the monumental essay titled *Ars Combinatoria* attempted at creating a universal method of observation not just of the physical world, but also of human psychology, structured theology and even metaphysical realities.

Everything was based on "sets" of objects: 9 predicates, 9 relations, 9 subjects, 9 virtues, 9 vices. All of them would be placed on rotating "wheels" and the sequences deriving from the many different combinations would provide precious insights on the deepest recesses of existence, both human and divine.

Seen by our own modern eyes, all of this appears to be deeply influenced by esoteric disciplines like numerology, cabalistic reasoning, varied symbology, etc., but if we go beyond the single terms and categories used by Llull, we find the basis for modern matrix analysis advanced conceptual categorization, instruments of fundamental importance for many modern technological, anthropological, economic developments.

It would not come as a surprise then that both Al-Kharizmi's and Llull's works, aimed at reaching a better control and comprehension over the world, would also find many applications among the games that had the very same purpose: the definition of single operations and their orderly succession (game phases and general turn sequences), open-ended nature of input variables (all the possible moves on a map grid), orderly application of varied states in the single functions (terrain and combat modifiers), impact of relations among different objects of different nature (zones of control), definition of the ratio between two elements and the impact on the general depiction of events (combat results table), and so on and so on . . .

And yet, something else was still needed in order to solidify those gains and declaredly open the way for their application to the domain of games.

This opportunity came from the most unexpected of sources: not a mathematician, not a philosopher, not an artist . . . but a sovereign: King Alphonse X of Spain, much deservedly known as *El Sabio*, The Wise.

King Alphonse pursued two great hobbies in his life: the reunification of his country through military as well as political means, and games. Not necessarily in this order. And not totally unrelated between each other. It was he who conceived, sponsored and for the most part wrote one of the most amazing texts of the entire medieval period, *El Libro de los Juegos* (*The Book of Games*), defying the usual prejudice against games seen either as low and unworthy forms of leisure, or even objects of temptation that could distract the faithful from the right path.

The mixed cultural roots are evident from elements such as the allusion to distant realms of the Far East, by the constant mentions to games belonging to the Arab culture, but most of all by the drawing of many different miniatures depicting Muslims and Christians playing together at various games, including warriors in full set of armour and even members of religious knightly orders.[7]

Even more importantly, *El Libro* provided a conceptual structure that was fundamental to systematize the previous reasonings by many intellectuals as well as the popular traditions regarding games, considering them items of cultural and educational value, as postulated by Plato and Aristoteles.

King Alphonse obtained very cleverly this goal by dividing the study among games of "pure reason" (*Ajedrex*), those of "chance" (*Dados*) and those belonging to a third category, the boardgames (*Tabulas*) (Figure 1.1). Rather unsurprisingly, the king would favour this last group: games that were based on strategic and mindful risk-taking, quick and efficient answers to unforeseen difficulties, wise management of asymmetrical resources in order to pursuit one's final purpose.[8]

A couple of centuries later, in another area of the Mediterranean, a young and ambitious man began his observations of nature through what he knew best: art. If you ever asked Leonardo da Vinci, that was the name of the boy, what was his preferred thing to do in his pastime, the answer would have been probably just one, and fairly easy: drawing.

Once out of the city in his endless strolls in the countryside, he would start drawing just about everything that he saw around him, taking an image of every single animal, landscape, building, person that he happened to meet. His caricatures made on the spot were famous, and many of those sketches—even the smallest ones drawn at the very margin of his dense notes—are now auctioned for unbelievable sums of money. But for him, they were just his studies.

Now, Leonardo is probably the greatest and the latest representative of the use of emulation as a form of depiction of the world . . . but, even if all his work was later of inspiration for countless generations of scientists, he was no scientist at all. Or, at least, not in the modern sense of the term.

Let us take in consideration his technical drawings. Leonardo was perfectly capable of imagining and maybe even building most of the wonders he put on paper:

FIGURE 1.1 A game of astronomical tables, from *El Libro de los Juegos*.

Source: Public domain

tanks, mechanical wheels, water mills, multiple cannons, underwater vessels and, why not, helicopters, parachutes or gliding machines. But he was only copying them from his own imagination, in some ways hinting at the physical principles behind their operations, but never really understanding them. As we shall see in the next pages, he was not building models of the natural forces at work, he was just depicting them as he saw them. That is probably why, at his death, all his wonderful machines recessed into obscurity, with no one capable of replicating them through objective regulations and principles.

However, his *attitude* towards nature was probably more important than the actual results of his studies, inspiring future generations of thinkers and scientists.

One of them lived in the same area of Leonardo: a man called Galileo Galilei, from Pisa.

Galileo's approach to the depiction of the world was at the same time similar to Leonardo's and totally opposite. Just like his predecessor, the Pisan astronomer applied all his talent to gain a more accurate representation of the world, its laws and the dynamics of planets, satellites and stars. He was the one that first decided to observe the cosmos through a technical instrument, the telescope, to obtain better approximations of the movements of celestial bodies and the features of their structures. In the process, he created something much more relevant for future generations: a *method*, the scientific method.

Gone were allegories, symbology, philosophical speculations, literary descriptions of natural phenomena, elaborate structures that more served their own internal coherence than the actual research about the studied objects. The role of the scientist for Galileo was not to express answers and create a monolithic "system" that satisfied ideal premises. On the contrary, Galileo thought that the scientist had to find new questions, and proceed by trial and error in order to reach a plausible approximation that could be called a "theory".

To do this the scientist could rely only on the weapons of mathematics, logic, direct observation and experimental application. The only issue for Galileo's personal life was that mathematics is a neutral tool, and that sometimes the conclusions that were reached appeared to be quite unpleasant to hear for other, more important characters and social structures.

The seed was planted, though, and this had formidable repercussions also on the concept of using games as a rational way of depicting the world. A more extensive use of mathematical, combinatorial and even statistical tools in scientific research would be encouraged, leading us to thinkers like Girolamo Cardano, René Descartes, Baruch Spinoza, Blaise Pascal and finally Gottfried Wilhelm von Leibniz with, as we have already seen, his peculiar idea of using all these rational assets to create a game "for military colonels and captains".

For as much as we know, Leibniz's concept of using mathematical relations and not mere symbolic allegories to create a game about war remained just a hypothesis in his mind, never being put to practice. We will never know if this was because of Leibniz's lack of interest in such a peculiar experiment, or because the great scientist and philosopher did not truly possess the last two essential elements needed to obtain a successful "war simulation" of any kind: systematic collection and analysis of military statistics, and accurate topography, sciences that were moving their first steps in the days of the German intellectual.

This very concept, however, lingered on, and finally found its first practical application in the works of the pioneers of wargaming, such as Johann Hellwig, Johan Venturini and the two von Reisswitzes, father and son. With them, at last, the use of games based on rational representative functions in order to represent the world will finally come to the foreground, enjoying its first real opportunities for giving birth to something that we could call "simulation": not a static reproduction of an idea of reality through arcane symbology or vague generalizations, but the active interpretation of the dynamics of the world with the declared purpose of creating an interactive, open-ended, easily modifiable and infinitely reusable "model".

Of course, its first application was, once again, war.

Some differences were quite evident, though: Hellwig and Venturini's versions remained still close to the more eccentric versions of "military chessboards", Georg von Reisswitz Sr.'s game with his modular maps with adaptable squares each representing a different type of terrain would form the basis for modern day miniature board-wargaming, while the more open-ended structure of von Reisswitz Jr.'s system—based on dioramas, wooden blocks representing lines of troops each with its own tactical features and dice with special symbols used to introduce Friction in the general picture—can be easily considered the ideal precursor of modern-day miniature wargames. A new set of categories was forming, a sub-division that is still felt today, two and a half centuries afterward.[9]

It will then suffice to say here that the works of the very first generation of wargames were essentially first-hand applications of all the methodology described until now, stretching its roots to Aristoteles' *Petteia* and even farther before. Their collective name, however, hid much of these heritages behind a veil of illusory simplicity: *Kriegsspiel*, "The Game of War" or, if you prefer, "Wargame".

This first wargames would be hypothetical in nature, depicting not one specific historical situation, but many generic and stereotypical ones.[10] This would lend them easily to their use in a professional environment both for educational purposes as well as powerful planning tools, and this is exactly what happened when the new *Kriegsspiel* was taken out of the royal palace, included in the training programs and strategical activities of the armed forces and transformed into a true "secret weapon" in the hands of the Prussian, later German, High Command.

Successive generations of wargame designers would further refine the instrument, of course. In particular, German colonel Julius von Verdy du Vernois would stretch to the utmost limit the role of a peculiar figure, developed over the years: the referee.

Originally his role was restricted to giving actual knowledge of the enemy forces to the players only at the time of visual contact, defining some parameters of the various scenarios and in general guaranteeing the respect of the mutually accepted rules. Du Vernois, instead, delegated the entire adjudication process to him, thus creating a much more dynamic game asset, capable of representing higher levels of Friction as well as more elaborated events. This new version took the name of "Free *Kriegsspiel*".

This would open the untapped potential of hybrid political-military simulations, paving the way for tools very familiar to modern analysts such as matrix games (and, incidentally, create the premises for the development of today's role-playing games). However, this would also leave everything into the hands of the referee or referees that had to establish the outcome of the players' decisions only trusting his or their own personal experience, with the ability of ignoring or outright bypassing the results of the dice. This is exactly the kind of critical issue at the basis of the famous debacle of the Imperial Japanese Navy simulations led by Admiral Matome Ugaki just before the Battle of Midway.

Anyway, the use of games as tools to gain a better knowledge of the world through mathematical and combinatorial dynamics (i.e. actual simulation, and not limited to military matters, but extending also into political, economic, social and even sport simulation) was finally established. The march still went on.

The war with Japan had been enacted in the game rooms at the War College by so many people and in so many different ways that nothing that happened during the war was a surprise—absolutely nothing except the kamikaze tactics toward the end of the war. We had not visualized these.[11]

That was the famous mention by Admiral Chester W. Nimitz, Commander-in-Chief of the US Pacific Forces, about his experience leading the main American effort against the Empire of Japan from the days immediately following Pearl Harbor up to the final surrender signed aboard the USS Missouri moored in Yokohama Harbor. And that quote shows quite well the importance of wargaming in World War Two, both for the Allied forces and for the Axis.[12] During that conflict, wargaming was not an option but a requisite for the planning and actuation of any meaningful operation that wanted to have the slightest possibility of success. Oftentimes, generals would be caught by the course of events while still in the middle of their routine wargaming sessions, such as many of the highest German officers during Operation Overlord in June 1944: in that case, the commanders would just continue playing "in the field" what they had already rehearsed countless times in their games.

With this in mind, it is not surprising that the two new great powers emerging from the ashes of that conflict, USA and USSR, continued practicing extensively the art of gaining strategic insights from realistic and detailed simulation games (Figure 1.2).

In the West, at the forefront of this technique was a new, very peculiar organization: the RAND Corporation. In this veritable ancestor of many modern-day

FIGURE 1.2 *Pacific Tide* (Compass Games). Card-driven simulations accurately portray the impact of many non-kinetic and unpredictable factors on military operations.

Source: Photograph by the author.

strategic studies centres, many of the greatest scientists and mathematicians gave their talents to the military to create more plausible, useful and accurate simulations about past, present and future conflicts.

Among them, two names should be remembered: John von Neumann and Nobel Prize winner John Nash. Their studies on min-maxing, logic dilemmas and decision processes would be at the foundation of the most part of modern-day economic, social and behavioural sciences. Also, both of them worked extensively on wargames and simulation games while at RAND, creating many conventions now taken almost for granted in the hobby: maps based on hexes (von Neumann) and counters with accurate numerical combat values written on top of them (Nash).

Imagine their surprise when one day the intelligence service brought an unknown civilian inside the buildings of RAND: a civilian that had just created in a few week-ends of leisure time a combat results table not unlike those designed by the entire institution after years of research, and had already published a couple of games using those same top-secret assets!

The name of the civilian was Charles S. Roberts, the printing company was Avalon Hill, and those titles were the very first modern commercial wargames ever produced: *Tactics II* and *Gettysburg* (1958). The gentleman told the secret service that he had created his results-adjudicating table (combat results table, CRT) starting from common sense and his own personal wartime experience suggesting that the ideal force ratio for an attack is 3:1. He then convinced everybody that he was no Communist spy and was finally led back to his home to the amazement of all the top RAND scientists—not before, however, having taken with him the idea of converting his square-grid-based games to a much more practical hex-grid representation of the terrain.

Thus, the era of modern commercial wargaming was born, with titles both based on hypothetical "Red vs. Blue" scenarios as well as historical reconstructions and a very close relation between civilian game designers and strategic institutions. Charles S. Roberts would then continue to produce titles, leaning more and more towards historical games with the American Civil War and recently ended World War Two among the favourite themes.

This remained until in the mid-1960s when a young wargamer by the name of James F. Dunnigan wrote a piece about Avalon Hill's latest and much-appreciated *Battle of the Bulge* (1965) title. In it, he praised the games of the company for their playability and their dynamic style, but also put forward some very direct questions about the true historical value of the titles. Could this great instrument of simulation games be pushed a bit more to really fulfil its greatest potential? Could different CRTs be more accurately tailored and combined with clever game mechanics in order to better represent the actual features of all those diverse conflicts? Could the same game system reproduce the different nature of World War One attritional combat and World War Two much more mobile operational art of war, without adding too much complexity to the final system?

Dunnigan would find answers to his questions first inside Avalon Hill itself, designing great masterpieces like *Jutland* (1967) and *PanzerBlitz* (1970), and later founding his own game company with the help of his friend, graphic artist Redmond A. Simonsen: Simulation Publications Inc., or SPI. With them came a new generation of bright, young authors and developers destined to form the backbone of modern commercial wargaming: names like Al Nofi, John Butterfield, Kevin Zucker, John Young, Mark Herman and many others.

Dunnigan put forward his own idea of what simulation games could and should be, veritable "paper time machines" that could easily transport their players back into the real past events, the possible alternative worlds of the present as well as into the many plausible (or even implausible) futures.

But Dunnigan's open-ended vision was not just limited to practical game design techniques, since he gathered his experience and his thoughts on wargames and their relationship with the different kinds of historical research in a fundamental essay, *The Complete Wargames Handbook*. Among its pages, we find what still today can be considered one of the best description of wargames:

> A simulation is a model, or collection of models, that can be more easily manipulated to test "what if" questions. A simulation is a model that can move in many different directions. A wargame is a playable simulation.[13]

It is from this origin that a second generation of game designers will begin their career from inside the SPI cradle. After the demise of the great company, in fact, some of its game developers and younger, more promising authors started their own venture by founding other brands such as GDW, Victory Games and the like.

One of them, considered by many to be the real "pupil" of Dunnigan, was Mark Herman. A true genius of game design as well as a profoundly competent historian, Herman brought forward some of the most advanced and ambitious experiments already started in the SPI "thinking rooms", by adding a new dimension to traditional wargaming: cards. From such a versatile game element, already present in some of the most innovative game designs already on the market but never so much at the functional centre of a simulation, would begin an entirely new category of wargames: the CDG (or "card-driven games"), that had their first recognized example in *We the People* (1993), a game that would combine military, political, economic and also ethnic elements in its ground-breaking simulation of the American War for Independence.

Herman himself would have his own pupil, someone that would bring forward his personal conception to new levels. In 2001, Volko Ruhnke published *Wilderness War*, an incredibly asymmetrical and yet extremely well balanced CDG about the French and Indian War. Nine years later, in 2010, still Ruhnke would apply his professional experience as a CIA analyst to the design of *Labyrinth: War on Terror*, another CDG partly inspired by the great success of *Twilight Struggle* (2005), a masterful and incredibly successful pol-mil simulation about the Cold War. This new game would be totally different from any of its predecessors, though, and would pave the way for the next of Ruhnke's creations: *Andean Abyss* (2012), the first title of the *COIN* series, a system based on irregular warfare conflicts and counter-insurgent operations, with deep ties to political issues as well as many other non-kinetic elements. Finally, in 2019, Ruhnke seemed to get back to conventional wargame designs with *Nevsky*, a game about the Teuton crusades against thirteenth-century Rus of Novgorod: this new series, called *Levy & Campaign*, would totally re-set the very specialist niche of medieval wargames, with its particular attention to logistical issues and fluctuating loyalties typical of the period.

Ruhnke's work inspired countless other game designers and was, together with the titles and contributions of many other authors, instrumental in the emergence of new trends in the wargaming hobby. New lines of development and research bloomed, such as the many simulations created by Cole Wehrle, not strictly "historical" in their nature but undoubtedly dedicated to the concept of warfare and history themselves: titles like *Root* and *Oath*, very well known even outside traditional wargaming circles.

With this our short travel through the history of the games that wanted to recreate history gets to our own days. This path will not end here, of course, and we shall see much of its features in the following pages, studying how those titles will confirm the validity of two of the fundamental principles highlighted by one of the fathers of modern ludology, Johan Huizinga, in his highly influential essay *Homo Ludens*.

The fact that all culture, starting from the cave paintings up to the judicial proceedings, is just a derivation of the greatest human activity of them all: gaming. Also, how all gaming is, in some measure and notwithstanding its necessary ideal detachment from the many duties of normal life and the unconquerable limits of reality, nothing else than a constant attempt at recreating the world itself.

1.3 HOW TO MODEL REALITY: BEYOND THE CHESSBOARD

In the last portion of Leibniz's writing we find an interesting sentence in which he says that this hypothetical military boardgame could be practiced "*instead* of the chessboard". The word "instead" is of the utmost importance, since Leibniz is expressly putting this game in a totally different domain than the many "military chess games" that began proliferating at the beginning of the eighteenth century.

Those games were no more than simple variations and not-so-useful complications of the classic *Chess* rules. Bigger gameboards, terrain tiles with specific rules, allegorical game pieces such as cannons and grenadiers, even the first rudimentary "scenarios" that had some vague resemblance to ancient battles like Gaugamela, Cannae or Zama.

They found their origins in what can be considered a widely accepted, yet conceptually incorrect premise: that is, the fact that *Chess* is a game that represents the basic dynamic of an open field battle, a somewhat universal model of war. Yet, after having considered even the most basic Clausewitzian doctrine combined with simple historical observation, it becomes quite evident that in this classic game so many crucial elements of warfare are so abstracted that they become totally unrecognizable, or even outright absent. Friction, as an expression of unforeseen negative (or positive) events, socio-economic factors, political objectives and limitations, diffuse asymmetries, divergent victory conditions, individual leaders . . . that is a long list, indeed.

However, for its universal value, *Chess* has been regarded for centuries as the epitome of the "game of acute minds and profound intellectuals". Significantly, though, even this conclusion was refuted by a very thoughtful author such as Edgar Allan Poe, when in the introduction to his collection of tales *The Murders in the Rue Morgue*, he wrote:

[T]o calculate is not in itself to analyse. A chess-player, for example, does the one without effort at the other. It follows that the game of chess, in its effects upon mental character, is greatly misunderstood.[14]

The issue highlighted by Poe here is that *Chess* is such a sublimed, distilled game that it has lost every connection to the many facets of true analysis, that is the collection of different, incoherent data and their manipulation to reach a complex goal: in other words, intelligence itself.[15]

Just to add other fuel to his diatribe, Poe considers *Draughts* a better strategic game thanks to its innate simplicity, but above all he reaches a curious (possibly deliberate?) agreement with Clausewitz, by considering a game of cards such as *Whist* a much more evolved rendition of real-world strategy:

The best chess-player in Christendom may be little more than the best player of chess; but proficiency in whist implies a capacity for success in all these more important undertakings where mind struggles with mind. When I say proficiency, I mean that perfection in the game which includes a comprehension of all the sources whence legitimate advantage may be derived. These are not only manifold but multiform, and lie frequently among recesses of thought altogether inaccessible to the ordinary understanding.[16]

Echoes of King Alphonse X inclination towards games of *Tabula*, combining luck elements with resource management, abound.

Yet, at the same time, the mere existence of military chess games is of great relevance to our study, because it shows how much eighteenth-century society and culture was striving to find a new way to represent reality in games, renouncing the universal symbolisms and idealistic approach of the past. They tried to do the right thing, unfortunately in the wrong way.

This happened because, all their efforts notwithstanding, they remained *emulation* games. Their interplay dynamics tried to copy reality for their effects, Poe would have said, not inquiring about their true nature; that is, their causes. In so doing, they created perfectly harmonious and balanced renditions of their own visions of reality, which were, however, not at all related to actual field conditions, and so of no use whatsoever in reaching a comprehensive reproduction of the world in a truly dynamic and plausible environment.

Something else was needed to have truly representative games, systems that could reproduce reality in meaningful and manipulable elements, algorithms ready to accept the input of different data and player decisions to create an output of usable insights. In other words, real *simulation* games.

Military chess games created impressions; the new wargames created models.

But what is a model, anyway, and how is it such an important reference point in the theory of wargames and simulation?

The answer to that theorical question comes from one of the very fathers of modern wargaming, James F. Dunnigan, through the full formula of an already mentioned paragraph of his *The Complete Wargames Handbook*:

Wargames are, like most games, also models and simulations of real life events. . . . Wargames are usually simpler than models and simulations because, as the names imply, a wargame is something of a competitive game that is played while a model is a more detailed representation of a specific military event. A model duplicates a function in great detail and exactitude. A simulation is a model, or collection of models, that can be more easily manipulated to test "what if" questions. A simulation is a model that can move in many different directions. A wargame is a playable simulation.[17]

The relationship between models, simulation and wargames is clearly and very effectively described here. A model is a scientific (not artistic, nor symbolic, nor allegorical) representation of reality in univocal terms and values. That model can be included in a more general simulation in order to "make it move", so to say, and use it to depict different yet plausible outcomes through algorithms of various complexities. That simulation can become a wargame when it is simplified (*not* abstracted!) enough to make it capable of producing believable results every time it is played.

Later theorists have even perfected this original definition, and in particular Matthew Caffrey in his fundamental *On Wargaming* essay gives particular importance to the actual "flow" of operations taking us from an accurate, yet still raw and unusable, model to a structured simulation and finally to a playable wargame. The functional key to transform models into simulations is their constant repetition and adaptation, while what makes a simulation a truly playable wargame is the stress on players' interactions. Given these elements the true "magic" can happen.

This also allows us to understand why it is impossible to consider Aristoteles' *Petteia* a wargame of any practical use to his pupil, Alexander. That game could rightfully be used as a valuable metaphor for a philosophical essay, but its many abstractions and most of all its fundamental nature prevented it from being a simulation of actual warfare of any kind. In other words, it did not create a model of field tactics with actual considerations of the behaviour of Macedonian phalanxes when confronted with Persian infantry lines, war chariots or elephants. What happened during each play did not give reusable insights that could give sudden inspirations to a commander, supporting his decision process with empowered awareness of all tactical factors. Even the most constant practice of the game would never bring new ideas for military developments in the use of formations, weapons or maneuvers of any level.

It was a game inspired by war, a very good and clever game of course . . . but in that case, literally, just a game.

And this crucial difference also explains why military chess games, for all their ingenuity and also their undeniable entertainment value, cannot be considered precursors of wargames and simulations of any kind.

This is true, even if something of the old allure of *Chess* remained, even at the dawn of modern day wargaming. The game box Avalon Hill's seminal *Tactics II* (conventionally regarded as the first "true wargame" in the current sense of the term, even if not based on historical events) reported the following statement:

Now YOU Command an Army Group in this Classic Game of Military Chess[18]

The somewhat surprising affirmation would still be retained in various forms in ads, game descriptions and articles of the very first period of civilian board-wargaming:

from the late 1950s to the mid-1960s. That is, until James F. Dunnigan, in his famous letter, asked for a much higher adherence to historical dynamics while still maintaining the same dimension of rules complexity.

Yet, almost a couple of decades after, the very same Dunnigan would describe wargames in these terms:

> Basically, it's glorified chess. If you've never encountered a wargame before, it's easiest to think of it as chess with a more complicated playing board and a more complex way of moving your pieces and taking your opponents.[19]

Probably Dunnigan's intent was to give a reference point for the uninitiated reader that really had no previous idea of what a wargame is, but this statement still testifies the strength of the image of *Chess* as the quintessential simple but highly intellectual strategy game.[20]

So, the next field of enquiry would be the definition of the general nature of those approaches used to shift from emulation to simulation games.

The first and most intuitive one relies on a direct mathematical transposition of the material factors involved in a certain situation. Military matters are the perfect field of application for such a method and as we have seen accurate operational statistics such as march distances, ammo and supply consumption, technical data on weapons range and characteristics were crucial for the creation of the first wargames since the early days of the *Kriegsspiel*.

Those directly proportional renditions form the *quantitative* approach in simulation design, extensively used by Charles S. Roberts, Avalon Hill's founder and the creator of the very first civilian wargames, in *Tactics II* as well as the first edition of the historical boardgame *Gettysburg* (1958). Those simple calculations allowed him to design the first CRT, or *Combat Results Table*, based on the different force ratios between the combat factors of attacking and defending units.

Those factors themselves were the fruits of a quantitative approach, since Roberts created simple formulas to translate troop numbers and fighting capabilities into numerical values that could be written on the different units. Other elements such as weapons range could be expressed in the quantity of squares (later hexes) that could be covered by an artillery battery, as well as the differing march speed of infantry and cavalry formations. More eccentric elements, such as the commanders' efficiency, could be expressed in numbers, to be inserted as inputs in the various operations of the open-ended algorithms defining the conduct of the game.

It was all very basic mathematics, clearly readable (and even easily modifiable, if the players agreed), easily manageable and written very quickly by the designers starting from historical interpretation, as well as common sense or direct personal military experience. Also, after just a few plays and a bit of mathematical study, inherent probabilities of success or failure could be immediately calculated, giving players a comfortable sense of general control and risk containment.

Even this randomness, and this is a fundamental aspect, was not at all arbitrary. We are not speaking of *Risk!*-like combat resolution in which the highest roll always wins, regardless of tactical conditions and in a totally symmetrical environment. Statistics in simulation games, be they historical or fictional, is always pondered and moderated by the historical vision of the events followed by the game designer himself: that is why, for example, WWI games' CRTs are very different from those of wargames set in the Napoleonic era or during WWII. Or should be, as Dunnigan had pointed out.

For all its practical value and immediate accessibility, however, a purely quantitative approach could not produce totally satisfactory results all by itself. In war, and more generally in the real world, there are countless irrational elements that have a profound consequence over the course of the events, and true simulation games could not ignore this fundamental aspect. After all, Friction cannot be expressed just by modifying a numerical value or a generic modifier, since even the most capable units have a single tactical weak point and sometimes the very same terrain can have totally different effects on the behaviour of the military formations operating over it.

All of these "vagaries" form the second, *qualitative* approach. This is a method of defining the simulation parameters much more tied to personal interpretations of the historical factors by the game designers.

As such, it leads to a much more flexible and extensive representation of the varied dynamics leading to the final succession of events. This allows authors to include non-kinetic factors, divergent political objectives, asymmetrical tactical behaviours, imponderable events with deep consequences, even psychological deviations of single individuals.

One of the very first applications of the qualitative approach came into the refusal of a tacit "golden rule" of the first generations of wargames: the 3:1 ratio. Considered in conventional doctrine to be the best balance between attacking and defending forces, this ratio has become something of a goal in itself for old-time wargamers, trying their best to obtain the fatidic last combat point needed to reach this magic proportion in a CRT. The qualitative approach broke this convention, responding to the multiple doctrinal doubts about its universal validity and the possibility of determining with sufficient certainty what really constitutes that "3" and that "1" in a force ratio, considering elements such as force multipliers, contingency modifiers and more elaborated forms of Friction.

Another qualitative element in wargames is the fog of war, which is limited or distorted intelligence over the actual position and composition of the enemy (and in some cases even friendly!) forces. This mechanic is at the base of block games like *Hammer of the Scots* (Columbia Games) or *Holdfast: Eastfront* (Worthington) in which the features of the units are discovered only at the moment of actual contact, and it could also be used to determine the actual tactical capabilities of units on the battlefield at the very last moment, like in *Sekigahara* (GMT Games) or *Friedrich* (Histogame, Figure 1.3).

The real value, however, is much greater than that of a simple expedient to introduce other, more extravagant forms of Friction or uncertainty. British historian and game scholar Philip Sabin expertly described in his essay *Simulating Wars* how simulation games contribute to forming an interpretation of events not tied to rigid and simplistic quantitative estimates, regularly confuted by the final developments of many historical conflicts.[21]

This fundamental paradigm shift, however, does not come without its distinctive set of pitfalls. The most glaring critical issue is that with all its flexibility and the

FIGURE 1.3 *Holdfast: Eastfront* (Worthington). Block-games use a simple mechanic to recreate fog of war on traditional wargame maps.

Source: Photograph by the author.

mere extension of its possible applications, it is also the most susceptible to distortions, false interpretations or historiographical *lacunae*.

With all these advantages and disadvantages in mind, it could then be hard to understand in which cases a quantitative approach is better used rather than a qualitative one, and even when the obvious solution of combining them into a single simulation design process come to mind, how could we determine a good balance point between them?

By following Caffrey's conclusions about the nature of simulation and adopting a third, unexpected and comprehensive approach, of course: a *functional* approach.

With this term we can define a design method focused on conscious and cleverly established joint action of quantitative as well as qualitative elements in the Flow of simulation. To put it more simply, game designers will choose what solution to adopt judging on a case-by-case basis, in an effort to reach a "best of both worlds" scenario.

Obvious as it might seem, this approach is surely the hardest one to follow, especially if an author wants to create a properly balanced yet historically satisfying system.

Sure, an attractive solution could be the adoption of a rigorous "design for effect" approach (trying to represent in the game only the consequences of the player decisions, with only an indirect depiction of all the intermediate steps of the events) instead of a "design for detail" (creating rules for the purpose of directly reproducing every single moment of the action) style.

Chrome, the technical term for all the mass of these modifiers and small rules specifications, is a very crucial element in simulation design: too much chrome will kill you, as many players say, but also too little does no good to a simulation.[22]

Other designers decided to adopt something of a middle road, the so-called hidden complexity. Formally theorized for the first time by Italian designer Andrea Angiolino, game scholar and among other things author of the highly successful *Wings of Glory* aerial combat series, this specific style is based on a clever combination of game elements, rules economy and components distribution in order to make the games more intuitive, apparently simpler and more accessible for the player, while maintaining a lot of historical detail hidden "under the hood" of the single mechanics. For example, in Angiolino's system, all the planes have specific sets of maneuver cards that include characteristic moves depending on the single model: in this way, the player's spectrum of choices will be limited to the actual historical flying behaviour of that plane, without the need for clunky additional rules and sub-conditions. It goes without saying that good hidden complexity games are exponentially harder to design than highly detailed and openly complex titles.

Other solutions for obtaining a better functional result are advanced visual interfaces, immersive elements borrowed from role-playing or highly narrative games, even hybridization with specific Eurogames mechanics . . . but it is never simple to create a playable and involving game avoiding rigid quantitative rules and uncharacteristic qualitative elements, while also maintaining both a high accessibility and a sufficient historical value.

And, by introducing more innovative solutions, sometimes even inspired by the much dreaded "Eurogames bunch", there always is a great danger lurking in the dark: the "Is it a wargame or not?" dilemma, a persistent and regularly recurring debate within the wargaming community which will be extensively covered in the chapter dedicated to the many different approaches of wargame design.

Thus, the struggle for new forms of simulation, that is more effective algorithms through which reproduce the features and dynamics of past historical events, still carries on. A testament, as well as an ongoing challenge, for the most ancient and at the same time the most advanced form of games ever devised by the human mind: those games that want to take their players out of the material world with the declared purpose of depicting those same worlds.

A paradox we have yet to solve.

1.4 THE SIMULATION FLOW

As we have seen, it is fairly easy to describe Aristoteles' *Petteia* as an interesting allegory for the Greek hoplitic style of linear warfare, as well as a fun and engaging boardgame, but by no means could it be considered a proper simulation, not even as a remote precursor.

In the same way, it would be quite hard to indicate *Chess* as a direct representation of linear warfare, going beyond just some evocative similitudes. At the very best, one could say that some military episodes might be defined as "*Chess*-like confrontations": that is, that the battle itself could get close to a *Chess* match in a curious reversal process between reality and games, or even better that the general experience of *Chess* (a broadly symmetrical confrontation, wherein the final outcome might depend on a single easily identifiable move and its subsequent chain of consequences) might be used as a narrative instrument to describe the specific features of that single event.

No one would then venture to say that *Chess* is a perfect representation of all linear battles of human history, since *intuitively* we invariably come to the conclusion that there is so much more in warfare and military history than perfect, clockwork maneuvers and clear fixed chains of events, even without the need for thinkers like von Clausewitz or great commanders like von Moltke.

This method, however, while quick at telling us what simulation is not, suffers from the disadvantage of not being equally accurate at describing what simulation really is. We could understand that the game is just an emulation of a given situation, or at the very most an allegory of some of its dynamics . . . but in order to realize at first glance, starting from no previous data, that a certain game we have just met is a simulation of any kind we need a more powerful approach: an *analytical* method.

In other words, we have to define a conceptual structure of how a simulation works, some formal parameters to face with our direct experience of the game in question, with requirements to be met and steps to be present.

It would be very tempting to solve this problem by indicating single "features" that a game must have to gain the coveted title of simulation. Those features might be as broad as documented historical research, orders of battle, bibliographies, topographical representations . . . or very specific like hexes, rigid or non-rigid zones of control, force ratios, chain of command modifiers, linear supply rules . . . and so on, and so on.

This fragmented and granular approach, however, fails at recognizing the immense diversity of the wargaming and simulation hobby by basing its results only on the search for this or that specific mechanic. Once again, we get back to the old "It's not a wargame" conclusion, with the consequence of describing *COIN* titles just as "thematic boardgames" and not "proper simulations of actual conflicts" only because the players move generic wooden blocks without specific unit IDs on the map.

What we need, instead, is a careful scientific instrument targeted at consciously broadening, rather than arbitrarily restricting, the field of simulation games in order to include even the more eccentric, hybrid, multidimensional and non-linear titles.

Possibly, the best way to reach this result is by adopting a formal structure of concepts, based only on universal elements of the simulation experience, framed into a single cohesive cognitive and emotive process: what we could call "The Simulation Flow".[23]

Our first step consists of creating a sequence of isolated moments that, put together, give us the image and feeling of the intellectual and psychological motion created by playing simulation games. A motion that is not to be regarded as a rigid line of discreet events, exclusively dependent on the previous "step", but rather as an ongoing process with a constant back and forth oscillation, with the various elements of a game having different "development speeds" in this flow and even different perceptions by the single players who might enjoy totally different and even diverging experiences even during the same game.

In essence, the Flow starts with the most intuitive aspect of simulation, also present in the primal form of emulation: *Reproduction* of the reference events. This is what we get when we first look at the very cover art of a wargame box, with an attractive picture dominated by a mix of historical soldiers, vehicles, battle scenes accompanied by a catching title not dissimilar to what we would find in a hypothetical war movie. By opening the box, then, we would be faced with an even stronger sense of historical reconstruction, thanks to very specific objects that we immediately identify with military activity such as maps, counters with NATO symbols, statistical tables, a rulebook, scenario briefings and so on.

This tactile and visual first impact has a strong effect on our conscious perceptions and even more on our unconscious mental processes, because we are immediately pulled inside that specific event. By laying out the maps, placing the counters on the fixed setup positions, examining the battle lines and pondering over the results tables we have a gigantic picture of the "real" situation, feeling and even more expecting it to be "just like the actual thing" of the Battle of Zama, the Wars of the Roses or Operation Barbarossa.

For however delusionary, fallible and even outright misleading this approach might be, considering the impossibility of having sufficiently accurate and reliable historical information and of including all those data in a playable model, it is useless to hide the fact that it is precisely this irresistible pull that attracts people into historical gaming since the early days of childhood: the idea of having a powerful instrument capable of recreating the historical reality in order to transport you back to a past that you are curious to discover or feel a particular emotional attachment to.

This first, strong moment is, however, left behind when a player starts moving units and rolling dice: that is when the game is finally on, the players start making decisions and the static initial Reproduction gives way to the more mobile and interactive *Representation*.

This is a crucial passage, however, that must not be interpreted in an excessively literal way. In a sense, the formal historical value of a wargame ends with the very first move of the very first turn since that move will invariably be different from its historical counterpart. And even if that first move were just the same as the historical one, the second move will be different, or the third one . . . unless the players mechanically repeat the historical decisions one by one from the start to the end of the scenario, creating a "re-enactment" and betraying the fundamental element of games enunciated by Huizinga in *Homo Ludens*: freedom of choice.

What is left, then, is something much more important than simple recreation of past events. Representation allows players to act in a very different way but still within the boundaries of actual historical dynamics, at least as the author knows and interprets those dynamics. Their actions will stay free and not predetermined by anyone, but still in the realm of feasibility and coherent within the given scenario, as regulated by the game mechanics and the mathematical interactions of all the game elements. For however much this can depress me, I will never be able to obtain an Italian breakthrough of the Austro-Hungarian lines when I am playing a wargame about Caporetto.

The study of these dynamics not through their historically verified applications, but through the verification of alternative decision paths still following those same premises and cause-consequence processes, gives to simulation games their counterfactual value, which is also one of their most interesting features from an historiographic point of view. Through those alternative yet extensively documented and convincingly demonstrated processes, simulation games use the decision-making freedom given to their players not to "reverse" or "change" history, but rather to know it and understand it better from different perspectives.

This is because Representation is by definition a free application of human behaviour, yet included in a clearly recognizable and conceptually coherent framework. In our case, the ruleset inspired and aimed at reproducing historical elements, and the accurately designed and thoroughly researched scenario parameters like setup, orders of battle, specific contingencies and victory conditions form the "stage" upon which players move to fulfil their roles as they see fit, while still inside an acceptably plausible environment.

It is precisely in this moment that we leave emulation behind, and begin seeing the very first traces of simulation.

In order to get free of allegory and deep symbolism, even if their cultural value and importance should not be ignored nor understated,[24] however, the Simulation Flow has to take a final step: *Repetition*.

With this term, at last, we indicate exactly what distinguishes *Petteia* from a module of the *Great Battles of History* (GMT) series: that is the fact that the results of a game can be carried out from one session to the next, carefully evaluated, thoroughly studied, and later re-verified through other sessions with similar or opposite parameters. In a word, repeated.

This possibility is the great gift of the statistical base of simulation games, however simple or complex they may be. This happens since all game values, their reciprocate relations and the instruments given to the players in order to manipulate them with the purpose of satisfying pre-set victory conditions all have a mathematical nature in common, that allows them to be re-executed as many times as needed.

In this way the players will be able to exploit their game experiences in the real world, transporting the conclusions obtained during the game into the actual reality (with all due caution . . .). This reapplication apparently breaks Huizinga's fundamental law of separation between the game world and the real world, but at a closer study it can be easily reconducted in his notion of games as the quintessential form of culture, a powerful instrument devised by human beings to gain a much better and higher understanding of how reality and life actually work. All games create separate worlds, but those same games are still played by people who live in this world, and some games have this world as their object.

This process is of course much more important in a professional wargame environment, wherein the hypothetical scenarios provide their player with very specific insights that could be immediately reapplied into the actual reference situations: in other words, teaching the young Alexander how to best use his phalanxes long before the Granicus or Gaugamela.

Speaking of civilian hobby wargaming, of course learning the best way to keep your hold on the Imperial Crown as the Habsburgs during the Thirty Years War, or how to destroy the US Navy carrier fleet in the Battle of Midway as Admiral Yamamoto has no direct utility in our real world . . . and, yet, keeping your head straight when Gustavus Adolphus obtains victory after victory over you and staying focused to your true objectives in a limited and constantly changing situation are virtues and teachings directly applicable into real situations: their utility should not be summarily dismissed (Figure 1.4).

Reproduction → Representation → Repetition

FIGURE 1.4   The basic Simulation Flow.

So, Reproduction, Representation and Repetition form the Flow that can be seen as an exclusive feature of simulation, so much that they can be regarded as a good tell-tale sign of the nature of a game: if you have all three, you have a simulation. Yet, as we have said, considering them just as three separate A-B-C sequenced moments would give much too rigid and linear an image of this fundamental process.

To get things moving, we then need another subset of forces driving forward our Flow and creating a truly dynamic experience, worthy to be called a "game" and not just a theorical (and, frankly, quite boring) re-enactment of historical events. These forces operate before, between and even after the three main steps, linking them and taking the player from one to another during the course of one or even multiple different sessions.

The first one acts even before the beginning of the Flow, as a fundamental premise: the *historical research* that lays the foundation for the creation of the game itself by the designer and developers . . . but also creates the required mindset by the players for choosing to begin the experience. It is, in fact, this often overlooked fragment of the simulation game experience that provides the fundamental first spark, the intellectual stimulus (be it cultural curiosity, the desire for entertainment, the drive for this specific form of inter-personal aggregation . . .) that leads people to dedicate time to a hobby that implies leaving the real world for a parallel, imaginary one, as well as to choose a specific wargame instead of another. However deep the level of this research might be, it is undeniable that recreating historical dynamics with a variable yet always sufficient level of accuracy is considered a necessity for historical simulation games enthusiasts, up to the point of preferring an imbalanced yet well-researched game truly reflecting the actual asymmetrical field conditions rather than a more "fun" but excessively abstracted ruleset.

While historical research is a fundamental part of the introduction of historical elements in a simulation, another passage is required to transition from static Reproduction to more dynamic Representation. Something that more directly involves the human factors of the equation, giving them the necessary freedom of action shifting everything towards a proper game environment: *player agency*. It is only through the creation of a not-predetermined decision space that we pass from just re-enacting historical events in a dry emulation process to having a true interactive simulation of them. This decision space moves and operates by the rules set in the system (rules that can be freely changed if all players agree, by the way . . .), but those rules at most dictate the ways in which the Flow should move and adjudicate the consequences of the various tactical and strategic choices of all players involved. Those choices remain up to the players themselves, though, since this is the fundamental feature of having a game. On the opposite, a game with too few meaningful decisions to make, or even worse too much scripting due to obvious and unavoidable player choices that clearly must be made in order to win, is often considered "not a game anymore".

This, however, helps us understand why even the more indiscriminate and personally satisfying freedom of action in a simulation game would be totally useless if the next transition passage from Representation to Repetition is missed: receiving *plausible outcomes* from the game. This is the real objective of the players' decision to play in the first place, seeing the situation develop in meaningful and believable ways according to their own knowledge and understanding of the simulated events: you can accept losing, but you should lose in an historically sound way. Those outcomes might even be heavily biased in favour of a specific faction (once again, think of Caporetto, Waterloo, the last days of World War Two . . .), but even this seemingly negative feature is welcomed by experienced players if the situation requires and those biases reflect the historical reality: a fundamental distinction of simulation games in respect to other forms of boardgames usually having balanced victory probabilities as an indispensable landmark.

Eventually, the repeated use of simulation games leads them to obtain the status of "reference titles" for a specific battle or historical event, or even to the much coveted "classic game" status: this is the perceived *validity as a model* for a simulation that truly marks its success, inspires successive variations and evolutions, ensures and in a way starts the entire Flow again for the new players taking their turn at the gaming table.

The expanded Flow diagram truly reflects this optimal situation and can finally give us an adequate, even if just conceptual, image of what a simulation looks like (Figure 1.5).

This is by no means the only way to depict the nature of this very elusive beast, and one of the most amazing aspects of simulation games is that many more alternative structures might be easily traced and should be regarded as equally valid. They also serve as another testament to the high internal diversity of the nature of simulation games and of the many parallel approaches to their study.

In some of my previous works on the subject, for example, I proposed a much simpler set of general "Rules" pertaining to the simulation experience, that are still good at drawing an outline of the subjective, psychological aspect of the issue.

By this framework, wargames and simulation games in general should give three positive things to the those who play them: Engagement, Knowledge and Awareness.[25] *Engagement* is what drives people to begin their journey into the world of simulation games and to carry on walking in a substantially more difficult path than those of other kinds of boardgames: expecting strong emotions, compelling narrations and interactive decision-making processes with constant challenges to overcome. *Knowledge* is at the same time a fundamental prerequisite as a very positive by-product of the simulative experience, prompting people to read historical essays and make personal research on the events before, during and even after the gaming

Historical Research   *Validity as a Model*

Reproduction → **Representation** → **Repetition**

Player Agency   *Plausible Outcomes*

FIGURE 1.5 A more complete rendition of the Simulation Flow.

sessions themselves. *Awareness* is a much broader form of comprehending not just the historical facts and dynamics materially depicted in a specific game, but to obtain deeper insights even on similar contemporary situations and get access to cognitive instruments useful at deciphering our own modern reality by a better understanding of analog events that occurred in the past.

Those three elements are typical features of a simulation, and their collective framework provides an interesting corollary to the Simulation Flow theory just described, with a particular attention to subjective and psychological issues.

On the other hand, focusing even more on what a wargame (but in a broader sense any game that effectively tries to simulate history) is and, especially, what it can do, Philip Sabin proposes still another set of factors:

> It is this combination of mathematical modelling and active decision inputs that gives wargames their unique potential as a source of insight into armed conflict, since the combination mirrors the dual character of war itself as a set of physical realities in terms of force capabilities that is given life only by the interacting strategies of the competing antagonists.[26]

Mathematical relations and players' decision spaces are here considered by Sabin in a functional approach, as instruments for gaining a better knowledge of historical dynamics and cause-consequence chains. The human element, however, remains central because it is the interplay of "the interacting strategies of the competing antagonists" that really gives life to what instead would remain just a bunch of statistical data, no more interesting than a lifeless spreadsheet. Further theories would expand this definition to include not just the utilitarian choices made by the participants in order to simply reach the objective of satisfying victory conditions, but also an intertwined mutual narration of the same events.

A reciprocal storytelling like this has been seldom seen in such strength in the entire history of games, but it should come as no surprise since telling stories is exactly what simulation games excel in, and in some respects is the actual main purpose for their existence.[27] It should also be said that, unlike in other purely narrative games, this storytelling is not necessarily shared by all players, both in quality and quantity: the same game can give very different images of the simulated to each of its players, leaving them free to elaborate in their own way all the inputs received during play.

Sabin, however, very aptly takes the reader back to the true purpose of simulation games: recreating history and giving precious insights about it to those who play them, stimulating both their intellectual curiosity as well as their creative imagination.

The last and most effective synthesis of all, anyway, has been made by none other than James F. Dunnigan himself:

> A wargame is a combination of "game," history, and science. It is a paper time machine.[28]

With these three elements, the freedom of games, the accuracy of history and the clever use of applied statistical sciences, wargames and historical games in general reach their highest point of perfection. Crafting them is indeed "just a kind of magic", and another great expert on their nature, game designer and researcher Greg

Costikyan, justly described this activity as nothing short of "a form of art", different from any other:[29] a perfect expression combining study, experience and plain creativity, in a sense closing the great circle initiated by Johan Huizinga and his definition of art as the highest form of what we sometimes derisively call "just a game".

In these essential sentences we see once again the base elements of simulation games in action, randomness, allegory and combinations: elements moving by mutual relations dictated by pondered randomness inspired by a study of past events and put together with the clear purpose of recreating it, even by proposing alternative versions of what is perceived as "real history".

Whatever these two last words may stand for.

1.5 THE THREE REALMS OF SIMULATION

After having given a broad image of the concept of simulation both from an historical and an analytical point of view, it would seem that this particular element of our study has been sufficiently exposed. Leaving things like that, however, would give a fragmented and frankly inconclusive image of the issue, since those two methods, while being valuable and adequately accurate *per se*, would still be unconnected and sometimes even contradictory. Even worse, we could be led to think that the shift between qualitative, quantitative and functional conceptions of simulation pertains to a specific chronological succession, so that for example Aristoteles had no idea of how a simulation really worked in an organic logical structure, or that it was only Leibniz that really put all the elements together thanks to his mathematical genius.

In other words, it is much more complicated than a simple series of different phases: as in every other part of human culture there is no direct and linear evolution even regarding the concept of simulation, only unending discussion and re-elaboration.

We then need a third, more synthetic approach to the matter, something that could transcend both time and logic of our study, and for this we have to call to the scene another aspect of human perception: poetic imagery.

As our ancestors of old, when we are at a loss at describing a very complex object of our existence, we need to resort to our greatest creative assets and try to create a new mythology. Thus, by using rationalized allegories and similitudes, we could obtain a coherent picture from where to start our successive reasoning: in a sense, we could create a simulation of simulation itself.

We could then start to imagine ourselves as engaged in a long and always surprising journey through remote, unknown lands with the task of understanding what this strange wonder of simulation actually is.

In our travel, not unlike Ulysses or Marco Polo, we would face many perils and deviations—as the tradition of epic poems requires—but in the end we will be able to visit three mysterious kingdoms, the Three Realms of Simulation.[30]

The first one to encounter is the Realm of Deterministic Simulation. Perfectly rational and totally devoid of any random deviation due to dice rolling or card drawing, this kind of simulation relies on purely mathematical relations, so abstract that even statistics functions cannot touch them. The usual form of games of this Realm is that of a grid board, just like *Chess* or *Checkers* and thus the square could be seen as their ideal symbol.

Here the game proceeds through distinct and very easily recognizable stages, thanks to perfectly defined and usually identical moves available to the pieces of the two players. A black rook would move just as a white rook, a single white piece in *Go* has the same value as every other black piece and this would be valid also for single pieces making seemingly "eccentric" maneuvers such as the knight's "jump" or entire games in which the single pieces have different fighting values such as in *Shoji*, in which however every player has the same exact distribution of forces. True, there will always be interesting variations like the deeply asymmetrical *Hnefatafl*, the so-called *Viking Chess* game in which the two players have very different victory conditions to satisfy . . . but almost all the pieces will still be allowed to make the very same moves.

The most essential feature of this kind of simulation, however, is the almost total absence of external randomness—the inclusion of unexpected outcomes for the players' decisions outside the same players' abilities themselves. A piece will always capture another piece no matter what, a move will always be executed in the planned way, a turn will always be carried out in the exact same sequence, as long as everyone dutifully follows the rules of the game.

In formal yet simple terms, given the prerequisite conditions determined by the rules, A will eliminate B: no die roll or special card will be there to include any variation, whether directly or indirectly manipulable by any of the players, or even represented through totally independent "special events". This is a very deliberate choice made when *Chaturaji* lost its dice and went on to become *Shatranji*, then *Shamat*, then *Chess*.

The by-product of this development, however, is a total (almost fatal) detachment of this kind of simulation from reality itself, since randomness and unexpected deviations are essential parts of what we call "real life", and this is true for individual human beings as well as for entire nations and empires. So big is this detachment that in many cases these games could not be considered true simulations, but mere allegorical or at best emulation games.[31]

This does not mean that they are deprived of any strategic value, nor that they are not intellectually challenging experiences. For all their usual relative simplicity (even if there are numerous exceptions on this regard) those games tend to be perceived as very complex forms of entertainment, so much that—for example, and regardless of what Edgar Allan Poe would argue—*Chess* is still today considered the "thinking man's game", the intellectual challenge *par excellence*. And the same could be said for many much more recent German-style boardgames, usually considered higher forms of strategy because the absence of dice allegedly avoids random and totally uncontrollable events ruining the perfect rational thinking of the players.

Their complexity, however, is purely *mechanical*, that is relying only on the mere quantity of fixed variations to be considered in order to play them at an adequate level of competency, and the involved virtue for the players would be that of *resistance*, that is applying a direct opposition to the other players' will with their own open moves.

Still taking *Chess* as the perfect example for this Realm, the different combinations of moves on the board after a single decision by your opponent can be perfectly calculated up to the very last number . . . the only problem is that this number is almost infinite and only very few individuals (and high-efficiency computers) can elaborate all these variations. But in this gigantic "decision tree" there will always be an optimal move and finding it while at the same time hoping that your opponent fails to do the same is what keeps *Chess* from becoming just a very sophisticated and much more tedious version of *Tic-Tac-Toe*.

But what if you want to go beyond abstraction and idealized visions of what a conflict is, and especially what if you want to reproduce not "any" conflict—real or hypothetical—but a single, very specific and historically recognizable one? In that case you need to provide for some conditional modifiers other than symbolic special moves, pieces or terrain cases: you need dice or cards (or both) . . . even better, you need randomness.

As we have seen, we are not dealing with any arbitrary randomness à la *Risk!* here, but with a rationalized, pondered set of statistical variables, defined by the features of the represented (or "simulated") period in question. And since those features are often not universally known, but the subject for endless historiographical debates themselves, you will define them at the best of your knowledge, but also under the lens of your personal interpretation of the period itself. You, as the game designer, will be in charge, you will be responsible for deciding the distribution of results on a 3:1 force ratio column, a +1 or +2 modifier for rough terrain and its effect on the line of sight of long-range weapons, whether a wood grants one or two column shifts on the CRT and if that variable applies to every kind of unit.

In short, it is clear that we have entered the second Realm, the one of Probabilistic Simulation. This is the home country of traditional wargames, a sub-genre of simulation games graced by a very strong following still today and the symbol of which cannot be anything else but the classic hexagon of the "hex and counter" games.

Here, contrary to what it seems, nothing is left to chance, not even chance itself, since what we have seen so far is not the arbitrary *alea* to which Eurogames and German-style boardgames players point out as a factor of a general "lack of strategic value" in wargames, but a very thorough and scientifically sound historical interpretation of the simulated events by the game designer.

In this Realm, A will eliminate B . . . but only at certain conditions that depend on the internal coherence of the proposed scenario, be it historical, hypothetical or even fictional. Was the offensive equipment effective and accurate enough? Was the training of the attacking unit high enough to overtake a position within a certain range of probabilities? Was the unit in supply?

Yes, you always need to throw just a die on a table . . . but that table is constantly changing before your eyes, as well as the distribution of all the different results, and this depends not on arbitrary combinations but on the actual characteristics of the specific tactical situation represented on the table. A perfect example of this kind of simulation game is the venerable *Advanced Squad Leader* system (Avalon Hill), in which essentially every possible event has its own rule, probabilistic table and specific modifier to a die roll somewhere, up to the overheating of a machine gun barrel, a tank engine stopping to work or an Allied soldier being capable of crossing a river on a raft without drowning during Operation Market Garden: it's no surprise that *ASL* is considered the quintessential classical wargame treatment of WWII.

That was precisely Dunnigan's goal in writing that fateful piece to Avalon Hill: giving new relevance to the human factor of the game designer. His later company SPI would be famous for the importance given to its authors as well as to all those developers and playtesters that contributed to the many successful titles in its catalogue. This would spring an atmosphere of great artistic freedom, as well as extreme experimentalism personified by great characters like John Young and Al Nofi. Avalon Hill and other companies indirectly benefitted from this approach, too, nurturing real talents like John Hill, John Prados and others.[32]

But Dunnigan also provided room for yet another factor in the simulation equation: that of the players themselves. Since this randomness is not at all arbitrary, thus subject to direct human manipulation, and most of all is totally known to all the parties involved, it is clear that the players will do whatever they can in order to obtain a more favourable outcome distribution.

Sometimes there will be no all-encompassing optimized solution, forcing the players to accept varying degrees of calculated risk management or even daring push-your-luck moments . . . but the manipulation of the different variables to minimize the possibilities of failure while maximizing those of success, and even the provision of back-up plans in case everything goes wrong, constitute the true intellectual value of those games.[33]

All this constitutes the real complexity of those games, notwithstanding the actual weight of their rules: a *dynamic* complexity, that involves the balance of many different factors inside the statistical environment defined by the game designer and his or her personal interpretation of the simulated historical events. Considering the immense possibilities granted by an open map covered by tens of different counters, each of them with its peculiar set of values and abilities, will lead to the necessity of showing a great *resilience* to find as many different solutions as possible against the opponent's equally variable and meditated attempts to do the same in his or her advantage. This overall flexibility in players' behaviours, compounded with the availability of multiple lines of action of comparable effectiveness in an extensive decision space for all the participants to the games, holds true even if some of those parameters are freely changed by the players themselves through variations and house rules.

The argument of variations and diversified player input, however, brings us to the borders of the Second Realm . . . and beyond. Now we are entering a very dark, mysterious and somewhat undecipherable land, indeed.

This is where the many facets of world perception converge and diverge at the same time, where the infinite diversities and similarities of reality add up, multiply and nullify themselves. Where a victory on the battlefield leads to a final defeat on a peace table, where the economic trend of a country might depend on the action of an almost unknown political agent in another.

In short, this is the third, most elusive country we will be visiting in our journey: the Realm of Non-Linear Simulation. By this term we allude to all those games that are based on highly innovative and alternative game systems, whose inspiration comes from the most recent historical as well as strategic studies on the many connections between military, political, economic and cultural issues. Here you will find titles like *Twilight Struggle* (GMT), in which every single move supporting this local leader or provoking this specific brush war might lead you to gain political hegemony in South America or detonating the final thermonuclear apocalypse on Earth, on a domino effect of global proportions. Or a game belonging to the *COIN* series (still by GMT), in which you will find unsuspected analogies between the Viet Cong and the American revolutionaries, or between the Gaul resistance against Julius Caesar and the unending conflicts troubling Afghanistan.

The great strength of these titles, as it is evident, is their ability to simulate events and dynamics at various levels, often interconnected with one another and always subject to the most variegated player decision processes, whose intent will be to exploit every possible opportunity and discover unexpected crossings between highly inhomogeneous assets. That is why a good symbol for this Realm might be the all-encompassing circle, whereby even the smallest element is tied together with a whole world and capable of generating unpredictable changes all over the board.

The challenge coming into play here is then an *organic complexity* of not just understanding the precise nature of all those relations between the diverse factors, nor just trying to make profit of the various probabilistic occurrences of certain events and sub-events . . . rather to "feel" the trends of what is happening on the board at different levels and "catch the moment" to turn the opponent's apparent advantage into his or her fatal weak point.

Card-driven games such as *We the People* and *Hannibal: Rome vs. Carthage* (Avalon Hill), negotiation titles like *Churchill* and *Versailles 1919* (GMT), as well as hybrid boardgames like *Wallenstein* (Queen Games) or *300: Earth and Water* (Bonsai Games) are all part of this weird and incredibly interesting family of simulations in which A will be able to eliminate B . . . but only if A's position on the political track is sufficiently higher than B's predominance in the economic field. If it sounds confusing, it is because it actually is, and one of the greatest problems of these titles is avoiding muddling the water too much for their players' "situational awareness".

All these strategic reasonings require a very peculiar talent from the players: that of *adaptation* of their own strategies to infinite surprises, opportunities and setbacks that will be the norm.

In the end, and maintaining *Chess* as our reference point, we have shifted from the classic game of white and black pieces, to a much more dynamic and challenging probabilistic version of the game with pieces of varied quality and strength, to a very weird game played on three parallel chessboards, each with its own set of rules and victory conditions. All these three different types of simulation games are just as fun, only they provide very different kinds of fun and, most of all, very different (but not at all incompatible, and even quite often complimentary with each other) renditions of reality and history.

At this point of the study, the reader might be excused in thinking that all those domains, as different and contradictory as they seem to be, are discreet portions of the greater category of simulation games. That is, a game could be firmly established into one of those "boxes", without having any meaningful relationship with games outside it, nor being in any way comparable to titles belonging to other types.

The fact is, however, that reality is not known for its love of small conceptual "boxes" of any kind.

In other words, those games do enjoy constant comparisons, confrontations and evaluations against their counterparts living in other Realms, often finding ideal correspondences, whether universally recognized or not. A very probabilistic Napoleonic wargame like the relevant title of the *La Bataille* series might find itself compared to a *Jours de Gloire* series module, characterized by a more non-linear random activation mechanic. And, yes, there will always be someone who will compare (rightfully or not, your choice) the aforementioned *ASL* to the much lighter, and yet no less simulative, even if for unexpected reasons, *Undaunted* (Osprey Games).

This confirms, rather than refuting, the highly versatile and diversified nature of simulation games that can, through very different game design solutions and stylistic choices, represent the same exact event under many different (yet equally valid, from an historiographical point of view) aspects, now highlighting this or that other element. Once again, how many totally different games can we have on the Battle of the Bulge? At least as many as the history books dedicated to this crucial military campaign we have available on the market, right now.

But the highest proof of it all is the fact that sometimes even the same game can belong to different domains!

A very recent example on this regard is *Fighters of the Pacific* (Capsicum Games). In this simple and attractive wargame, players move their planes over the enemy carriers and bases to torpedo or bomb one after the other through fixed moves, dealing pre-established amounts of damage to their targets. The result is a mass of apparently totally deterministic dogfights and bombing runs, with no possible unpredictable or randomized variation possible . . . but there is so much more than what meets the eye in this amazing system.

The trick here is that each fighter has access to specific moves and attacks related to its historical performance, that the ever-crucial initiative order can be decided and manipulated by clever players, that the disaggregation or concentration of flying formations can lead to greater flexibility or better coordination all over the gigantic "furball" fights developing on a very classic hex-grid map. With no die in sight over the horizon.

The net result is a game with deterministic mechanics yet fundamentally inspired by probabilistic renditions of the aircraft flying and offensive features, and also so many of these different details playing all at once generating an undeniably non-linear experience. It's just like playing classic *Chess* with asymmetrical pieces and so many different levels of decision making that you cannot go hunting for the perfect optimal move: you have to decide where to commit a mistake at every single impulse of play, hoping that the opponent does not notice it and does not exploit your error . . . but in order to do so, even the enemy will have to expose his or her forces in another way.

All this harmonious coexistence of diverse simulation domains in a single title is explicable if we consider the fundamental distinction between *mechanics* and *dynamics* in game design. The former is created by the single rule that governs a specific aspect of the simulation such as a CRT for combat, a terrain chart for moving, a command span for dealing with army control and communication, hidden block games to recreate fog of war, et cetera. The latter happen when the single mechanics are put into relationship with each other and constitute the most evident part of the gaming experience, forming the veritable "flow of the game": CRTs and terrain charts create the ebb and flow of classic hex and counters wargames, variable sequence of turn and action menu give you the unpredictability of *COIN* titles, deck-building and a bucket of dice take you back to the typically late Roman power gathering and constant backstabbing of *Time of Crisis* (GMT), and so on. Mechanics are the carefully calibrated gears of a rules system, dynamics are the interaction of those gears creating the movement of the game itself.

And, as we have just seen, it is then possible for a game to have totally deterministic mechanics, inspired by probabilistic representations of the general behaviour of your assets and producing non-linear game dynamics in order to represent the historical nature of the simulated events.

In conclusion, the final challenges for the three different categories of simulation games (deterministic, probabilistic and non-linear) might be very different from each other—respectively, resource optimization, calculated risk management and interaction with other players and general strategic situation—but their three Realms have many hidden passages between them, are much more interconnected than what it seems, sometimes are even overlapping one above the other . . . and sometimes they are just the same single territory: the Unified Realm of Simulation.

NOTES

1 Such was the conviction of the great anthropologist and ludologist Roger Caillois: "Je commencerai par le jeu. On peut définir le jeu comme une activité libre, réglée, conventionnelle, aléatoire, improductive et limitée, c'est-à-dire nettement séparée de la vie ordinaire et éprouvée comme telle. Or, si l'on s'en tient aux termes de cette définition, due d'abord à Huizinga et que j'ai eu l'occasion de discuter et de compléter, il est incontestable que les animaux jouent." ("I will begin with games. Games can be described as a free, regulated, conventional, aleatory, unproductive and limited—that is clearly separated from ordinary life and accepted as such—activity. Now, if we stand by the terms of this definition, as established by Huizinga and which I had the occasion to discuss and integrate, it is undeniable that animals play games"). Passing after that on describing the various forms of games played by games, related to general categories including among others "representational games". See Caillois, R., L'univers de l'animal et celui de l'homme (The universe of animals and the universe of men), *International Conference Le robot, la bête et l'homme* (*Robots, animals and men*) (Genève, 1965), but also his great work *Les jeux et les hommes*.

2 This comprises all diverse forms of acting, from religious ceremonies (for example, imitation crucifixions during the Easter festivities or "living" Nativities during Christmas, so common in Mediterranean cultures and clearly derived from previous more ancient, pre-Christian practices), to artistic and theatrical performances up to cosplaying anime figures.

3 Once again, Latin language makes a very definite distinction between informal and regulated play: the former is indicated by the term *lusus* while the latter by the word *ludus*. This fundamental divergence has been highlighted by many ludologists and anthropologists, starting with the aforementioned Roger Caillois.

4 You just need to look at the mass of sourcebooks and reference material dedicated to just a single setting of a fantasy or sci-fi role-playing game, often comparable if not superior in quantity and depth of analysis to historiographic material about real events, to appreciate the conceptual proximity between historical and fictional simulation.

5 A casual look to the many *Facebook* boardgaming groups or the first *BoardGameGeek* forum will be sufficient to understand that this prejudice against *alea* (i.e. dice rolling) is alive and well even a couple of millennia afterward.

6   The term *grognard* derives from the nickname of Napoleon Bonaparte's veteran soldiers.
    It stands for "grumbler", since only those soldiers fighting under the Little Corsican Cor-
    poral since the days of the first Campaign of Italy enjoyed the privilege of expressing their
    doubts and concerns about the emperor's decisions openly and in his presence. The term
    was later adopted in wargaming circles to indicate the truly dedicated and long-time war-
    gamers; nowadays it is (once again) considered a great honourific title for long-standing
    (and long-grumbling) members of the community.

7   This in an era in which the Templar Knights Rule written by Bernard of Clairvaux strongly
    limits the access to games for the members of the order, expressly forbidding the use of
    chessboards (Rule 317).

8   This is just a very general and cursory study of the many writings of these giants of human
    thinking, and their possible applications to modern game history. A more comprehen-
    sive explanation is included in Masini, R., From chessboard to mapboard, in *Conflicts of
    Interest Magazine*, n. 1, https://sdhist.com/conflicts-of-interest-zine/. Of course, further
    studies on such an extensive subject are needed.

9   A much more exhaustive analysis of these early versions as well as a useful classification
    of "wargame generations" can be found, respectively, in Peterson, J., A game out of all
    proportions: How a hobby miniaturized war, in *Zones of control: Perspectives on war-
    gaming*, The MIT Press (Cambridge, 2016) and Caffrey, M., *On wargaming*, U.S. Naval
    College, https://digital-commons.usnwc.edu/newport-papers/43/ (Newport, 2019).

10 Interestingly, apart from a few initial experiments by the Reisswitzes, the use of war-
    games to recreate historical battles dates to many decades after the birth of the original
    systems and was typical of civilian wargaming clubs.

11 Nimitz, C. W., *An address to NWC*, Chester W. Nimitz, USNWC Naval History Collec-
    tion (1960).

12 Angiolino very acutely traces a direct line of ideal continuity from Girolamo Cardano's
    De Ludo Aleae treaty on combinatorial statistics applied to a game of dice, up to Admiral
    Nimitz's famous and declared application of the "calculated risk" principle in operational
    planning. See Angiolino, A., Chi ha paura del dado cattivo? (Who's afraid of the big bad
    die?), in *ioGioco*, n. 30 (May 2023).

13 Dunnigan, J., *The complete wargames handbook*, p. 225.

14 Poe, E. A., *The murders in the rue Morgue*, Demetra (Colognola ai Colli, 2023).

15 It is worth remembering here that the Latin term *intelligo* means literally, "I gather differ-
    ent things together".

16 Poe, E. A., *The murders in the rue Morgue*.

17 Dunnigan, J., *The complete wargames handbook*, p. 225.

18 Recurrent phrase on the first-generation of Avalon Hill wargames, sometimes used also in
    later productions.

19 Dunnigan, J., *The complete wargames handbook*, p. 13.

20 On the limits of *Chess* not just as a simulation but also as a believable "image" of actual
    warfare, you can read Masini, R., *Gli scacchi e l'arte della guerra: mito e realtà* (*Chess
    and the art of war: Myth and reality*), https://www.goblins.net/articoli/scacchi-e-arte-
    della-guerra-mito-e-realta (2020). To the benefit of non-Italian language readers, in this
    article I used the Battle of Antietam as an example of the impossibility for *Chess* to rep-
    resent in their game dynamics the premises (the fortuitous fall of Robert E. Lee's march
    orders into Union hands), actual development (the incomprehensible tactical behaviour of
    Union commander, General MacClellan) and political consequences (the transformation
    of a draw into a "victory" by President Lincoln, in order to obtain a plausible precondition
    for the Emancipation Proclamation) of the historical military campaign.

21 Sabin described the results of a purely quantitative approach as "Lanchestrian equations",
    from the name of traditional historian Frederick Lanchester that in 1916 published a set
    of mathematical formulae capable of explaining the outcomes of every possible military

confrontation. For a more extensive study of a quality vs. quantity approach, see Sabin, P., *Simulating war: Studying conflict through simulation games*, Bloomsbury Academic (New York, 2012).

22 Sometimes, "chrome rules" are so extensive that they become a distinctive feature of a particular title. Such is the case of *Barbarossa Deluxe*, a game in which every turn begins with a series of different specific rules used to portrait the evolution of the Eastern Front campaign in WWII.

23 We are deeply in debt to Mihály Csíkszentmihályi's famous game Flow theory, here applied to simulation games.

24 On the relationship between games, allegories and symbols, Italian-speaking readers can find a very thorough and stimulating study in Sciarra, E., *Il simbolismo dei giochi* (*Symbolism and games*), Unicopli (Milano, 2017).

25 I understand that this sounds much better in Italian: *Coinvolgimento, Conoscenza e Consapevolezza*. Consequently I called this structure "The Three Cs Law" in Masini, S., Masini, R., *Le guerre di carta 2.0* (*Paper wars 2.0*), Unicopli (Milan, 2018).

26 Sabin, P., *Simulating war: Studying conflict through simulation games*, Bloomsbury Academic (New York, 2012), p. 75.

27 Not coincidentally, from this storytelling aspect of simulation came role-playing games, an offspring of wargames and historical boardgames in general. For more on this aspect, see Arnaudo, M., *Storytelling in the modern boardgame: Narrative trends from the late 1960s to today*, McFarland Publishing (Jefferson, 2018). As we will see, Arnaudo declaredly excludes wargames from his study, considering their narrative aspects highly peculiar and somewhat incomparable to those of other games.

28 Dunnigan, J., *The complete wargames handbook*, p. 13.

29 Costikyan, G., *I have no words & I must design*, contribution to the 2002 Computer Games and Digital Culture Conference [text available on www.costik.com].

30 Italian-speaking readers of my previous essay, *Il gioco di Arianna* (cit.), and those who were present during my online talk for the Georgetown University Wargaming Society, *Crossing the line: The hidden realm of non-linear simulation*, https://youtu.be/IqWMMg-gTGMY (2022), would find many already known elements in the following paragraphs, even if somewhat evolved thanks to later studies and experiences.

31 Interestingly enough, *Knightmare Chess* (Steve Jackson Games), a small format card game introducing random elements that change the rules of the game all over the entire play, totally transforms the experience getting much closer to what we usually call wargames or even simulation games.

32 Many of those first-generation wargame designers are sadly no longer with us, but they were exemplary figures to a second generation of great authors. Some of them can be found in a collective debate included on the video *Ghosts of SPI*, https://www.youtube.com/live/RU8nTHsGktY hosted in the *Ardwulf's Lair* YouTube channel. The strength of the heritage of the first pioneers of civilian wargame design is evident.

33 This is a central element of Mark Herman's extensive studies on the impact of randomness in simulation games, as defined in many of his articles on the prestigious *C3i* game magazine, as well as in many other essays. A comprehensive vision of this aspect of pre-emptive risk management can be found in Herman, M., Frost, D., *Wargaming for leaders: Strategic decision making from the battlefield to the boardroom*, McGraw-Hill Education (New York, 2008).

2 How it is Done
Common Simulation Game Mechanics

"In the whole range of human activities,
war most closely resembles
a game of cards."

Carl von Clausewitz, On War

What we have seen so far could be considered the fundamental parts of a general theory of simulation games. In other words, a conceptual framework is needed to understand both the nature and the boundaries of what a simulation is and is not, what it can accomplish and what lies beyond its immediate sphere of influence.

There is another step to take, though, if we don't want this study to remain too vague and abstract, an evident contradiction to the nature of simulation itself. We now need to adopt a much more practical approach, studying not just what a simulation does, but *how* this incredibly peculiar family of games manages to do it.

Of course, it would be next to impossible to create a thorough and exhaustive list of all the different game design solutions adopted by the authors and developers in the last decades of board-wargaming history. Also, the history of game design development is not a linear process, going from less efficient traditional approaches to more elegant innovations: almost all the game mechanics used today have their roots firmly planted in recognizable previous incarnations already used at the dawn of modern simulation gaming, and many of them are recurrent over the years. Some even have their "phases", periodically coming into and going out of fashion.

In other words, this history is much more cyclic than we believe and, as we will see, much less prone to the excessive categorization that seems to be a persistent obsession of modern game critics.

Even with that in mind, however, knowing the core elements of what practically makes a simulation a simulation is a fundamental step into understanding what goes on "under the hood" of those games and understand how they manage to recreate history only through a clever combination of pieces of paper and titbits of applied mathematics.

Utterly fascinating generations of gamers and history buffs in the process, of course.

2.1 THE PIECES AND THE BOARD

Just as we did with our first introduction to simulation game theory, we will start this exploration of its many practical components from the real basics. So, let us open the

DOI: 10.1201/9781003429098-3

lid of a game box (or a Ziploc, depending on the format), then, take the game pieces into our hands one at a time and put them on the table to examine them a bit closer.

The one that will immediately catch our eyes is also the largest: the map. There are few components of a simulation game so defining as this cartographic rendition of the terrain where the events are taking place, so much that it provides the first half of the very definition of what a classic wargame is (or, according to some, should be): hex and counters. By hex we mean a contraption for the word "hexagon", the geometric figure used since the time of the RAND Corporation and later Charles S. Roberts to divide the ground into an easily readable grid, capable of managing the calculations of distance, heading and effects of the different locations present on a battlefield.

Hexes supplanted the more traditional squares, derived from the classic chessboards, because they are the highest-sided geometric figure that can provide a homogeneous grid: thus, they can also be described as "squares with rounded corners", used to avoid complex mathematical operations or excessive abstractions to include also diagonal movement while representing discreet portions of different terrain types. Finally, and this not a minor advantage, agglomerations of hexes can create roughly circular areas of proximity from each unit, leading to the fundamental concept of "zone of control", creating a much greater interaction between the different units.

In fact, board wargames were devised primarily to simplify the gaming experience, while guaranteeing a greater topographic accuracy and minimizing the margins of error, as a much more manageable alternative to the 3D wargames and their dioramas of Wellsian memory.[1]

It is no surprise then that hexes and their grids, also known with the contraption "hexgrids", have been a trademark feature of kinetic and probabilistic simulations for so long that by now a hexagon shape is still universally recognized as the main symbol for board-wargaming and countless examples can be taken from the catalogues of first-generation publishers like Avalon Hill or SPI. Even today, many introductory hex-based titles can be found online, available in print-and-play free format (Jim Dunnigan's *Napoleon at Waterloo*) or as digital freeware (Frank Chadwick's *Battle for Moscow*).

For all their virtues, however, hexes do suffer from several shortcomings as a simulation tool. Even without the inevitable distortions due to the reproduction of irregular terrain features like riverbeds or forest extension through a strictly geometric grid, one of the most serious problems comes with scale: the different capabilities of rendering different situations of different scope. One thing is to use a scale of one hex equal to 100 feet to recreate a tactical engagement, quite another to adopt a one-hex-equals-100-miles scale to obtain a strategic simulation.

This upscaling, while being a major advantage of board wargames over their miniature counterparts, imposes a much higher level of abstraction with a consequent loss in granularity. In other words, short of having multiple maps attached together, a strategic game about the final years of World War Two in Europe such as *Battle for Germany* (SPI) has to cope with a much less accurate rendition of the geographic locations of big cities like Berlin or Warsaw, as well as the actual profile of mountain chains like the Italian Alps (Figure 2.1).[2]

FIGURE 2.1   *Battle for Germany* (SPI/Decision Games), a typical hex and counter wargame.

Source: Photograph by the author.

The first solution to this has been the use of so-called "area maps", maps divided into irregular but contiguous portions inside which counters could be freely placed, à la *Risk!*. The obvious advantage of this is the higher flexibility in terrain rendition, as well as an added ease of management for the players. Terrain difference could still be represented by having areas identified by the predominant type belonging to their "territory". That is why this scale is much more used into strategic simulations, like *Time of Crisis* (GMT, about the crisis of the third century AD) or the *Downfall* series (Do It Games, about the two world wars).

It should be said, however, that this simplified approach has also had many applications at the tactical level, often coupled with original activation rules. The "area impulse" family of games, in fact, with its alternate activations by area and maps divided by irregular sectors, has been quite successful at depicting fragmented and unconventional conflicts like the urban warfare of *Storm Over Arnhem* (Avalon Hill, the very first recognized area impulse title), as well as the challenges in army coordination in *Waterloo: Napoleon's Last Battle* (CWG). A very original game designer, Brien J. Miller, has also used maps with sectors delineated according to topographic features such as rivers or hill crests as the basis for his *Eagles of the Empire* series, a hybridized form of board wargame in which the facings of units are determined by the physical orientation of their counters inside the borders of those areas.

A step up from the area maps can be found in their direct evolution: point-to-point maps. In these game boards, the action occurs over a succession of "points" connected by lines, and corresponding to the relative positions of all the more significant locations. Those crossings are often divided by fixed distances, like in the map of *Napoléon, the Waterloo Campaign* (Gamma Two Games, Columbia Games) or *Lee's Invincibles* (Worthington) in which each point is divided by a pre-set number of march hours.

Conceptually not so different from area maps, this approach obviously emphasizes the succession of marches and counter marches typical of operational games. However, many strategic titles like *A House Divided* (GDW, Mayfair) have used it in order to further simplify their rulesets to keep players focused also on not strictly military issues in their management of the conflict.

Point-to-point maps have become in fact highly popular among card-driven games, since their high flexibility and potential for interaction have allowed to represent complex maneuvers in a very intuitive way, coupling them very well with the variation in command points and the unpredictable events created by the special cards used by the players. Titles like *We the People* (Avalon Hill), *Hannibal: Rome vs. Carthage* (Avalon Hill, Phalanx Games), the block game *Julius Caesar* (Columbia Games), the *Tide* series (Compass Games) or the much-celebrated *Paths of Glory* (GMT) have regularly exploited the advantages of this specific solution, with great results both in their playability and in their historical simulation value. Sometimes, even the map itself is not the same for every player, just like in *No Peace Without Spain!* (Compass Games), in which some of the intersections between the different points are only usable by a specific faction, thus introducing further elements of strategic asymmetry.

Proceeding with the simplification and abstraction of map conventions, we arrive at the outer border of board wargames. In this "grey zone", the pieces are sometimes still made of bi-dimensional paper or wood, sometimes made of miniatures with specifically shaped bases, and while all the rules are still typical of "flat" wargames including the massive use of counters, markers, cards and so on, the movement and ranging procedures are based on actual free measuring on the table.

Two of the most well-known examples in that respect are the historical hybrid wargames by Andrea Angiolino: *Wings of Glory* (which in its first version used cards instead of miniature planes) and *Sails of Glory*, both published by Ares Games. Those games carry on the tradition inaugurated by Jim Dunnigan's 1967 naval wargame *Jutland* (Avalon Hill), but instead of using fixed templates for movement, they are based on decks of maneuver cards secretly chosen by the players during a special planning phase, and then placed in front of the miniature stands to execute the various maneuvers allowed by the plane or ship features. The cards have arrows and shapes telling their owner where their piece is going to end up and with which orientation, according to the interaction of different factors like speed, wind direction and type of movement. All of this happens on a completely free playing surface, with firing ranges estimated by the use of special rulers placed inside the arcs of fire delineated on the pieces themselves.

Other companies have used similar solutions in other historical contexts, like Draco Ideas with the ancient wargame *Onus!* and Trafalgar Editions with their Napoleonic titles *Austerlitz 1805* and *Waterloo 1815*, or also Sir Chester Cobblepot's *Waterloo: Enemy Mistakes*.

Is it possible to go even further? Can there be historical simulations with still different kinds of maps, or even with no map at all?

First of all, maps do not have to be "fixed", staying the same for all the duration of a gaming session. To represent the changes in military, political or economic situations with cities flourishing or burning, fortresses appearing and being destroyed, trades routes alternatively opened or closed, games like *Medieval* (GMT), *Pax Renaissance* (Sierra Madre Games) and *Blue vs. Gray* (GMT, as well as the other titles using the same *Enigma* variable map system) have recurred to special tiles to place over certain elements of the map, altering the nature and distribution of the different areas accordingly to what happens during the game, based on special events as well as the outcomes of players' strategic decisions.[3]

Secondly, game maps can include geographical as well as metaphorical "spaces" in their composition. This is especially true for political-cultural simulations as *1989* (GMT), *Europe in Turmoil* or *Prelude to Revolution* (both by Compass Games), in which players compete for the control of social blocks, power centres and intellectual circles physically represented on the map and even tied by a network of symbolic connections.

And, finally, there are plenty of simulation wargames which come without a map inside the box. Most commonly they are card games in which the engagements are resolved by defining relative positions (such as the planes in the *Down in Flames* series), abstract locations (World War Two tactical games like *Up Front!*, *Tank Duel*, *Point Blank: V is for Victory*, *Fields of Fire*), pre-determined combinations of orders and maneuvers (*Table Battles*, Hollandspiele) or generic "areas" of the battlefield (the *Lightning* series by Decision Games, *Milito* by PSC, or *Napoleon Saga* by L'Oeuf Cube).

In effect, the high narrative value of card games is a recognized fact since the Renaissance, when in the courts of Northern Italy the first versions of Tarot decks were used not for gaming or divinatory purposes, but as storytelling devices to inspire brief tales or philosophical elucubrations: today this tradition continues to push forward narrative solitaire or multiplayer card games such as the *Warfighter* series (DVG), or the RPG-like experience of living the life and adventures of a Napoleonic era officer through *Legion of Honor* (Clash of Arms).

Finally, speaking of narrative elements, maps contribute to the general "suspension of disbelief" by their iconography, visual style, artistic impression and many other subtle and not-so-subtle suggestions disseminated in their colours, fonts, drawings and countless other elements. To fully appreciate this point, one just has to look at the "weird" map of Japan in *Sekigahara* (GMT) based on the twelve cardinal points of classic Japanese mapmaking,[4] or to the elaborate desk complete with leather inserts and contemporary images and photographs that compose the conceptual game board of *Versailles 1919* (GMT).

What cannot be missed from a game, however, are the forces in play, be they physical or ideal, identified or generic, military or complex. And those are almost invariably represented by specific game pieces, paper chits, wooden blocks or even cards.

Those small bits represent the mobile portion of a simulation, as opposed to the (not always, as we have seen) fixed component of maps. In fact, it is by moving them around, creating positive or detrimental interactions between them, getting them to specific positions or avoiding the same by the opponents' pieces that players impose their will on the general situation through their strategic decisions. This aspect makes them one of the most crucial components of a classical wargame (the second half of the "hex and counter" definition), and as such also the subject of endless debates about their graphical design, material production, functional use and even colour choices![5]

To be more accurate, the word "counter" identifies only the game pieces that have specific identification numbers and significant factors (movement, attack, defense, range, etc.) written on them for practical purposes, as the word itself ("counter": to "count" factors) suggests.

The counter stands as a highly flexible game component, and it is not by chance that it has remained a general standard in simulation games for so many decades. For example, in classic wargames when a unit suffers a loss in its cohesion or status, the counter can be reversed showing a damaged or reduced side.[6] Also, according to the rules, those counters can be combined with others, broken down into smaller units, or piled one over the other (a technique called "stacking"), in order to indicate the tactical status and general position on the map.

All the other pieces can thus be included in the general category of "markers", that is mobile components used for various game purposes, like victory points and turn tracking, resource accounting and active special events reminding. Markers are generally used to show indirect effects like the mounting of losses leading to a pre-established demoralization level, a sudden disorganized status for a defeated regiment or the use of a special card determining a change in weather conditions.

In recent times, new game design trends have reinforced a practice already present in classical wargames: the use of "generic" counters represented by anonymous wooden pieces. This has generated lots of discussions between the old *aficionados* of historical simulation, since those "tokens" inevitably lose the fundamental element of unit identification, which is for some an essential part of "proper" wargames.[7]

What is sometimes missed by those critics, however, is that the lack of identification of specific units has often as much an historical value as its presence. The reduction of accurate military formations, with all of their story and personal soldier narrations included, to generic and faceless "assets" is perfectly suited in games about the global war on terrorism like *Labyrinth* (GMT) or World War One slaughterhouses as in *Verdun 1916: Steel Inferno* (Fellowship of Simulations) . . . and there is an undeniable sense of self-identification when you move nameless pieces on a Vietnam map from your far-off headquarter in *Fire in the Lake* (GMT) or *Saigon 75* (Nuts! Publishing). Also, some of the more evolved forms of wooden tokens do have special markings on one side or the other, for example to highlight an underground or active status of insurrectional cells in *COIN* titles, and finally the use of wooden game pieces has a strong evocative value in games set during the Middle Ages like the *Levy & Campaign* series (GMT).

A somewhat different reasoning should be made for the use of plastic miniatures that, while undoubtedly adding to the aesthetic value and accessibility level of lighter wargames such as *Memoir '44* (Days of Wonder) or *Hold the Line* (Worthington), sometimes have had a detrimental effect on the ease of play and visual interface quality, due to the lack of any game factor and distinguishing features. It is not by chance that titles like *Hannibal* (Phalanx Games) or *Britannia* (PSC) include both miniatures and conventional paper counters in their boxes, leaving the players free to decide which solution suits them best.

Speaking of "mobile" game elements usually included in a simulation game, it is easy to understand how the third component can be easily recognizable as a trademark feature of this family of games.

Here comes the bane and delice of every wargamer: the die. Usually six-sided, sometimes present in couples or in greater numbers, often (but not always) used in conjunction with tables and modifiers, these small pieces of plastic or wood are the door through which randomness enters into our scene as a very powerful simulative device.

The most classic dice-based mechanic is the force ratio calculation: you take the attacker's combat value, divide it by the defender's combat value and obtain an approximate ratio for them, like 2:1 or 1:3, corresponding to a specific column on a CRT, or *Combat Results Table*. A die roll would then be made, identifying a specific row of results, and the intersection between the ratio column and the die roll row determines the final effect of the action (losses, no effects, retreats etc.). Other contingent elements like terrain, line of sight quality, troops efficiency and the like might impose modifiers both to the column to be used (known as "column shifts") or to the actual die roll. Variations on the mechanic include the use of more easily calculable (but less accurate) differentials, use of multiple tables for example to disaggregate morale degradation and physical casualties, various forms of approximation.

Of particular note is the fact that force ratios beyond a certain point in favour of or against the attacker respectively have no further consequences (there is a limit to how many forces can actually assault a smaller force in the amount of time represented by the single game turn) or make the attack impossible (outright inconsequential for disparity of forces).[8]

This CRT was precisely the "top secret" device that got Charles S. Roberts in so much trouble with the US Government in the late 1950s, and even if it is susceptible to serious distortions (such as the obsessive "factor counting" practice, with players hunting for that last precious attack point leading up to the much-celebrated "golden ratio" of 3:1[9]) it is still today a very effective game mechanic from a simulative point of view.

Another technique is the use of the so-called "bucket of dice", which is the rolling of a number of dice determined by unit quality, terrain conditions and other factors: every die that obtains a certain roll, like a "6" or a specific target number, determines a "hit" on the target. Those hits might be negated by similar defensive dice rolls, like in the *World at War 85* series (LnL). Some highly innovative titles, such as *Give Us Victories* (Dissimula), go so far as to adopt hybrid mechanics, determining the number of dice used in the "bucket" according to the force ratios in the assault.

Another solution is the use of "special dice", which are dice with specific sets of symbols representing the various consequences of the assaults, depending on the types of units involved and other situations that make some of the more conditional symbols capable of inflicting losses on the enemy. This highly readable solution, statistically equivalent to the use of a CRT, is what makes lighter games such as the *Commands & Colors* series surprisingly "traditional" in their game design approach, since it was included in many original forms of *Kriegsspiel*! (Figure 2.2)

Variations in this mechanic include specific sets of dice for specific factions, as in the highly asymmetrical *1775: Rebellion* title (Academy Games) with the elusive

FIGURE 2.2 *Commands and Colors: Napoleonics* (GMT Games). The combined use of unit symbols and special dice avoids overly complicated CRTs.

Source: Photograph by the author.

American militiamen not terribly effective due to scarcity of "HIT" results on their dice, but much more capable of escaping to fight another day than regular British forces thanks to the many "WITHDRAW" sides, as well as the combination with bucket of dice procedures as in *1944: Battle of the Bulge* (Worthington) or even column shifts with the variously effective "column dice" with different results distribution of *Modern Warfare* (WBS).

To connect all those elements, fixed or mobile as they are, simulations use many functional "assets", other game components whose purpose is to make the rules move along the intended course and give the necessary outputs to the equations formulated by the participants: in simpler words, adjudicate the consequences of the players' decisions.

The most evident of these supports is, of course, the great bunch of tables, charts, order of battle sheets and so on that so frequently come with a wargame or a historical simulation of any kind. These long and apparently random series of numbers and symbols, be they included in CRTs or TECs (Terrain Effect Charts), are indeed the very heart of a game algorithms and have been subject to constant evolutions for all the decades of the hobby and professional history of simulations.

They are not alone in the game box, however, since they are often accompanied by other tracks of various kinds, sometimes depicted near the map, sometimes presented in separate sheets. Those tracks range from the more conventional game turn or morale level point scores to more eccentric categories, often depicting the level of collateral elements such as supply, economic resources, political stability and so on: in essence, many elements that we can define as "non-kinetic factors".

Finally, we come to the main component itself: last but not least, the rule manual.

Rulebook writing has become quite an independent art in the simulation gaming world.[10] Manuals are usually divided into basic and advanced levels, depending on the degree of complexity and "realism", oftentimes also including optional rules to be used at discretion by the players. The most advanced rulebooks also follow a "programmed learning format", gradually introducing new players to single elements of the system, offering specifically focused scenarios.

By convention, most rulebooks follow the so-called "legal format", being divided into paragraphs and sub-paragraphs, creating a (hopefully) intuitive structure exposing the game procedures in detail and with efficacy, in conjunction with other specific player aids. Other than the rules themselves and the related diagrams or tables, rulebooks might contain other elements such as illustrated examples of play, game strategy advice, the all-important designer's notes and the always appreciated bibliography of reference texts consulted during the design process. In recent times, playbooks have appeared also, as an accompanying support for game manuals, including extended historical notes, alternative modes of play, components lists and analysis and other useful or at least attractive stuff.

Conclusively, the physical components of a game speak volumes about the design approach followed by the author of the title, but also exert a strong influence over the practical enjoyment of the simulation by the players. They do so both with their contents and with their exterior form: their "visual interface".

Not at all a secondary aspect as some in the wargaming hobby tend to believe, the efficacy and readability of these supports, from the map and counters to the rulebook and the player aids, is a crucial element of the experience. A good interface is capable of conveying lots and lots of information to the players, both overtly and indirectly, allowing them to stay focused on the game situation, "in the flow" we might say, rather than having to constantly go hunting for a procedure hidden in a random sub-paragraph or the umpteenth exception to a (not so) general rule.

This was true in the classic "golden age" of SPI and Avalon Hill 1970s productions, when graphical designers such as Redmond A. Simonsen pushed the existing quality levels to their limit, creating very effective solutions in terms of readability and information providing.

The resurgence of wargaming and historical gaming in general, together with the various forms of hybridization with more recent forms of gaming, has also led to a renewed attention to the efficacy of visual systems, a crucial aspect of analog games in which the engine of the entire experience is not a digital hardware but the brains and sensibilities of the players themselves, what Dunnigan aptly called "the mushware". Decades after, the objective remains always the same: making playing with history an accessible and enjoyable hobby for the broader public of potential players.

2.2 C3I . . . AND MORE

After having exposed all the single material elements constituting a game in their greatest potential, one would be excused in thinking that this kind of experience allows its participants to truly "see" the historical events with the utmost accuracy, a surprisingly precise representation of all their different phases of evolution, based on a perfect depiction of the position in space, time and cause-effect chains of all their related elements.

Sadly, this is not at all true, since all this detail remains unavoidably distorted.

This lack or even distortion of detail is sometimes due to physical constraints coming from production issues (you can print only so many counters and maps . . .) or conscious game designer decisions (who might want to create a mainly economic simulation of the industrial effort during World War One, in which military matters stay in the far background, such as *Wings for the Baron*, VPG). In other instances, however, those deviations are caused by more specific reasons, tied to the actual inner workings of simulation.

The truest aspect of wargames and historical games, one which displeases some of their more hardcore enthusiasts, is that at their heart they still are games, not by chance the second "unsavoury term" mentioned by Dunnigan in his classic definition. To be as such, a game has to be free (even if somewhat regulated) in its results, decisional space left to the players, variability of consequences of individual events during its duration and so on. So, in order to preserve that essential freedom and stay "playable" without becoming a fixed "reenactment" of the events, a functional simulation must reach a cleverly balanced compromise between the "real thing" and at least a certain degree of deviation from it.

But here another aspect literally comes into play. One of the bigger strengths of simulation is its powerful narrative element: its ability to tell so many amazing stories during play through purely mathematic and statistic elements, such as a CRT or the value on a counter. So much that the average player might easily fall into the illusion that the simulated events are taking place just as they are depicted on the gameboard, in the exact same succession of time and spaces.

One might then believe in the truest honesty that a certain regiment is located on the top of a certain hill on hex 2214, and that turn after turn those men have heroically repulsed three successive assault waves of numerically superior enemy troops, while on the other side of the battlefield their comrades finally managed to mount a powerful counterattack, get to that crucial hill and save the entire situation at the very last moment . . . except that this is not what happens during a simulation game. Or, at least, not necessarily with those specific details and in that order.

To fully understand this crucial and yet elusive aspect of simulation, we have to resort to the words of two very influential game designers: Kevin Zucker and Amabel Holland.

In the first case, the author of the classic *Napoleon's Last Battles* (SPI) and curator of the *Library of Napoleonic Battles* series (OSG) repeatedly discusses the concept of "true accurate locations" even in the most traditional family of wargames, dear old hex and counters titles. In the online magazine *Wargame Design*, hosted on the OSG website,[11] Zucker responds to some critics of his uncomplicated systems by saying that the combination of movement, combat and interaction between enemy units more than compensates the apparently "scattered" and not contiguous positions of units all over the map. That is because all those rules represent the general influence areas of fighting formations during the period of time corresponding to a game turn, not the actual physical locations up to the last meter. In this essentially "quantistic" representation, a unit might actually be on a certain hex at the end of the movement phase, but then be deployed on the side of that hex or even on an adjacent position during the combat phase, or on a third spot to interdict an enemy retreat during the opponent's turn . . . What really matters about spatial representation in simulation games is not the material status of a unit, but its interactions with the terrain, the chain of command, enemy forces and so on.

This is true about space, but what about time representation? Here comes the second designer: Amabel Holland, creator of the highly appreciated Hollandspiele publishing house.

In the article *Time distortion in wargames* hosted on her website blog, she proposes a radically different approach to the matter. Game turns in simulation games give to the players a perfect sequence of events, but in reality those events happen in a totally non-linear fashion. Not only units do not follow a rigid sequence of move/fire/retreat maneuvers in different and clearly recognizable "game turns", but that whatever happens in those same turns might be verified in a very different order, especially if the events are not closely related to one another. Unit A might be retreating during turn 3 and unit B might be advancing on turn 5. . . but those two events could actually be happening at the same time or on the opposite order than what the game turn track suggests. They are just materially presented as such by the game system only to make things understandable to the players.

This somewhat confusing state of affairs is even truer in political, economic or hybrid simulations, in which non-kinetic elements are included in much more abundance than in strictly military wargames.

Luckily for us, as both Zucker and Holland suggest, all of this could be of no practical relevance to our enjoying of the simulation experience, no more than the knowledge that whenever we are watching a movie we are actually seeing a very rapid sequence of still pictures: our eye is deceived and so our mind, even if we rationally know what is happening.

Understanding however that things are not so rigid and clearly defined in simulation helps us immensely in tackling the sometimes erratic and contradictory representations of the single processes that compose a "historical event".

Yet, unable to trust traditional categories such as time and space, we need some new key to understand how historical simulation games manage to represent highly diversified events in their ever-changing universe. A good case to study on this regard is the application of a classic military concept: C3i, or Command, Control, Communications and Intelligence.

Command and control, the first two tenets of the formula, can be defined as "The exercise of authority and direction by a properly designated commander over assigned and attached forces in the accomplishment of the mission."[12] To differentiate a bit further, we can define command as the formal exercise of authority, while control is the capability of assessing the practical efficacy of the orders and directly influencing their practical execution.

Regarding command, military simulation games over the decades have used a lot of different solutions, with the primary (often declared) objective of guaranteeing a good decisional space to the players, thus avoiding perceptions of excessive "scripting" on one side and arbitrary randomness on the other, while however limiting the unrealistic idea of full and total control over the behavior of up to the smallest force in the order of battle.

The first basic IGOUGO dynamics ("I go, you go": totally linear activation structures, with one player moving all his or her pieces, and then the opponent doing likewise) have been coupled since the earliest days of wargaming by much more dynamic forms of WEGO (alternate movement, one piece or a portion of pieces per activation "impulse"), sometimes even carried out by previous secret planning phases with simultaneous execution *à la Diplomacy* or by the possibility of interrupting the opponent's chain of activations and seize the initiative, as in *Simple Great Battles of History* or *Men of Iron* (GMT).

Other, even more radical attempts in representing the grievous issue of coordinating different formations on a single battlefield have been highly asymmetrical sequences of play, forced limitations in the number of units activated per turn, or multiple activations of the same unit in a single turn (as in the highly innovative *Waterloo Campaign 1815* by Mark Herman, for RBM Studio).

An alternative is represented by randomizing the activation order through the adoption of "chit pull" mechanics. These rules assign a specific "chit" or "card" to a certain formation, then ask players to pull one of them at random from a common opaque mug or deck: the formation represented by the drawn chit will then perform its actions and after that a new chit would be taken out of the mug. Since the first recognized title using the chit pull mechanic, the American Civil War title *Across 5 Aprils* (Victory Games), this device has become quite a favourite of many wargamers, even if with countless variations. Separate pull groups for the different armies, dummy counters, preliminary chit selection (for example, in *Give Us Victories*, Dissimula), special events and repeated activation impulses for the same formation (*Jours de Gloire* series), even placement of the drawn chit on the map with localized activation of all eligible units within a certain range (*A Victory Lost* series and *PanzerBlitz: Hill of Death*, both by MMP), or the use of cards to introduce further elaborations on command management (*A Most Fearful Sacrifice*, Flying Pig Games, *Tank Leader* series, West End Games)—all of these adaptations have been tried in several titles and appreciated, also for the easy conversion of this system for solitaire play.

Another way to represent the difficulties in formulating orders and seeing them executed at the proper time has been found in limiting if not the quality of the orders expressed over a game turn, their quantity. This method relies on a variable sum of "action points", determined by circumstances like leadership levels, that are used to move, fight or rally formations all over the battlefield. Much less aleatory than chit pull activation, this mechanic allows a more precise (even if limited) management of the respective order of battle, and it has become a trademark of lightweight wargame systems such as the *Hold the Line* series and its derivate, *Horse & Musket*.

The greatest distortion here, however, is that since the quantity of action points is limited, it is often too tempting to carry on fighting on only one portion of the battlefield, since it would be necessary to spend at least a couple of precious game turns to move the "forgotten" units into the fray, and all of this while suffering the opponent's active defense. A possible solution is to actually "force" the involvement of the entire army by adopting a card-assisted activation mechanic, in which players are dealt a fixed and not always symmetrical number of order cards, which will dictate how many units on the left flank or how many cavalry formations can be activated once it is our turn.

This system looks a bit more harmonic, at least on paper, and encourages a clever hand management behavior by the players, forcing them to plan in advance their offensive all while "building" a good set of cards to sustain a prolonged offensive in a specific sector without leaving too many troops behind. This solution has become the core mechanic of series such as *Commands & Colors* and *Combat Commander* (GMT), with all the advantages and the flaws involved.

Other more elaborate, even if less intuitive, design features are based on the adoption of different "attitudes" on the battlefield by individual units, which grant specific advantages. At the tactical level they could be called "missions", prepared maneuvers and actions on the smaller scale (such as in the Poland 1939 game by Brian Train *Summer Lightning*, LnL), while at the greater operational and strategic size they often take the name of "postures" (*Kursk: The Tigers Are Burning* and *Desert Victory*, RBM Studio, by Trevor Bender). Other games set during earlier periods like the American Revolution (the dedicated series by Mark Miklos, published by GMT) or Napoleonic battles (games by Enrico Acerbi such as *Caldiero* or *Tolentino*, inserts of *Para Bellum* magazine) use similar mechanics under the guise of "general orders" given to smaller formations.

Closely related to command, we have the element of control, defined as the decision maker's ability to see his or her orders promptly executed by the subordinates on the field. In other words, the art of "getting things done", for better or for worse, since sometimes individual initiative by those on the spot can supersede the most well-thought and rational commands coming from above. Most of the time, however, it is simply a recipe for disaster.

Control in simulation games lives, it has to be said, in a very delicate balance: too much of it and the system will be overly complicated and introduce unrealistic "God-like" direct micromanagement by the players; too little of it and the game will look totally arbitrary and in effect "play on its own", relegating its participants to the role of mere spectators.

Classic historical game design has found many ways to deal with this issue, the main one of which surely is the (properly called) "zone of control" (ZoCs), a mechanic through which actions are prohibited or reactions are allowed based on the respective proximity of the opponents' units. This solution is so effective that, while being born on the hexgrid, it has been successfully applied also to point-to-point games with the "interception" mechanic.

Units are not separate entities that "float" on a battlefield, totally unaware of each other, each confined in its own little hex or area. On the contrary, as further proof that their position in space and time is not as deterministic as what appears on the map, they have a proximity area through which they can exert a sort of "control" and influence the actions and function of enemy as well as other friendly forces in various ways, negative or positive.

There are different kind of treatment for this proximity: rigid ZoCs interrupt every enemy movement and force a mandatory close combat, semi-rigid ZoCs cause a greater expense in movement points to enter or exit the interested area, flexible

ZoCs have close to no effect. Some units might follow different rules for ZoCs, with light units generally exerting them also through woods or commando formations capable of ignoring the enemy ones. To use a real-life example as a reference, just consider the difference between rugby, American football and soccer matches as, respectively, rigid, semi-rigid and flexible ZoC systems.

Beyond the ZoCs, there may be larger even if less invasive areas of interaction between units.

Usually set at *two* hexes of distance from the active units we find the zone of influence (ZoI). This is a very interesting solution for representing a somewhat extended area of interaction, less restrictive than a ZoC, based both on actual capabilities of the active unit and on the general attitude of the passive units aware of their approach to an enemy position.

Game designer Mark Herman has given us two perfect examples of both of these dynamics. The first one is found in his *magnum opus* about the Pacific War, *Empire of the Sun* (GMT), and essentially represents the ability of reaction of air and naval units through the range of their recon assets; the second is a fundamental part of his already mentioned *Waterloo* game, which forms the basis for the Rebel Fury American Civil War series, published by GMT. In this system, whenever a unit enters a ZoI of an enemy force, it has to shift from marching to combat formation, reducing its movement capabilities and consuming many more activations (a measure of time and command transmission) to keep it advancing.

There is even a third zone, that could conventionally be defined as zone of engagement (ZoE). In this even broader area the effects are naturally more vague, but potentially no less crucial in the chaos and frenzy of a battlefield. In Enrico Acerbi's *Piacenza 1746* (Europa Simulazioni) the control of units getting up to three hexes close to the enemy becomes exponentially much more difficult, while Peter Perla's Napoleonic tactical wargame *The Pratzen* (CTP) has units rolling on a special table with modifiers due to their competence and other contingencies whenever they get inside eight hexes from the enemy: the roll will determine if they will still remain under the general control of the player, or if they will abruptly stop, retreat, fire, charge to melee or adopt other erratic behaviours.

Games like Herman Luttmann's *A Most Fearful Sacrifice* and *Blind Swords* series (Revolution Games) will frustrate dreams of total control and expand the element of unpredictability even further through special and disruptive events happening on the battlefield, creating what can be considered to be practical treaties on Friction in tactical warfare—also known as "No battleplan survives contact with the enemy".

Another fundamental aspect of the management of military assets is the third C: Communications, defined as the capability of transmitting your orders to the force on the field as well as receiving a good flow of information about the shape of the engagement taking place. These data, both inputs and outputs, will be the key for the establishment a well-informed and optimal decisional cycle, capable of achieving the mission objectives with a minimal loss of forces.

A nice bunch of words that could be much more easily and much more effectively resumed by the immortal maxim: "If an order can be misunderstood, it *will be* misunderstood."

Since the days of early *Kriegsspiel* rulesets, order transmission and its many misfortunes are a traditional feature of miniature wargaming, which has found expression over the years through formally written orders, sometimes reported on small pieces of paper put under special messenger figures with their individual movement factor: when the small rider gets physically in touch with the miniature of the subordinate leader (if he is not captured, or worse, during the trip . . .) the new order can substitute the old one.

Board wargames used various mechanics simulating this fundamental aspect of warfare. Earlier forms of order communication mechanics included hidden planning systems with players writing down their plotted moves and then executing them simultaneously, or games with "order chits" with more general directives needing some game turns and often a close proximity to the overall commander to be changed. The modern warfare *World at War* (LnL) series justly simulates electronic warfare by decrementing the control capabilities on the players' units due to the action of specialized ECW assets deployed by the enemy and used with varied effects.

Hybrid miniature and board wargame series *Battleground Historical Warfare* (YMG) has fixed orders written on the card units themselves that can be changed only through the expenditure of limited command points; in the *TLNB* system (OSG) certain formations can move much faster when put on written "march orders" towards pre-established destinations; while the *Tactical Combat Series* titles (MMP) allow players to actually draw their designated attack maneuvers on special Op Sheets.

If communication is all about the transmission and reception of information in a direct engagement situation, intelligence stands for the actual previous collection of that information in such a chaotic and difficult environment.

Intelligence can take various forms in simulation games, but it is usually related to the famous "fog of war" expression found in von Clausewitz's *On War*: a sort of "screen" that keeps a commander from having a complete knowledge of the battlefield.

One of the most frequent and direct solutions adopted to represent this peculiar and yet fundamental aspect of warfare is the use of "hidden forces" on the mapboard, epitomized by the "hidden block" mechanic. Born with the Gamma Two titles *Quebec 1759* and *Napoléon*, this system transforms the usual paper counters into much more solid wooden blocks held upright on the table and with the unit values written only on the side towards their owner: thus, the real nature of forces will be revealed only at the moment of their contact with the enemy, allowing the use of complex diversional strategies and preserving a certain element of surprise. This has become a trademark feature in all the titles present in the Columbia Games catalogue (the true heir to the Gamma Two line), like *Hammer of the Scots* or *Julius Caesar*, as well as in some series published by Worthington Games (*Lee's Invincibles*, *Trenton 1776*, *Holdfast* and as an optional rule in *1944: Battle of the Bulge*).

A similar effect is reached by just having a special neutral counter cover the usual carboard counters until in close proximity with enemy forces, as in *The Library of Napoleonic Battles* titles. The *SCS* series published by MMP uses other solutions like forbidding the examination of multiple unit stacks beyond the first counter in the pile, while Mike Nagel's *Ancient Battles Deluxe* (VPG) deliberately uses highly intricate combat ratio calculation procedures just to muddle things up and force players to play instinctively, without necessarily going hunting for that last precious combat point that guarantees the optimal probability of success.[13]

On top of this we can also find games almost exclusively dedicated to the hidden "spy wars" which represent such a fundamental aspect of military events. Titles like John Prados's *Spies!* (SPI) and *Bodyguard Overlord* (Spearhead Games) deal with such elusive topics as information gathering and counterespionage.

To make matters even more interesting and "foggy", in a dedicated article on the *C3i* magazine[14] game designer Jeremy White describes how the actual *On War* passage might be much more accurately translated as a reference not to simply sight-obscuring "fog" but to the distorted perception of things due to the "moonlight" produced by battlefield conditions.

In other words, instead of having a "toggle switch of information" such as the one present in *Stratego*-like games, military commanders have to make their decisions on a highly unreliable information base, absolutely unaware of the degree of trust they can have on every single intelligence datapoint reaching their desk and infiltrating their decision process: in a sense, sometimes the issue is not the absence of reports but their excessive *abundance*.

Reminiscent of the crucial importance of intelligence in great naval engagements like Pearl Harbor or Midway, naval simulations like the recently revised *Task Force* (Kokusai-Tsushin/VUCA) by Japanese master designer Ginichiro Suzuki adopted very simple and effective systems to represent this rather elusive aspect: flood the map with dummy markers alongside the real ones and force players to undergo extensive recon missions to distinguish between good, misdirecting and outright fake info.

But a step more could be taken, since in certain conditions the "moonlight" can make even the position and nature of your own forces as well.

White himself designed his highly innovative and thought-provoking *Atlantic Chase* game (GMT), about the naval war between the German *Kriegsmarine* and the British Royal Navy, starting from this intriguing premise. Here all task forces and other assets, including your own, are represented by long lines stretching all over the map ("trajectories"); and the players, representing top-level commanders giving their orders from their headquarters situated hundreds of miles away from their forces, strive to reduce those lines into more precise locations ("stations") through recon operations, air missions, tactical movements and interception attempts.

Interestingly, something similar to this (even if not so outright revolutionary) had already been established as a proven mechanic of several classic hex and counters titles. In 1976, SPI published Dunnigan's *Panzergruppe Guderian*, a title introducing the use of "untried" units, Soviet army formations so badly trained and tactically unpredictable that their actual combat values remain hidden on the reverse side of the counter until the very last . . . even to their own commanders!

This solution allowed the insertion of another level of simulation, keeping the rules still easy and intuitive enough and incidentally granting a very high level of replayability, as well as a very good solitaire suitability. So much that countless successive titles used this mechanic, elaborating sophistications like general classes of efficiency, partial use of the mechanic only for specific groups of units inside an army, chit pull draw of different combat values for every single combat and so on.

The fight against perfect information in simulation games did not start in 1976, however. Classical *Kriegsspiel* was in fact based on the "double blind" mechanic, with players making their decisions in separate rooms over maps giving incomplete or inaccurate renditions of the tactical situation, position and nature of enemy forces, actual terrain conditions of unexplored terrain and so on.

All of this granted a very good level of plausibility to the simulation, but at the cost of satisfying two essential conditions: having a good referee feeding correct or incorrect information to the players, and being able to rely on a very large gaming space. Since those two assets could not be taken for granted by all players, wargames and simulation games in general have usually "flirted" with this mechanic, including it as an optional rule (like in Columbia Games latest *Napoléon* re-edition—demanding, however, the use of two full copies of the game), but very rarely have used it as an integral part of their basic mechanics.

There are exceptions of course. Yasushi Nakaguro's latest edition of *Fury at Midway* (Revolution Games) uses double maps to hide the movements and positions of the engaged forces, while *Pacific Fury: Guadalcanal* (Revolution Games) resorts to closed boxes to make players bluff about the beaches chosen for the landings of US Marines. The classic *Midway* by Avalon Hill adopted hidden movement mechanics as well, and also the aforementioned secret planning games could be considered to be forms of "fog of war" titles.

Another device regularly used is the "game screen", a sheet of cardboard put in front of the players' positions to hide them from sight of the opponents. This solution is generally used to conceal the identity and distribution of assets, or during the setup phase to guarantee the reciprocal surprise effect of simultaneous deployments. However, in Maurice Suckling's *Chancellorsville 1863* (Worthington), through a clever combination of simple yet effective game rules and the small number of game pieces involved, double game screens provided in peripheral areas of the map have notably returned as a suitable solution for describing approach to battle movements.

Finally, the use of cards is another good way to include another layer of intelligence uncertainty in simulations. This can happen at the strategic or operational level, in which action cards represent all those crucial non-kinetic dimensions that go beyond the simple physical location of armed forces on a map and also allow the use of elaborated bluffing dynamics, but also at the tactical dimension: an apparently simple game like *Undaunted* includes "Fog of War" cards that clog up the players' hand, while demanding the use of specific recon actions by Scout units to "open" map tiles to the movement of more conventional forces.

Lastly, adding to the C3i concept itself, a mention must be made about what still today remains perhaps the least appreciated but nonetheless ever so crucial domain of military sciences: supply and logistics. Also known as the art of getting bullets and beans to the soldiers on the battlefield, this essential portion of military strategy has been the key to success (as well as the fatal bane) of countless commanders over the centuries, with similar analogies possible also on the political and economic fields.

Actually, for wargames as well, supply has been one of the elements that decided the failure or the success of several rules systems as believable (and playable . . .) simulations.

The topic has been represented through highly diversified systems, ranging from simple automatic distribution of ammo and food to all units operating inside a predetermined range of roads and wagon trains, to almost maniacally detailed accounting of "supply points" to be distributed all over the map, with subsystems dealing with the administration of truck convoys or the actual capacity of depots and caches that could be captured or destroyed.

Of course, many simplified simulations such as Dunnigan's *Battle for Germany* (SPI) simply ignored the issue for playability's sake or considered the action so condensed in time that all units would be carrying with them enough supply to operate for the simulated duration of the scenario (*Iron Curtain*, MMP, in most included scenarios). These solutions, however, have been regularly criticized by some players, since they make the attack on transport routes—the actual "lifelines" of an army on the march, since the earliest days of warfare—a much less important tactic than in real life.

The level of simulation most influenced by supply issues surely is the operational one (tactical engagement actions are usually too short, while strategic games tend to treat the matter with more abstracted solutions), and at this level one cannot find a more accurate treatment of logistics than in the highly regarded *Operational Combat Series* titles (MMP). However, it has to be considered that comparable results have also been reached by much less elaborate titles like *Warsaw 1920*: here Yasushi Nakaguro has represented the crushing supply problems of the campaign by giving a very limited reserve of supply points to the Soviet player, a very simple device forcing to "shut down" one of the two fronts at least temporarily in order to keep the other operating against the gradually mobilizing Polish forces.

As with the Polish campaign of 1920, there are also other environments in which supply has represented a very major issues for military leaders, and one of them undoubtedly is the North African theater. Since the days of the monumental *Campaign for North Africa* (SPI) by Richard Berg (such a detailed and elaborate simulation that some consider it more a design experiment than an actually playable game . . .), a true catalogue of different design solutions have been adopted to represent this aspect. Just to mention a single notable title, *Desert Victory* (RBM Studio) combines the essences of most of these systems with an asymmetrical supply point accounting mechanic that takes into consideration the higher efficiency of the Allied logistics network and the back-and-forth movement of "supply heads" allowing units to operate much better and much longer in advanced positions.

A very peculiar scenario in this regard is medieval operational warfare, and game designer Volko Ruhnke decided to fill this void by creating a dedicated series of titles called *Levy & Campaign* (GMT). As the title itself suggests, the system is based on two crucial aspects of medieval warfare: recruiting and then keeping on the field armed forces bound only by personal loyalties, maintaining them effective with a reasonable number of supplies.

The segment of the rules dedicated to logistics is particularly enlightening about the characteristics of warfare in the period. Every Lord leads his own independent formation of troops (in essence, the precursor to modern day army corps) and has to provide for their supply; this is done in a special phase when a certain quantity of "provender" points are accumulated on the Lord's individual mat and later consumed by the troops . . . but those supplies have to be transported over the treacherous road and river network, and so our Lord would need carts, sleds, even ships. All of this

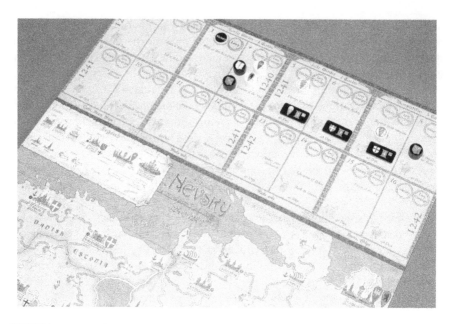

FIGURE 2.3 *Nevsky* (GMT Games). The *Levy & Campaign* series introduced innovative mechanics to make complex logistic problems much more manageable by the players.

Source: Photograph by the author.

is obviously seen through the lens of the specific events portrayed: campaigning in frozen Russia with the Teutons of *Nevsky* (Figure 2.3), rampaging through the treacherous Spanish mountain passes of *Almoravid*, or cavalcading around the fertile lands of Tuscany torn by the eternal struggle between Guelphs and Ghibellines in *Inferno* are very diverse experiences, as they should be.[15]

Other wargames went even further and dedicated themselves almost totally to the treatment of logistics as an essential premise of operational warfare, so much that they apparently betrayed the conventional image of what a wargame should be, assuming the shape of asset-management Eurogames. Two of these tiles are *Race to the Rhine* and *Race to Moscow*, published by Phalanx, in which the advance of World War Two Allied armies towards Berlin as well as German *Wehrmacht* units towards Moscow are seen as a function of the maintenance of a stable supply flow into the main attack drives entrusted to the players themselves, faced with logistical nightmares as well as direct enemy action.

In conclusion, this cursory examination of how games deal with the elements of the C3i concept, while focused on military wargames, is of course applicable to all forms of simulation and still take us back to the same point: there are countless different game mechanics available to authors and players, each of which is focused on the specific representation of this or that historical dynamic, but all of which are to be considered equally valid and sources of full of interesting insights—just as there are countless historical essays and treatments about the same event, seen from different points of view.

However, exactly as is the case of a diversified historiographical approach, there is still more to be said (and simulated) regarding past events ... but this requires the use of a very peculiar and powerful game component, at the same time as old as gaming itself and as new as one of the most revolutionary innovations of recent game design.

Cards. Lots of them.

2.3 THE TURN OF (SO MANY) FRIENDLY CARD(S)

There is a single game element we have already met, and actually not the biggest one included in our game boxes. It is an integral part of the gaming world for entire millennia, combining in it the randomizing powers of dice, the complex statistics of tables, the informational values of counters in what author Volko Ruhnke aptly defined as "real estate on your table" during a dedicated presentation.[16] That component is, of course, cards.

Those "simple" pieces of paper have gone through what could possibly be considered the most dramatic changes in simulation games regarding their components. This section will deal with the importance of cards as game elements, and as such a mention to their history in modern boardgaming is necessary.

The very first uses of cards inside map-and-counters-based simulation boardgames started in the 1970s with titles in which these elements were often complimentary to the main rules, almost considered as pieces of "eccentric" taste. They were usually relegated to the representation of fortuitous special events whose excessive randomness could not be properly represented through conventional tables, such as the plague outbreaks or the various revolts in *Kingmaker* (Ariel Productions), a role not so unlike what they already had in classic family games like *Monopoly*.

And yet, the same *Kingmaker* testified how the innovative trends in game design of the 1970s were beginning to understand the need for the inclusion of diversified types of randomness, by using cards also as game pieces representing nobiliary titles, additional mercenary troops and even as devices to adjudicate the unpredictable outcomes of the many field battles, even if combined with a much more traditional force ratio base systems.

The many groundbreaking elements of such a relevant title, for many years the reference simulation for the Wars of the Roses and still today considered a true classic, paved the way for a new role of cards in game design: diversified and more elaborate conflict resolution and resource collection, as in the epic title *Empires of the Middle Ages* (SPI).

The time was right then in the early 1990s for the new phase in the history of cards: that of becoming not an ancillary, nor a complementary element in game engines ... but an *essential* part of that engine.

Thus began the age of cards as the core component, the age of so-called *card-driven games*. "CDG" for short.

With this term we indicate simulation games in which the action is effectively driven by the use of special cards giving to the players a variable quantity of flexible "Operation Points" (or Ops) to be used for conventional actions, or alternatively the ability to unleash more focused "Events" operating on other dimensions of the conflict (politics, economy, diplomacy etc.) and breaking the usual arithmetic dynamics of force ratios, modifiers and the like.

Endless variations of this design solution have been conceived, experimented, appreciated and criticized over the decades, but one thing is considered certain—the name of the first recognized title of the sub-genre: *We the People* (Avalon Hill), created in 1993 by master game designer Mark Herman.

The genesis of this classic is quite a story, considering that Herman was looking for a new system capable of including non-kinetic, multidimensional, political events in a more historically convincing narration of the American Revolution. Herman knew that a broader approach was needed, drawing from his deep personal knowledge on the subject as well as from his experience as a former SPI author while Jim Dunnigan himself created some very unorthodox and experimental titles like *The American Revolution: 1775–1783* already in the early 1970s.

Other titles like *1776* (Avalon Hill) already used cards in their typical early auxiliary role, but Herman needed something more to recreate the intricate web of military actions, on field deceptions, irregular warfare, asymmetric confrontations, political intrigues, international entanglements and the like. And he found that from the most improbable of all sources: playing in representing the grievous issue of coordinating different formations on a single battlefield in the collectible card game *Magic: The Gathering* with his daughter.[17]

In so doing, he started from some of the most innovative traditional titles, exploited the versatility of the blooming card games, combined everything with a typical point-to-point map . . . and obtained a totally original and ground-breaking, eminently playable and highly accessible, hybrid pol-mil simulation of one of the most peculiar conflicts of modern world history. Incidentally, in so doing, he started his own little revolution.

In just a few years, players were taken away by the amazing depth of this attractive game, that managed to include simulative dimensions in a single streamlined flow, avoiding unnecessary complexities and distilling all the exceptions to the cards themselves, while covering peculiar aspects such as the political impact of military victories on popular support for a cause . . . in short, everything made this game a joy to play and an example for an entire generation of game designers.

The CDG was now "the thing" and new similar titles began to pop up: more elaborate *Hannibal: Rome vs Carthage* (Valley Games), multiplayer *Successors* (Avalon Hill), more military oriented and "wargamey" *Paths of Glory* (GMT) and many others. By the mid-2000s card-driven games were so common that almost every major publisher had at least one such title in its catalogue, with a constant request for new offers covering more and more conflicts.

It was clear that the new subgenre was there to stay, even when some of the newest titles had begun to depart from the original approach and find innovative ways of their own. The emerging game designer Volko Ruhnke used his knowledge of the French and Indian War as well as his personal competence of intelligence analyst to push the original asymmetries to the extreme with *Wilderness War* (GMT), considered an instant classic since its first inception. Ananda Gupta and Jason Matthews combined their academic and political analysis experiences to create the supreme pol-mil simulation that almost redefined the concept of CDG and even of its historical subject, the

Cold War: *Twilight Struggle* (GMT), one of the best-selling boardgames of all time. Charles Vasey used his deep knowledge of the English Civil War and internal politics dynamics to create *Unhappy King Charles!* (GMT). And so on.

This did not keep Herman from continuing to work on his creation, a simplified and streamlined version in *Washington's War*, as well as adapting his previous much more complex game designs to the new medium with the highly sophisticated CDGs *Empire of the Sun* (World War Two in the Pacific) and *For the People* (American Civil War), all published by GMT.

Ruhnke in the meantime continued his work and recombined the original CDG approach with the new solutions proposed by *Twilight Struggle*, by creating *Labyrinth* (GMT), an encyclopaedic game system on the war between Western democracies and international terrorism regularly updated year after year with expansions, revisions and additional cards inspired by the latest global events.

After that, Ruhnke reinvented the genre once again by proposing his seminal *COIN* series (GMT), dedicated to non-linear, asymmetrical, non-conventional, counter-insurrectional warfare ranging through various titles from Central America (*Andean Abyss*) to the ancient Gallic Wars (*Falling Sky*), with a specific title by Harold Buchanan dedicated to the American Revolution (*Liberty or Death*) paying proper homage to *We the People* itself in the shape of the leader's stand-up counters. The circle was ideally complete (Figure 2.4).

In *COIN* games (usually conceived for 4 players, but many variations are present) cards are not dealt to players and kept in a hand, since the depicted situations are so irregular and unpredictable that even their decision makers can count on a limited

FIGURE 2.4   *Liberty or Death* (GMT Games), a typical *COIN* game.

Source: Photograph by the author.

knowledge and control of those complex and interconnected events. Rather, they are presented in a common deck for all players, with a fixed initiative order on them: starting with the first player, one can decide to activate it for the event or just to use the peculiar abilities of his or her faction. The trick is that the more powerful the action, the greater will be the reactions available to the opponents, and that the active player will skip the next turn, leaving many openings to the adversaries or even to unreliable allies. Also, every card represents the same historical fact, but its consequences can be very differently nuanced depending on which faction uses it for the event: quite an effective way of depicting the "spin" that savvy political leadership can give to the news.

The resulting effect is a convincing description of action and reaction dynamics and OpTempo management so typical of modern irregular conflicts, as well as of many similar confrontations that have happened in the past centuries and that are now revised in that sense by the more modern and elaborate historiography.[18]

The game design solution has thus led to the definition of *card-assisted games*: games in which cards are not the almost exclusive driving mechanic of the system but are still one of the elements essential to its working.

All the while, the CDG breakthrough has inspired and is inspiring still today many other rulesets, vindicating the use of cards in historical titles so much that now even several traditional wargames include regularly include supplementary card-driven like mechanics. These new elements are more similar to the use of cards in traditional 1970s and 1980s wargames, but are much more influential on the overall decisional process and so are generally described as *card-enhanced games.*

Whatever their definition may be, and also considering the possibility of having different types of cards in the same title (through action, combat, event decks and more, all coexisting under unified sets of rules), games with cards as one of their main elements are now the rule rather than the exception, and it is easy to see why this is the case even outside the realm of strictly CDG titles.

On the side of game mechanics, several examples may be made regarding the versatility of cards as a basic pillar of the deeper processes in more recent simulation games.

In general, cards allow for a much more accurate randomness distribution than dice. Basic statistics tells us that the limited number of dice rolls might not lead that distribution to the probabilistic average; card decks, however, "remember" the already drawn results by leaving them in the discard pile. Of course, periodic reshuffles and other forms of manipulation can shake the situation up a little, like in *Combat Commander* (GMT) and *Great War Commander* (Hexasim), but also those events can be part of the simulation itself, representing pauses in the combat and the periodic reorganization of forces.

In effect, different levels of randomness can be included in a single card. Every card, in fact, includes possible basic orders to be given to the troops, modifying actions to those same orders, reaction impulses, random events activated by special "triggers" once again determined by other cards! Even though the many diverse options offered to a player by cards may seem a bit daunting at first, they represent a spectrum of possible choices: instead of intimidating newcomers to the genre, cards narrow down the almost infinite variable moves that are a trademark feature of hex and counter games to a much more manageable subgroup, avoiding the dreadful stall of analysis paralysis.

However, in many traditional hex and counters cards are nowadays present in many forms, too.

Sometimes they can be just an optional component, with varying degrees of importance: *The Library of Napoleonic Battles* (OSG) entrusts cards with the representation of the unpredictable reinforcement flow, the *Napoleonic 20* series (VPG) uses them as a quite powerful random event generator, Peter Perla's *The Pratzen* (Canvas Temple) has them as purely optional devices. Other games adopt cards as much more essential elements of their engine, like the battle games series by the Historical Game Company in which every turn a random card is drawn to indicate special events occurring and how many units can move and fight, or Hermann Luttmann's *Blind Swords* series (Revolution Games) and *A Most Fearful Sacrifice* (Flying Pig Games) in which cards control command activations, random events and general Friction on the battlefield.

Other sub-categories of classic wargaming use cards in extensive measure. Area impulse games like the *Storm* series (MMP) include cards for representing the fluctuating condition of battlefield control, while very basic forms of point-to-point CDGs like *The Struggle for New France* (THGC) provide for cards without the familiar Event/Ops dichotomy to guarantee a much simpler and accessible turn management by beginning players. Not to mention the several light CDGs like *Flashpoint: South China Sea* and the *Lunchtime* series titles *Fort Sumter* and *Red Flag Over Paris* (GMT), or *13 Days* and *13 Minutes* (Jolly Roger Games), in which cards are once again streamlined to help players focus on very complex geopolitical contingencies and multiple simulated "dimensions", without damaging the overall playability of the experience.

Cards can also become powerful tools with which even highly conventional and codified elements of wargames, like combat, can be reinterpreted at the light of a very different approach. We have already seen how the unpredictable battles of the War of the Roses are perfectly depicted in *Kingmaker*'s volatile cards, but this is just a rudimentary first attempt compared to the highly differentiated CRTs included in every single card of *Dawn of Battle* (Worthington). Much simpler, but no less effective, systems can be found in *Hannibal: Rome vs Carthage* and *1815: Napoleon Returns* (Worthington), in which the resolution of combat is based on a matching card dynamic. Interestingly, the many variables of air combat have found a precious asset in cards, such as in solitaire titles *Skies Above Britain* (GMT) and *Western Front Ace* (Compass Games), where cards adjudicate the consequences of the different offensive and defensive maneuvers by the involved planes, while in the *Wings of Glory* series cards are used to determine the actual damages (conventional and special) inflicted on the targeted enemy planes.

Speaking of solo titles, cards have demonstrated an unsuspected value in that peculiar environment, by parcelling out information and guaranteeing a much higher replayability over different sessions.

Cards can determine orders for the "automated" units of the "bot", like in *Stalingrad: Inferno on the Volga* (VentoNuovo) or the *D-Day* (Decision Games) and the *Enemy Action* (Compass Games) series. Those actions can be quite simple or much more elaborate and multi-layered priority ladders, as in *Nights of Fire* (Mighty Boards) or in the card-based bots of the *COIN* series (for example, the *Arjuna* deck in *Gandhi*). Game designers can also take profit of the aforementioned multiple uses on each of them, as is the case of the *Leader* series (DVG) cards with pre-, during and post-events, the many asset management dilemmas in *Campaign: Fall Blau* (Catastrophe Games) or John Butterfield's masterpiece *RAF* in which the different cards have info on detection levels, entity and tactical choices by the Luftwaffe raids all over Britain in 1940.

This peculiar capability of cards has also been exploited by renowned game expert and content creator José Ruiz (also known as "Stuka Joe") to create a universal method for playing non-solitaire CDGs in solitaire mode, through a clever combination of dice-based activation of cards and selective hiding of portions of the "players'" hands.

All these different uses of cards are stipulated by precise rules, structured in their respective game systems. As always happens with the single mechanics, their combinations and interactions deeply influence both the general representation flow and the players' decisional process, creating what should by now be a familiar term: dynamics.

The game features thus called are dependent on the amount of the involved card, as well as on the type of behaviour asked of the players in order to exploit them with the objective of satisfying the final victory conditions, and thus succeeding in the game against other players or, in solitaire and cooperative games, the system itself.

The first dynamic we can find is, of course, also the simplest.

In game systems like *Commands & Colors* or *Combat Commander* you may or may not have the right cards to perform just that exact type of maneuver that you consider essential to victory. The bad news is that, as we have already seen, limitations like these are actually more realistic than systems granting you total or almost total control over your troops. The good news is that there is, however, a way to still maintain a broader sense of control also in CDGs: hand management.

With this term we describe all the techniques used to obtain just the perfect combination of card that you need to execute just the perfect combination of orders that you think are needed to obtain the final victory (if all your tactical calculations are correct and Friction does not have its say, of course). You can then discard unnecessary cards, use dilatory tactics until you get enough useful assets, bluff the enemy with diversions and false attacks. Also, neutral or offensive cards can be included in this management, with jammed weapons, bad weather or command uncertainties that can be unleashed on your opponent, with you temporarily impersonating Friction itself!

The only real problem is that you cannot be sure of the timing in which you will obtain these favourable conditions, and so you need to keep at least one or two cards in reserve to buy you the needed margin to improvise a counterattack . . . and so on, and so on, creating a deeply interactive cycle of decisions that really make the game.

Hand management is thus deeply tied to a similar dynamic, regarding the entire quantity of cards included in a game: deck management.

Here is where deckbuilding games like *A Few Acres of Snow* (Warfrog), *Hands in the Sea* (Knight Works), *Time of Crisis* (GMT) or the *Undaunted* series truly shine. In all these titles players begin with a preset deck that they can increment, turn after turn, by choosing additional cards from a common or individual pool. The new "assets" are then added to the original ones, effectively customizing the amount and quality of strategic choices, as well as the "speed" with which cards are cycled over through the reshuffles: do you prefer to have a wider, more versatile but also much "slower" and less controllable deck, or a more limited and yet much more focused and effective group of cards? The design solution is so flexible that also its conceptual opposite, deck destruction games, has been successfully used to represent more attritional conflicts like in *Lincoln* (PSC Games) for the American Civil War, in which players have to "burn" potentially valuable cards from their hand in order to "finance" complex tactical maneuvers or strategic actions.

In games belonging to the medieval operational wargame system *Levy & Campaign* the order of activations of the different Lord and their respective armies is decided by drawing cards out of two decks pre-formed (and *not* randomly shuffled) at the beginning of a turn, a system declaredly inspired by the classic *Angola* (MMP). Activation decks are also a part of *A Most Fearful Slaughter*, in which players can include a certain quantity of favourable cards to a deck that, unlike the *L&C* system, is shuffled at every turn. When card activation escapes direct players' choices and is entrusted to random draws, you get systems like *Commands & Colors*, *Onus!* (Draco Ideas) and *Quartermaster General* (Griggling Games), with all the tactical problems that they pose.

In still another *L&C* title, *Inferno* (GMT), players gain Treachery cards through various sources or as a consequence of game events: in medieval Tuscany devastated by continuing conflicts of Guelph and Ghibelline cities, these cards can determine random revolts on the map, changes of allegiance, quick surrender of castles and other isolated and unpredictable events, whose succession may decide the fate of an entire war. Alternatively, in the *Undaunted* series special orders add useless "Fog of War" or "Discord" cards to the deck, thus slowing it down and inducing dangerous uncertainties in leadership just at the most crucial moment of the engagement.

In conclusion, it should be clear by now that cards offer a lot of advantages to the game designer and the players, too, even if they pose just as many problems to game balance, replayability, players' experience discrepancies, scripting and many other issues that will be fully exposed in a dedicated chapter.

Here and now, suffice it to say that few components have influenced so much simulation gaming over the decades. Their flexibility and capability for including so much information in such a little space, exception management, original dynamics and much more is unsurpassed, and has represented an innovation at the very least fully comparable to the introduction of the combat results table or the zones of control. They have opened the market, introduced and retained large quotas of today's wargaming world, contributed to the rebirth of historical boardgaming after the darkest moments of the 1990s and much else.

This is because cards have repeatedly demonstrated their potential in creating games that are at the same time more accessible and attractive even to players not belonging to strict wargaming circles, as well as much more accurate and broadly scoped simulations encompassing kinetic and non-kinetic elements in a more believable narration of the many diversified and interconnected aspects of past events, even those of predominantly military nature. They obtain this goal by introducing more reasoned and elaborate risk management dynamics, simply because cards operate through more reasoned and elaborate forms of randomness itself.

The fact that historical miniatures games have also begun using them in larger numbers in their rulesets should come not as a surprise but as a confirmation of their value, versatility and, above all, durability as a game component that will undoubtedly remain a fundamental part of the vast majority of new simulation games designs for decades to come.

Another great little piece of paper earning its rightful place among the other great little pieces of paper we find in a wargame box: maps, counters and tables.

2.4 ENDGAME: FROM MECHANICS TO DYNAMICS

To complete our journey into this introductory study of typical simulation game mechanics, we have to take one last step: go beyond them and get at least a cursory look at their reciprocal interaction; that is, at the main simulation dynamics.

In effect, the most fundamental aspect of analog games to always take into account when speaking about them is that they exist as such only when they are actually played. It is true that Jim Dunnigan theorized the virtues of observing the "dynamic potential" of a game, just through placing maps and pieces on the table, tallying up the combat and movement values of all the pieces on the board, studying the relative tables and obtaining a visual picture of all the possible variations that could happen during a session. This however was not to be intended as a study with an end to itself, but rather to be considered a first analysis of the represented situation or, even more frequently, a preliminary exercise of the simulation parameters with the purpose of defining more efficient decisions during the actual gameplay.

In other words, even in the most conceptual parts of Dunnigan's studies, simulation games maintained their primary purpose, sometimes even predominant over the reproduction of historical events itself: to exist as games, needing to be played in order to express their fullest potential and justify their own existence.

So, mechanics exist only to propel the game towards their own reciprocal and constant interactions, that is the dynamics. Those processes, equally based on their mathematical relations as well as the emotional impacts on the players' perceptions, would form the game itself and, when inspired by actual events and constrained by the notional limits defined by historical studies, would create that very special and paradoxical game that wants to effectively recreate the world while apparently escaping from it: simulation.

In this regard, with a curious oscillation from the study of historical simulation games to the analysis of the history of simulation games, many have argued that in the last decades a trend has formed going in the general direction of merging "traditional" wargame mechanics with "more modern" and "innovative" Eurogame or German-style design solutions and even physical components. Some, quite acutely it has to be said, have gone even beyond this and saw in this a general change in the historiographic approach to the study of past events, joining together different academic disciplines, focusing on deeper analyses of more diversified events, and thus requiring a more "open-minded" approach, defying conventions that look more and more obsolete with each passing day (and published game).

This is true, of course, but only in part.

On the theoretical side, in fact, it has to be noted that alternative and even eccentric historiographic approaches are not by any mean just recent news: the old diatribe between Marc Bloch's *Nouvelle Histoire*, with its greater attention to social and economic studies than to war events, and the traditional *Histoire Bataille*, based on the mechanical retelling of notions and information about the mere kinetic aspects of military history, is itself a thing of the past, made obsolete at the end of the last millennium by the growth of studies focused on the social and economic aspect of war, some of which have aptly taken the name of *la Nouvelle Histoire-Bataille!*[19]

On the more practical side, there are no such things as "traditional wargame mechanics" or "more modern Eurogame or German-style design solutions", nor can the drive towards "innovation" (as well as cyclic moments of conceptual conservationism) be found only in this or that kind of game. Actually, most of what we today call "Euro" mechanics are direct evolutions or even outright transpositions of solutions introduced and commonly used by wargames published the 1970s . . . or even before. Simulation games that were, in many cases, much more innovative and experimental than the nth worker placement and resource management re-themed clone appearing with an almost obsessive regularity every single week on the more general boardgame market.

Again, the evolution of game design does not happen in a linear fashion, nor through clearly defined evolutionary processes. We can only observe general trends in its development, rigorously abstaining from giving them a particularly positive or negative value, and limiting ourselves to the study of the reasons leading to the re-emergence or re-submergence of this or that cycle in a given historical moment of game production.

By applying this awareness to the study of historical simulation, we can easily come to the conclusion that yes, there is a growing tendency towards more elaborate game treatments of well-known historical events as well as a particular curiosity towards titles dedicated to more obscure or even forgotten conflicts . . . but that this tendency is not the result of an unstoppable and almost mythical "progress" of game design, nor that it is an improbable "betrayal" of unmovable ideological landmarks.

Much more simply, it is just a homecoming of what simulation games have always tried to do—that is, give a better and more believable depiction of past events—and that today manage to do better thanks to mechanics that are considered more effective. All of this without renouncing traditional systems (hex and counter first among all), but rather reinterpreting, combining and redesigning them, or limiting their application to the simulation of predominantly kinetic events, even if with fresher approaches including exotic dynamics such as asymmetrical and variable victory conditions, fluctuating morale levels, more elaborated treatment of chains of command and their deficiencies, depiction of various forms of Friction, and so on.

The real problem probably derives from the fact that in the past a physically recognizable mechanic such as the hex grid easily separated more "serious" wargames from all other family games. Now, the advent of mid-level Eurogames made that distinction no longer so clear-cut, even if all the game mechanics described so far have this in common in their evolution: the push towards the creation of game dynamics which could obtain a more complete and effective simulation of past events in all their aspects, kinetic and non-kinetic.

That is why we see the multiplication of what once was a very peripheric sub-category of historical games and their respective dynamics, political-military sim-ulations (or pol-mil, for short). At the same time and in roughly equal measure: because the public demands that sort of approach; because game designers have a legitimate interest in that sort of historical reconstruction; because more efficient design solutions pertaining to that sort of titles have been found.

As one can easily see, all these reasons are internal and not external to the needs and most rigorous principles of simulation: no improbable attempts at gaining a few players more through the introduction of a decks of cards here, or a bunch of wooden cubes there, as often highlighted by more traditionalist critics denouncing the "end of wargaming as we know it", just the dear old experimental attitude of historical game designers and players. Together with the satisfaction of a perfectly legitimate, growing demand by the public for broader-approach games (not mutually exclusive with the always popular more traditional titles, by the way).

In effect, one could define political-military simulation as games based on dynam-ics characterized by an equivalent focus on political as well as military issues in their reproduction of past events, but of equal importance are those titles that we could call "mil-pol" games: games much closer to traditional wargames like *Paths of Glory* or *Shifting Sands* (MMP), in which military events on the field remain predominant in the general economy of the experience, however at least partly tied to political and non-kinetic generations which can have significant effects on the conduit of opera-tions. And a very similar study could be made over almost exclusively "pol-pol" sim-ulations (like *Votes for Women*, Fort Circle Games), as well as alternative "mil-mil" simulations (like the *Undaunted* series (Figure 2.5), with its trademark take on purely tactical engagements).

This preliminary consideration on modern day simulation titles to see how it is not by looking at single isolated mechanics that we can define the nature of a game (distinguishing at first glance *Twilight Struggle from Barbarossa to Berlin*), but by studying their interplay as the game dynamics that really give sense to the approach chosen by the game designer. In other words: mechanics are just neutral tools, while dynamics resulting from their calibrated and deliberate combination are the "true colours" of a simulation game.

One of these key dynamics is the final element that defines the tone of game dynamics, which is also the end of the game itself, and for this reason is the last element analyzed here: victory conditions. While sometimes relegated to a second-ary paragraph in the rulebook, the endgame objectives (or even mid-game, in case of sudden death contingencies) are instead an essential portion of the simulation, orienting the players' behaviour, giving them the important landmarks to keep every-thing on course and most of all being what really defines the final adherence of a gaming experience to its historical authenticity. By overlooking victory conditions in the analysis of a game, you are essentially disregarding what really makes that game *historical*, or not.

For example, in real history, "body counts" may have made a great title on the next day's newspapers, but only through a very pragmatic change in strategic paradigms

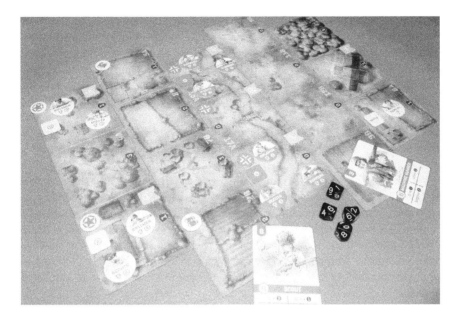

FIGURE 2.5   The *Undaunted* series (Osprey) provided a surprisingly convincing tactical simulation with a particular emphasis on command and control during combat engagements.

Source: Photograph by the author.

could one proclaim himself the true winner: in this, the destruction of the enemy armed forces is just one of the many possible meaningful events. In simulation games, the very first solution to avoid simplistic "last man standing" scenarios is the inclusion of geographic key positions to conquer and control, or the ability of keeping your army standing firm on the battlefield at the end of the last turn (preservation of your forces is the conceptual opposite of destruction of the enemy ones).

Having said that, there is a veritable plethora of much diversified options devised by game designers over the decades. Sometimes you just need to get as many of your troops off the map as soon as possible (*Breakthrough: Cambrai*, MMP or *A Distant Plain*, GMT), other times you lose points every time you "purchase" special non-linear effects (*The Library of Napoleonic Battles*, OSG). Sometimes you have your fixed score card in front of you from turn one, other times you get your points based on partial conditions as soon as a certain card is drawn or a certain pivotal contingency is verified thanks to your strategic decisions that you have to "build" turn after turn (*Twilight Struggle*, GMT, *Europe Divided*, Phalanx, *Prelude to Revolution*, Compass Games). And in some very interesting cases, victory conditions are not only asymmetrical in nature but also in knowledge, since only one of the players is fully aware of them, leaving the way open to bluff strategies and deceptions of varied kinds (*Dunkirk*, *Napoleon Returns, 1815*, *D-Day to the Rhine 1944*, *1944: Battle of the Bulge*, Worthington . . . all inspired by *Battles for the Ardennes*'s multiple victory choices, SPI).

Again, those conditions may be parallel and lead to possible alternative paths to victory (*Bravery in the Sand*, MMP),[20] forcedly contained (in *Churchill* and

Versailles, GMT, the delicate balance of the political portion of the game requires a victory, not a supremacy that would put the subsequent after-game peace phase at risk!), dependent on players' choices in activating or not a certain reinforcement formation (*Crisis on the Right: Plancenoit 1815*, White Dog Games) or, on the opposite, forcedly "pushed" through a system of growing set quantities of victory points to be satisfied every turn to avoid an exhaustion defeat, not unlike one of those 1980s car racing videogames (*The U.S. Civil War*, GMT, and *Lincoln*, PSC). There are also titles that offer as a victory condition the destruction of the enemy's will to fight even before its armies (*Empire of the Sun*, GMT), integrating deeply asymmetrical and non-kinetic factors in a predominantly military simulation.

And the victory conditions can be, or better usually are, asymmetrical between the two or more opponents, with individual goals, sometimes totally exclusive of each other, some other times interconnected with those of the other participants, like in *COIN* titles in which one player usually has an "ally" of some sort at his side sharing a part of his or her goals, or in the recent *The Barrack Emperors* (GMT), in which, in order to gain the favour of a candidate to the Roman Imperial throne, you have to manipulate the board and allow another player to obtain favour with another candidate . . .

Regarding other forms of games that are not strictly competitive, even the mere survival would be a victory in itself, especially in solitaire games whose real purpose is not to gather points but to tell a coherent story of "your" characters. There are of course even more possible examples, like many different aspects of victory conditions in cooperative and semi-cooperative games, that would require almost another entire paragraph.

Any way you put it, victory conditions provide the players with something like a "draft script" to adhere to and follow in order to fulfil not only their gaming goals, but also the historical vision of the game designer. There are even times in which one of the players knows that he or she cannot but "lose" (*Durchbruch*, Acies, about the battle of Caporetto, in World War One) and when the only satisfaction is to lose a bit less than the historical counterparts. Yet, this is the true force of historical simulation games in respect to German-style and even Eurogames: they don't need to be obsessively balanced in every single component, because history is imbalanced and the object of wargames and simulation games is not to gather mere "points", but rather to provide an engaging and believable storytelling experience, in which everyone wins by the mere fact of standing around the game table and reenact past events together. In this sense simulation games can be said to be much less competitive than more abstract titles, because the historical facts and their narration are much more important than the material game procedures used to give them a new life.[21]

Actually, victory conditions highlight the fact that in war there is not just one kind of victory or defeat, but a series of different "states" of final balances in which a "peace" could be much different than another, even when the identity of the "winner" and the "loser" stay the same. Would a triumph at Waterloo mean a full restoration of Napoleon's First Empire? Probably not, since there would still be many other powerful Coalition armies converging on the battered *Armée du Nord* . . . but the vanquishing of Anglo-Prussian forces might have radically changed the fate of Napoleon himself and with that also the balance of power in continental Europe for the next century. Or think to the very last stages of the Thirty Years War, when armies still fought an effectively ended war just to obtain a more favourable peace . . . perfectly represented by the agonizing joint military and diplomatic operations that are the real protagonists of pol-mil game *Westphalia*, Hollandspiele.

So, victory conditions satisfy two very precise and crucial functions in simulation: they help define the historical interpretation of the game designer regarding the depicted events, and they keep the players "on track" with that interpretation. Even in games in which competitivity is more apparent than real, the storytelling aspects of wargames and simulation games are considered to be of much greater importance.

With this, our dedicated analysis of game mechanics (and dynamics) ends here. They will be mentioned and analyzed even further, of course, but only as needed in order to obtain the true purpose of simulation games, transcending even the practical combination of their single pieces: the offering to the players of a playable, interactive and plausible historical model. Rather, a *possible* historical model, based on a certain choice of elements to be focused on and with a certain approach in mind by the author and the players themselves.

Inside this small, but fundamental, discrepancy between a mere reconstruction of historical events and their modelization through an open-ended game environment lies the true nature of simulation, distinguishing it from mere emulation or rigid re-enactment. So, get ready, because nothing that you have read so far, either theoretical or practical, would be of any use without what is coming in the next chapter: history and, even more, the image of history that we enjoy and express through books, art, movies, personal and national memory . . . and, of course, games.

NOTES

1   Interestingly, H. G. Wells's *Little Wars* itself was in part conceived as a declaredly pacifist "response" to the great celebrity enjoyed by the more militaristic German *Kriegsspiel*.

2   Of course, many so-called "monster wargames" did not accept this compromise and carried on in their accurate geographical depiction, leading to a multiplication of their table space and counter density. An example in that sense is the *Europa* series, published by GDW.

3   This does not include the use of "modular" tiles over plain mapboards to create single scenarios like in the *Commands & Colors* system. Some of these games, however, allow players to change the shape of the terrain through their actions, like *Undaunted: Stalingrad* (Osprey Games).

4   As mentioned in Mahaffey, M., Historical aesthetics in mapmaking, in Harrigan, P., Kirschenbaum, M. (curated by), *Zones of control: Perspectives on wargaming*, The MIT Press (Cambridge, 2016).

5   It may be of use to remember here the famous "black SS" debate over the frequent use of the colour black to identify SS troops in World War Two wargames. Some have considered this a not-so-well-hidden form of celebration of the supposed martial prowess of these German elite troops, seeing it as possible evidence of a revisionist approach. Much more simply, this colour choice might come from a classic Hollywood approach since in war movies, SS officers invariably appear in their spotless black uniforms . . . which were almost never used in actual combat! Game designer Brian Train has deliberately opted for a much different tint to depict these units in his Battle of the Bulge wargame *Winter Thunder* (Tiny Battle Publishing), inspired by the actual historical colour of the SS shoulder tabs: hot pink.

6   There are exceptions and further sophistications, of course. In the *Brigade Battle* series (Worthington), dedicated to the highly attritional American Civil War battles, losses are treated with much more granularity, with units having ten or more "steps" indicated by additional counters. Those components are called "Pollard markers", in honour of game designer Bob Pollard, that devised them in 1980 for *Forward to Richmond!* (3W), and have also inspired the rotating wooden blocks with different step losses on each side so commonly present in the Columbia Games titles and their derivations.

7   This might come as a surprise to the *connoisseurs* of classical *Kriegsspiel*, more often than not based on hypothetical, only vaguely defined "units" represented on the game map by . . . coloured wooden blocks.

8   For a more extensive analysis of CRTs as elements of game design, also see Herman, M., Wargame CRTs or how to resolve chaos, in *C3i Magazine*, n. 36 (2022).

9   A "golden ratio" reminiscent of the purely quantitative "Lanchestrian equations" used in conventional approaches to military history and analysis, so vehemently criticized by Philip Sabin in *Simulating Wars* (cit.).

10 For an in-depth analysis of some rules writing techniques, see also Delwood, R., *Writing war gaming rules correctly*, Medium, https://robertdelwood.medium.com/writing-war-gaming-rules-correctly-43e0428fd966 (2019).

11 Actually, Zucker reprises positions expressed all throughout his entire career such as in the articles *The image of battle* and *Accuracy vs playability* hosted in the *Fire & Movement* magazine, respectively in 1978 and 2005.

12 Stanton, N., Baber, C., Harris, D., *Modelling command and control: Event analysis of systemic teamwork*, Ashgate Publishing Ltd. (2008).

13 In the *Standard Combat Series* design notes, author Dean Essig explains that he devised this simplified and essential ruleset with the intended purpose of letting players "shoot from the hip".

14 White, J., Moonshine in Atlantic chase, in *C3i Magazine*, n. 35 (2021).

15 Rather unsurprisingly, Ruhnke himself presented an in-depth analysis of supply treatment in strategic, operational and even tactical level simulation games in Stock & flow in wargames, in *C3i Magazine*, n. 33 (2019).

16 Ruhnke, V., *Cards in wargames*, Georgetown University Wargame Society, https://www.youtu.be/WIBpCJ09KhA (2021). Several parts of this paragraph are directly inspired by Ruhnke's work on that presentation as well as in his other works, which explains in great depth the many advantages (as well as the potential issues) of the use of cards in game design.

17 For more in-depth and first-person accounts of the genesis of the first recognized CDG, see Herman's dedicated article on C3i issue n. 17, as well as the photos of the original notes shared on his personal Twitter account.

18 Yet, as we shall see in the next chapter, the system is not without its faults and its somewhat abstracted approach to the many facets of counterinsurgency warfare has been recently criticized by game designer and political relations expert Stephen Rangazas, in the video *Guerrilla Generation: COIN beyond COIN* on the YouTube channel *Homo Ludens*, https://www.youtube.com/watch?v=keUR15gYwSM&t.

19 Henninger, L., La nouvelle histoire-bataille, in *Espace Temps* (1999).

20 For a detailed analysis of the masterfully crafted victory conditions of this title, see Starkweather, A., On to victory—victory condition considerations in bravery in the sand, in *Operations Special Issue*, n. 2 (2009).

21 Interestingly, by stressing the importance of narration and self-recognition, as well as the innate complexity of some of the depicted events, one can reach the conclusion that maybe victory conditions are not so necessary, nor meaningful in the general experience of simulation games. Such is Amabel Holland's opinion in *Do board games need victory conditions?* Mary Holland, https://youtu.be/QxZcDZ1MUjk (2023).

3 In the Field
Historical Dynamics through the Gaming Lens

"Games are the most elevated form of investigation."

Albert Einstein

Having both the theorical principles as well as the practical founding blocks of a typical rule system in hand, we will now focus on the objective reasons why simulation games tend to be so elusive and constantly changing not just because of the players' fluctuating perceptions, but for the very mathematical and historiographical elements of their essence.

It has all to do with the protean nature of reality itself, our vision and interpretation of it, our collective memory of past events, how we deal with the consequences of those events, the corruption of primary sources, the extent of the exploitation of the past to change the present and the future, and so on and so on. All these eminently volatile factors are highlighted to the extreme in a game environment and, as we have seen, the underlying paradox is that the more elaborate and expressly "simulative" the game strives to be, the more potential deviations and personal interpretations it includes.

On top of all this, you get revolutions in historiography, as well as in the historical gaming world.

This definition could be easily applied to Mark Herman's great invention of card-driven games, how they demolished the 3:1 "golden ratio" fixation, their inclusion of non-linear and non-kinetic elements into the simulative equation, the fact that one could win all the possible military victories in the field, and yet lose the conflict on parallel political and diplomatic dimension—just like what happened during the American Revolution portrayed in the first recognized CDG, *We the People.*

This will be the subject of this chapter: starting with the past events themselves, how they are differently interpreted by different game authors and systems and how they are ultimately "modelled" inside those wonderful statistical machines that are simulations.

3.1 THE FACE(S) OF BATTLE

What's it like to venture into an open conflict—fully armed, trained and equipped—against other fellow similarly prepared human beings? To participate in that strange, almost ritual event which is a battle, fought on chosen material or ideological field, with pre-established objectives, summarily described "rules of engagement", a

DOI: 10.1201/9781003429098-4

peculiar rhythm of action, a set of accepted (and unaccepted) behaviours? All following the purpose of justifying one of the most distasteful and yet more innate elements
of our human nature: subjugating other people to our will.

So many military historians have tried to find an answer to these questions since
Herodotus and Thucydides. Of course, no one has found a way out of the dilemma.
What many have managed to do is just to purify the narration of military events from
all its pomp and circumstance, adopting a practical (not necessarily neutral) approach
to its description and trying to make their readers understand all the tragedy, suffering, infinite complications and outright terror faced by those that have fought in real
wars, regardless of their nationality, religion, political creed and personal opinions.

In a way, historical simulation games, followed a similar streamlining approach,
even if from a different and somewhat opposed direction: by focusing almost exclusively on material statistics—like force ratios and terrain effects—to show the true
"scientific" nature of war.

Of course, not all kinds of simulations faced the same challenges. Generally,
lower-level representations of reality at the tactical or grand-tactical dimension could
get along fairly well just by introducing some morale rules and a random events table
or two. Yet, already from the operational scale and even more at the strategic level of
representation (that is, entire campaigns or whole conflicts), it quickly became clear
that something else had to be there if the simulation aspired to be something more
than just "a fun game".

This was the core idea behind the famous observations by Jim Dunnigan, which
led to his early collaboration with Avalon Hill, a true turning point in simulation
games history. Games had not only the task of making playing with history fun or
even just informative . . . they had to make that playing "right", by giving it the fruits
of dedicated historical research and passionate refinements in the development process. They had to simulate the past, and to do so they had to *model* it.[1]

But what could be considered a model? And how could it be included in a game
by a more comprehensive activity called "historical modelling"?

Let's start with the odds. Their definition, as well as the definition of their interactions, are the sole responsibility of the game designer (and the game developers,
unsung heroes of the endless refinements of simulative systems). All this stuff, making up the bulk of the game itself, begins with a general idea by the author, itself
derived by his or her personal interpretation of the historical events. That interpretation is sharpened by successive research, calibrated by extensive playtesting and also
subjected to many changes during the game design process, whose main purpose
is—just like the historian's work—to ensure a better representation of the "true" (or
at least, passably believable) historical dynamics. The final goal of it all is duplic-
itous: create a fun "toy" with which a number of players can spend an enjoyable
amount of time, as well as provide a truly informative historical depiction of the
subject of the game itself.[2]

The resulting endless fluctuations in historical rendition have also another side-
effect, a small miracle almost unknown outside the inner circle of wargame connoisseurs: it is not true that every single hex and counter or card-driven wargame is just
the same as all other similar titles. They are just very closely related, since the core
structure of this kind of game is at the same time so compact and flexible that even

by changing a very small detail (a modifier here, a CRT entry there, the distribution of cards in the deck, the zone of control or interception mechanics . . .) the entire experience changes dramatically.

Maintaining all this diversity, creating believable historical models that are instantly recognizable as wargames as well as capable of effectively depicting all the specific period features is the real tell-tale sign of the good old art of wargame design. Something that only the true masters of the trade can achieve with almost jaw-dropping simplicity.[3]

Different periods call for different solutions in the games that are set to portray them. The much less granular operational style of ancient armies, for example, is better served by area movement or point-to-point map, while the more scientific and calculated art of warfare in the contemporary period from sixteenth century onward often requires the use of hex-based maps.

Changing a CRT or the nature of a map to introduce a different treatment for, let's say, small-unit tactics between the two World Wars is relatively easy.[4] But what happens when the diversity in simulative treatment is not "external" to the object itself (that is, due to different chronological periods covered), but *internal* to the situation itself?

This is generally true for games about irregular or asymmetrical conflicts between one or more factions who do not follow the same "rules of engagement", so to say. The thought here runs to *COIN* games, but even before such extreme examples of different, often opposed, treatments of multiple factions in the same game, one could look at one of the "ancestor titles" to the acclaimed series to find other just as equally interesting examples. The title of choice is, of course, *Labyrinth* (GMT), still by Volko Ruhnke (Figure 3.1), which very effectively depicts the two different tactical approaches by Coalition forces and Terrorist groups on the global scene of the War on Terror: while the former have to create an elaborate set of preconditions to see their actions implemented on the ground, the latter can act with much more speed and less formal constraints, being however subjected to dice rolls that introduces a very random element to the resolution of their decisions.

Contrary to what many believe, though, even less irregular conflicts may need a peculiar treatment not based on a simple IGOUGO symmetrical structure. The first phases of the Eastern Front actions in WWII, that is Operation Barbarossa in 1941, clearly showed not only the differing levels of readiness between German units and their Soviet counterparts, but also the very different operational doctrines of the two armies. To accurately reflect this in a simulation environment, game designers need to devise something more than simply changing a combat factor value on some of the counters.

That is why several wargames about very peculiar events resort to dynamic and asymmetric turn sequences. The idea is to depict the differences in military structures and foundational strategies in a simple and effective way, without overburdening the players with a myriad of arbitrary modifiers or special rules.

One of the most interesting examples lies in the *SCS* series titles *Heights of Courage* and *Yom Kippur* (MMP), dedicated to the Fourth Arab-Israeli War. Here, to depict the different levels of readiness by the different armies while maintaining the trademark simplicity of the series, the Israeli player can count on a deeply asymmetrical

FIGURE 3.1   Published in 2010, *Labyrinth* (GMT) has redefined many key concepts of simulation games, providing a highly original model depicting many features of modern global asymmetrical warfare.

Source: Photograph by the author.

turn sequence which grants him or her the possibility of conducting additional attacks right inside the Egyptian/Syrian player's decisional cycle. The Arab commanders can decide to "step up" their operational tempo to respond to the more effective Israeli command structure, but cannot do it for extended periods of time if they want to keep their fragile armies together: the decision of when to "push" and when to "hold back" becomes thus fundamental, adding another layer to the game.

Just by changing the conventional "movement and then combat" structure of classical wargames to a "combat and then movement" to incur in subtle, yet fundamental differences, *Caporetto & Italy 1917–1918* (Decision Games), an insert game to the popular *Strategy & Tactics* magazine, deliberately adopts this solution to depict the slow planning required in order to organize operational offensives in World War One, when you had to amass lots of troops and materials in a sector before even thinking about unleashing a general assault over a relevant portion of the frontline.

Other times, the succession of these two fundamental moments in a turn (movement and combat) can be left to the will of the players, becoming an integral part of their respective strategies. Renowned game designer Ty Bomba devised this general system in which a player decides the order between move and combat segments in his or her turn. Countless variations have been devised by Bomba's highly creative fantasy: *A Crowning Glory* (Battle of Austerlitz), *Bloody Retribution* (Battle of Inkerman, Crimean War), *Drive on Stalingrad* (WWII Eastern Front) and many others. This not only creates a highly dynamic player experience, but also provides for a very effective model of the disruptions in the strategic and tactical management of forces imposed by the chaos of the battlefield.

There are even instances in which differing historiographies create different solutions in game design. For example, military historians are not in agreement about the practical consequences of urban combat in the broader "economy" of large-scale battles of the American Civil War. Considering the linear small-unit tactics of the period, was it really an advantage for the defender to fight inside a town or a city? Or, rather, did military leaders of the era actively avoid these situations, leading to the disaggregation of their units, a loss in command and control, and a general decrease in efficiency?

We have differing testimonies supporting both visions during battles like Fredericksburg, Chancellorsville and Gettysburg, leading to divergent historical analysis . . . leading of course to differing treatments in simulation games. While the classic quad-game *Blue & Gray* (SPI, Decision Games) provides a fairly good defensive bonus in densely built urban areas, other more recent titles like *Gettysburg* (MMP), published as an insert game for *Special Ops* magazine, speculate that no real bonus could be had in fighting in such environment since the commanders actually tried to pull the troops out of the town areas and fight in the clear as soon as possible.

In short, all these examples constitute a true testimony to the very high internal diversity in wargames, at least as varied as the diversity in historiographic treatments of the same events. Which, by the way, should be considered as a very good thing for the hobby, keeping it alive and avoiding the stagnancy over repetitive models.[5]

As already noted, however, space and time rendition in the simulation have a strong influence over the choice of game design solutions.

An entire world of difference lies of course between the topics covered by a purely tactical game and a strategic one, as well as those simulated by an operational title. This happens not only because different decision-making spaces and dimensions are naturally introduced at higher levels of leadership (namely, with a progressive insertion of political, economic, social and other non-kinetic elements the more you climb that "ladder"), but also because the public expectations and sometimes even composition for such games are generally quite different: an *Advanced Squad Leader* player may be interested in strategic games like *Rise and Fall of the Third Reich* or *The Russian Campaign*, but what he or she will look for in a strategic title will be much different.

So, it comes as no surprise that the overall experience offered by man-to-man games like medieval *Guiscard* (Historic-One) and hypothetical modern *Firepower* (Avalon Hill) or *Warfare: Modern Tactical Combat* (WBS) are not at all comparable with titles dedicated to similar periods like *Nevsky* (GMT) or *Iron Curtain* (MMP). It is, however, always possible to introduce systems by which several games of distinct levels can be combined, in order to create a truly complete and seamless multi-level simulative experience.[6]

However, games at the same level of simulation can include or exclude elements that are typical of other equivalent titles, dealing with the exact same space or time scale, also when it comes to elements that are broadly considered a standard or a defining feature of a certain period.

There are few things as distinctive of a specific tactical approach in the history of warfare as Napoleonic-era formations (line, column, square . . .), so much that some traditional historians have come to treat them as something of an evolved form of rock-paper-scissors . . . and yet, renowned game designer Kevin Zucker has purposedly taken them away from his acclaimed *TLNB* series, considering the tactical choice of adopting specific formations well below the decision level of the portrayed commanders.[7]

Expert wargamers will surely indicate as a perfect exemplary case of this the amazing plethora of different systems dedicated to World War Two small-unit tactical engagements, of which there surely is no shortage!

Advanced Squad Leader is the best known of them, and undoubtedly one to be considered a reference point in the sub-genre. Yet even series like the much simpler but no less effective *Band of Brothers* (Worthington), innovative hybrid *Undaunted* (Osprey Games), highly streamlined *Old School Tactical* (Flying Pig Games) and the ideal heir to *ASL*, *Lock 'n Load Tactical System* (LnL), cannot be discounted, representing very different takes on the same subject.

Here the diverse focus possibilities of simulation games appear in all their strength. By highlighting this or that other element of tactical firefights (command and control, unit training, equipment capabilities, general doctrine . . .), those titles allow their players to have a much broader knowledge of the features of these deeply dramatic historical moments, as well as having access to a better awareness of what really means to be under fire, with a mission to accomplish and fellow comrades to protect.

Much less "kinetic" historical dynamics are subject to infinite variation in their simulation by analog titles as well. The very complex military, political and even cultural conflict by the empires of Russia and Great Britain in the Afghan Iranian area during the nineteenth century become to be known as "The Great Game", thanks to some contemporary newspaper articles and the adoption of the definition by writer Rudyard Kipling. The same title, *The Great Game*, belongs also to a card-driven simulation published by Legion Wargames in which the Russian and the British players compete in order to obtain the support of various local potentates, recruiting armies, expanding their sphere of influence and toppling down unwanted sovereigns in the area. This approach correctly highlights the ruthlessness of the colonizing powers of the era but has the problem of not giving enough agency to the complex tapestry of kingdoms, tribal societies and full-fledged nations flourishing in the region . . . something that game designer Cole Wehrle addressed in his *Pax Pamir* (Sierra Madre Games, Wehrlegig Games) in which the players instead take on the role of the many native clans of Afghanistan actually playing out the British and the Russians in order to promote their respective power interests against the other locals.

Are these two games mutually exclusive? Of course not, since both give different points of view over the same historical episode, and actually the comparison between those two very different experiences will give an enquiring player much more reference material and personal insight for his or her study on the subject. Just as two different and yet somewhat complimentary historical essays about the same event.

Some of these historical "traditions" have been with us across entire millennia and are present in totally different games. Think about Alexander of Macedon, whose nickname "the Great" is just the first sign of an almost immediate process of glorification, if not outright deification.

A similar testimony of his fame can be found in two very different and totally unrelated games, recently re-published *Alexandros* (XTR, Compass Games) and solitaire game *Field Commander: Alexander* (DVG). In both, a fundamental mechanic and victory point source for the players (or the single player . . .) are specific personal objectives that the simulated "Alexander" receives in the guise of material advantages or even mystical prophecies. Those goals assume the form of "missions" to be fulfilled in the best tradition of heroic literature, carrying forward that almost chivalrous depiction of the young Macedonian king and later "World Emperor".

The totally opposite case is represented by those game systems that, while keeping most of the rules unchanged, simulate different historical periods over several separate and autonomous titles. Here you can find a core of rules that are instantly recognizable and familiar to the series *aficionados*, and yet are somewhat calibrated with pervasive variations in order to better depict a specific event.

The most known example in the wargaming world is the *Commands & Colors* system that, even if published under different brands (Avalon Hill, GMT, Compass Games, Days of Wonder, PSC . . .) in a long list of titles (*Battle Cry, Memoir '44, Commands & Colors: Ancients, Commands & Colors: Tricorne, The Great War*), covers battles belonging to periods from antiquity up to World War Two and even beyond with dedicated fantasy and sci-fi versions.

Here, the "core" is simply constituted by the card-driven activation system and the special dice-based combat resolution. What distinguishes all the different titles is all the rest, with variations ranging from national characteristics (*Napoleonics*), preliminary bombardments (*The Great War*), special unit capabilities (*Medieval*), additional decks, varied card distribution or even a combination of some of these subsystems. In *Samurai Battles* there are even very "evocative" mechanics like honour and *seppuku* ritual suicides committed in order to preserve it!

All those simple and yet very significant from a gaming point of view features can be considered to be the "historical highlights" of the chosen period.[8]

Another case is represented by the games designed by Dan Verssen. This author has created some very unique series of card games like *Down in Flames* (air combat in the two world wars, as well as in the Cold War era), *Naval Battles* and also solitaire lines like the *Leader* series. Here players manage entire flight squadrons, composed by different pilots each with his or her own sets of skills and weaknesses, dealing with historically calibrated enemies over different missions and campaigns. While the similarities in the system over the different simulated eras are even stronger than with the battles of *C&C*, a simple variation in the cards' contents (and there are *lots* of cards in those games), as well as in the plane features, mission types, campaign parameters and single special rules is quite effective in showing the differences between leading a Cold War US Navy squadron (*Hornet Leader*), a close air support formation (*Thunderbolt Apache Leader*) or an Israeli flight group from 1948 onward (*IAF Leader*).

Similar considerations could be made for multi-period systems like *Wings of Glory* (Ares Games) with his different WWI and WWII rulesets, *Guiscard* and the special units and formation rules belonging to the different factions, classic *Ancients* (3W) system with his variations created to cover conflicts ranging from antiquity up to the Renaissance, Mark Simonitch's *194X* series of hex and counter wargames, every single title in the card game series *Lightning* (Decision Games) dedicated to a different World War Two campaign, and so on.

In order to maintain a proper simulative value, those series of similar titles, as well as those very different titles set in the same periods, need to find a delicate balance between rules familiarity, simplicity of play and believable reconstruction of the events. As a textbook example, one could consider the *Battle Cards* series of one-sheet mini-wargames about several famous World War Two campaigns and its minimalistic design approach: just by modifying a small rule here, adding a modifier there or adjusting a very essential CRT, those die-rolling based solitaires manage to create a valid modelling of the main tactical and logistic dynamics of their respective simulated operations.

The reverse of this, whatever their complexity and approach may be, is that all games always run the risk of failing in their simulative purpose, appearing in turn too bland and "generic", or too elaborate and demanding in terms of rules management. A good deal of experience and competence is then required from the game designers to have the necessary premises for a successful historical simulation . . . as well as the wilful and well-informed participation of the players themselves, whose main responsibility would be to "make the magic work"—the players being the ultimate game engine behind these paper time machines.

Letting this quantity of game designs become a quality in historical simulation is not an easy task but this is the true trademark of good designers wishing to create good open-ended, believable and easily understandable depictions of all the very different (and equally fascinating) historical events in a long series of good games.

3.2 SENSITIVE ISSUES AND INSENSITIVE GAMES

The fact that there may actually be a dozen or more titles dedicated to the same Napoleonic campaign or to the infinitely dissected Battle of the Bulge, each of which coming with its own peculiar centre of interest (be it essentially maneuvering, logistics, leadership, political consequences, or a mix of those aspects and even more . . .), is a testimony to the genius and multifaceted expertise of historical game designers. And some of them are more aware of this than others.

Actually, every author knows that his or her work is as much a work of art as a personal projection of some parts of themselves into material form. In this respect, boardgames are no different from books, movies, paintings et cetera, especially in more recent years when, finally, designers' names have begun to regularly appear on the game boxes, in some cases becoming selling points themselves. This tendency is very common in the broader boardgaming world, but even more felt in the forcedly more restricted niche of the historical simulation hobby, especially now that social media, information technology and global instant communications have decreased the distance separating players from designers.[9]

True, even in the "glory days" of the 1970s and early 1980s one could easily see some distinguishing telltale elements that the game in question belonged to this or other designer. This could become more evident when the said designers worked on different titles belonging to the same series: speaking of the two aforementioned designers, the *PRESTAGS* series (SPI) by John Young clearly appears as a comprehensive treaty on the evolution of battle tactics from ancient Egypt to the emergence of gunpowder in the late Middle Ages through early Renaissance period, while all the medieval warfare *Men of Iron* titles (GMT) by Richard Berg are introduced by a subtitle revealing a not-so-hidden message about said evolution: a very Delbrückian "The Rebirth of Infantry".[10]

As a circle-closing moment, Berg himself returned to ancient warfare with a comprehensive scientific treatment of its features through the *Great Battles of History* series (GMT), co-designed with Mark Herman and widely considered as one of the wargame systems that gave a fundamental contribution to the re-emergence of the hobby in the late 1990s. Herman himself would very often mix his academic studies with the design of many of his most famous titles, sometimes even explicitly mentioning them as in the playbook of the new GMT re-edition of *Peloponnesian War*; similarly, even the designer that could be considered Herman's *de facto* successor, Volko Ruhnke, included many elements of his works and personal conclusions as intelligence analyst for CIA in titles like *Labyrinth* and the *COIN* series, setting an example followed also by other designers; all the while, and operating in a totally different environment, Martin Wallace subjected his experience as history teacher to his passion for simulation, producing amazing hybrid Euro-wargames under the Warfrog label like *Liberté*, *Waterloo*, *Gettysburg* and most importantly *A Few Acres of Snow* with its ideal opposite "deck destruction" title *Lincoln*.

This need was felt also at the editorial level of entire magazines, and one of the best examples in this sense is surely represented by the *Against the Odds 2015 Annual*, *Four Roads to Paris*. In that anthology a player could find no less than four titles dedicated to four different aspects of the 1940 Fall of France campaign: *The Seeds of Destruction* (by John Prados, a "prequel" rendition of all the main military as well as political events leading to the 1940 debacle), *Springtime for Hitler* (by Michael Rinella, a classic simulation of the campaign itself focusing on the asymmetrical states of readiness between the different armies), *Betrayal!* (by Roger Nord, an interesting game stressing the misunderstandings and even sometimes divergent objectives of France and Great Britain) and *Strange Victory* (by Steven Cunliffe, a solitaire game in which the player fights at the head of the famous Panzer spearheads both against the enemy and against the mistrust of the German High Command regarding the new independent armoured formations). Indeed, four games and four different roads to finally get to Paris . . . and a broader comprehension of what really happened in that astounding May of 1940.[11]

In other cases, the same single designer provides for a similar collection, starting with a common theme and then dissecting it with different titles based on the very same systems but enough variation to appreciate the different ways for the treated historical dynamics to manifest themselves. In many cases, these titles are bundled together in the popular format of "quad games": four distinct but highly similar games sharing the bulk of their rules and offered inside a single box.

Appreciated author and renowned irregular warfare expert Brian Train managed a similar feat with *Brief Border Wars* (Compass Games), a simulation of four short and highly asymmetrical conflicts: El Salvador against Honduras (the so-called "Soccer War"), 1969; Cyprus, 1974; China's punitive expedition against Vietnam, 1979; Israeli raids against Hezbollah forces in southern Lebanon, 2006 (Figure 3.2). The simple central system allowed Train to expose both the similarities and the differences in these quick modern conflicts, often dominated by a gripping need of gaining the best possible advantages in the very short time allowed by possible peacekeeping international interventions.

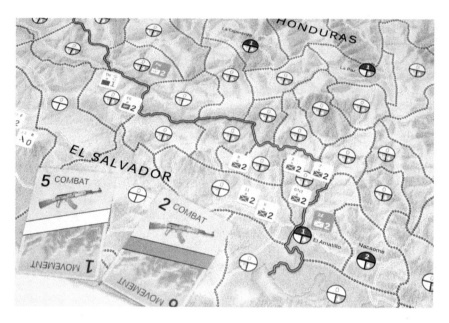

FIGURE 3.2   *Brief Border Wars* (Compass Games), by Brian Train, is focused on the simulation of highly unusual small conflicts whose outcome was deeply influenced by political consideration and that are still today regarded as highly controversial in all the nations involved.

Source: Photograph by the author.

In another case a much newer addition to the game designers fold, Stephen Rangazas, produced a highly stimulating re-interpretation of the by now classical *COIN* system by presenting four mini-scenarios for two players, all focused on different moments in the dissolution of the former British Empire after World War Two in *The British Way* (GMT): Malaya, Kenya, Cyprus and Israel (once again . . .). The entire game is presented as a historical essay about the ugliest aspects of British de-colonization, uncovering previously held myths about a "more peaceful" transition to independence than the one endured by former French-held colonies like Algeria or Vietnam.

None of the names already mentioned, however, can be considered superior in their attention to including academic treatments in their game designs than Phil Ecklund and Cole Wehrle.

The former created a whole line of games, the *Pax* series, in which every single title started from a very specific thesis and provided extensive scientific documentation throughout their game manuals. This documentation was not confined to a final and ignorable bibliography, as happens in many other fine historical simulations, but spread among the rules paragraphs, sometimes at the expense of their overall clarity.

The latter, starting as a co-designer for some of the later Ecklund titles, somewhat refreshed this approach by adopting some stylistic solutions derived from Eurogame designs, producing games with a very high level of historical detail, impressive originality and yet absolute accessibility with jewels like *Pax Pamir* and *John Company*.

It should be said, however, that with all the extension and sophistication of historical analysis required by academic-level games, their respective theses could easily deal with very sensitive issues, sometimes undermining the acceptance of those titles by the players.

It is a risk to be accepted when boardgames want to be not only "fun" (which is and will always remain one of their defining essential features) and not only "informative" (as any well-documented simulation worthy of the name should be), but also have a "meaningful" historiographic value. In short, history is full of bad moments, ugly things and very unpleasant events and if simulation games want (and they actually *should*) to deal with them, some dangers have to be faced.

Every artistic product, and regardless of what some game designers themselves have affirmed in the past, games do contain *messages.*

Of course, this does not mean that behind every message brought forward by a game there is a specific agenda. There have been cases, and not few in number, in which the great communication potential of boardgames has been used for identifiable causes, good or bad: educational games, environmental awareness games, explicitly didactic games, protest games (the highest example of which is the anti-capitalist *Monopoly*) . . . but also propaganda games created by totalitarian regimes to justify their actions and military enterprises among the younger and more manipulable public opinion (for example games published in Italy under the supervision of the Fascist government during the Italo-Ethiopian War of 1935, depicting International Red Cross structures as sympathizers for the local resistance[12]).

Actually, by choosing a universally recognized problematic event, a game designer and also the players have to be aware of the required delicacy in treating those tragic facts.

A good example can be found in a discussion on the *BoardGameGeek* website regarding a game about one of the most controversial and at the same time more simulated topics in simulation games history: the American Civil War, with all the issues related to slavery. The game in question is *In Magnificent Style* (VPG, Worthington), a solitaire title by Hermann Luttmann putting the player in the shoes of General Pickett during his famous charge at the battle of Gettysburg, in 1863.

Stuart Ellis-Gorman, an academic historian specializing in medieval hoplology, started an organic study dedicated to boardgames and historical narratives, with a specific focus on the American Civil War and its treatment in hobby wargames, considering the high narrative potential of them among the public. In his review of the mentioned title,[13] the scholar highlighted the possible risks of the game becoming instrumental in promoting revisionist "Lost Cause" historiography glorifying this military episode that is key to pro-Confederate positions, asking also why the designer precisely chose this event and most of all this peculiar point of view. Is the game an excuse for empathizing with Southern soldiers and their pro-slavery cause?

In the ensuing (and quite heated) discussion that followed under the thread, many positions emerged ranging from the supporting ones to those in contrast. In the middle stood Hermann himself, affirming that he chose this event only for its actual historical importance and how effectively it was simulated by the rules as designed.

Possibly the most interesting answer, however, came with a later review of the same game by another user,[14] stressing how the title not only omitted any glorification of the episode, but also put into stark evidence the absolute military incompetence of Confederate commander Robert E. Lee, who ordered his men into an advance comparable only to the worst World War One massacres against German entrenched positions on the Somme.

The relevant part of this review, though, lies in its final assumption that probably even this was not on Hermann's mind at the time of designing the game, but nonetheless that astounding final result came out as the true message of the game.

Even the experimental game *Trains*, apparently just another innocent railroad simulator but actually being a title about the logistical management of the Holocaust, has not only a message but a very specific agenda behind it, and a very good and valid one at that: helping people realize the simple horror of the systematic genocidal policies of the Third Reich, as seen from the point of view of their cold-blooded "organizers".

This is the true moral burden of historical-themed boardgames, with the added caveat that, unlike books or movies that put their readers and viewers into purely passive and receptive positions, analog boardgames ask their players to be the main engine of the game itself, leading to much higher interaction and even self-projection.

A comprehensive treatment of simulating controversial issues would go far beyond the purposes of this study and will most probably also be quite premature since the debate is currently ongoing. However, a cursory exposition of its main features is necessary to understand this specific and crucial aspect of historical gaming.

A good starting point for this could be the narrative mechanism of Sam Peckimpah's *Cross of Iron* movie, a thrilling narration of the Eastern Front as seen from the eyes of a German Wehrmacht NCO which, even avoiding revisionist myths such as the one putting all the blame on the shoulders of SS formations while exonerating "regular Army" German officers, just showed how the protagonist tried to survive the hellish experience and get as many of his soldiers as possible to come back home alive. Many wargames put you exactly in this position, without making any questions on the broader context of the war and all the tragedies involved.

Sometimes this is understandable and even historically correct; other times these elements and their partial but undeniable influence over the operational management are—knowingly or unknowingly—left out of the picture, in favour of more conventional and generally "kinetic" factors such as lines of advance, supply routes, air support availability and the like. Other times they are simply mentioned in separate playbooks, or in some cases included in the game itself. *Absolute War!* (GMT), explicitly puts war crime locations on the map, and even awards specific victory points to the player that reaches them, gathering information and publicizing it to the entire world.

Yet, the general context remains important, since no element of an historical episode, as small as it can be, happens in a totally secluded environment, isolated from the greater picture of it all. Our Sergeant Steiner might even be totally unaware of the atrocities committed on the whole Eastern Front by all parties involved, but could not avoid being a part of them and his actions would still have an impact over the general course of the conflict and its atrocities.

A good question to ask a game designer would then be how much those issues were relevant in the situation described by their games, how much of them would be effectively needed to include in the simulation not just for the sake of it being conceptually "fair", but for it to be historically "correct". How much slavery would be influential into Robert E. Lee's decision-making process at Gettysburg (quite little), and how much it influenced Jefferson Davis's political management of the entire conflict (much, much more)?

It always remains a matter of perspective, then, also considering the interaction between two fundamental dynamics.

On one side, if we want to maintain some sort of historical credibility to simulation titles, the usual objection that "games are just games" and thus one can suspend his or her moral sense when playing them cannot be accepted . . . at least no more than one does while watching a period movie or, even worse, while reading a history book. This is the state of mind needed for games about great moral and political issues like *Votes for Women* (Fort Circle Games), about the women's suffrage movement's first battles in America: it is the only way through which they can really deliver their important messages to the players' awareness, and not remain just an ultimately meaningless bunch of wooden cubes moving on a map like every other generic boardgame.

On the other, we should also avoid excessive projection of our own moral compass onto the past, forgetting that those people we see represented on the counters of our shiny new boardgame made their choices based on their vision of the world, unavoidably conditioned by the wider social and cultural environments in which they lived.

A further specific case study might be useful to better illustrate this aspect and one that has been dealt with quite extensively both in the past as well as in more recent productions: the long and painful phenomenon of colonization.

The domination of powerful countries over other portions of the globe, its cultural and social impact (eradication of traditions, veiled and not so veiled racism, law inequality . . .), its many economic repercussions (resources exploitation, lost development, social dependence from the "mother country" . . .) and even its military aspects have been at the centre of many heated debates.

Historical simulation games have always been sensible to the issue, even if with very diverse approaches.

The first titles, such as *Conquistador* (SPI) or *Pax Britannica* (SPI), were more often focused on the colonizers, while later productions such as the *COIN* title *The British Way* (GMT) or the lighter wargames *Plains Indian Wars* (GMT) switched the point of view towards those who fought for their nation's independence (the US included, remembering *Liberty or Death*, about the American Revolution, aptly called in the subtitle *The American Insurrection*).[15]

This is not to be taken as an absolute rule, since several classic games also gave much agency to the locals in their struggle against the European invaders (remembering the highly innovative *Geronimo*, Avalon Hill, in which you constantly switched roles between the two!) while many recent titles carry on the tradition of non-agency and pure exploitation (like *Struggle of Empires*, Warfrog).[16]

However, the dichotomy created some interesting confrontations between games about the same period and world location, even if with different focus. This is the case of the aforementioned *The Great Game* (Legion Wargames) and *Pax Pamir* (Wehrlegig).

In other cases, the same conflict has been simulated from both sides, but the switch lies in objective dynamics and not subjective impersonation. These games portray both sides, the colonizers and the independentist forces, but stress different parts of the insurgency equation. *Algeria* (One Small Step) deals primarily with the kinetic operational aspect, *Colonial Twilight* as every *COIN* has the military level subservient to the political and social events, while *Ici C'est la France* (Legion Wargames) tries to find a compromise between all these different dimensions. Yet, all of them are about the same struggle for independence in Algeria and by playing all three you can get a fairly comprehensive depiction of the entire historical episode in its many different facets.

Also, it should be noted that since not all decolonization processes follow predominantly violent dynamics, the treatment this peculiar topic should not be confined to wargames or direct conflict mechanics alone. One of the more prominent examples surely is the movement for independence of India from the British Empire, whose non-violent policies are correctly portrayed in the *COIN* title *Gandhi*, in which the Indian National Congress faction has no direct attack actions but only demonstrative and non-cooperation initiatives at its disposal. In the upcoming game *Kartini* (Ion Game Design), alphabetization and education become the primary weapons towards achieving social promotion and breaking the colonial ties with the Dutch masters in late 1800s and early 1900s Indonesia.

Domination itself, however, can take many other faces rather than pure territorial and political control. Colonialism is often linked to exploitation of natural and, even worse, human resources to the extreme, leading up to the historical plague of slavery which has become the subject of many games, each with its own particular take.

There surely is no shortage of alternative titles dealing with these matters.

One could endlessly debate over the validity of Phil Ecklund's opinion represented in *Pax Emancipation* (Sierra Madre Games) considering the Western social bodies (religious individuals, philanthropists and politicians) as fundamental subjects in the process towards the global abolition of slavery in the last three centuries. Or discern over the social consequences of European penetration into Chinese society during the Opium Wars portrayed by Cole Wehrle's *An Infamous Traffic* (Hollandspiele), in which players have to manage the delicate but highly profitable trade routes into Asia making their personal fortunes over the blood and flesh of countless locals. Or understand the many hidden aspects of political and legislative processes, with all their most cynical elements, especially when related to such a deeply moral issue as the abolition of slavery, depicted in *This Guilty Land* (Hollandspiele). Or, eventually, learn much about the almost forgotten deeds and the unsung bravery of the incredibly motivated people who maintained the secret routes allowing enslaved families escape the Southern United States towards the North, avoiding the inhuman hunt of the professional slave catchers in the solitaire/cooperative title *Freedom: The Underground Railroad* (Academy Games).

To really sum up and simplify things, it could be argued that these titles tend to suffer from two negative dynamics in their simulation value: being "too much" or being "too little".

In the first instance, we have games dealing with significant episodes, but that are also objectively related to historical events very far from the collective conscience of the public, being effectively penalized by a reproduction too isolated from the wider picture. I can and should have a game about the Mau Mau Rebellion in Kenya, but that very peculiar event should be considered in its greater impact over all global history, to take it out from the highly specialized territory and have a functional (not only "formal") resonance over the greatest possible public. In this case, the interest of the internal game mechanics and that of transmitting an important message to the wider audience are totally aligned.[17]

In the second case, we are faced with an excess of a very specific dynamic: gamification. With this term we can define processes in which highly complex elements are translated into game form to make them more understandable to the observers, also allowing their manipulation and the accurate quantification of the relative success by a certain sum of "game points" and the satisfaction of easily recognizable victory conditions. The problem of this is that, up to a certain degree, gamification remains a very capable instrument for vehiculating elaborate content into a comprehensible form . . . but, if present in excess, it can banalize and oversimplify the messages of the simulation, pushing people to live the entire experience as a mere "game", gathering victory points but disregarding the true nature of the represented content.

This is a critic often moved against lighter simulations, as for example *Bleeding Kansas* (Decision Games) and *Plains Indian Wars* (GMT), believed to reduce respectively the fight between pro- and anti-slavery factions in the Western territories and the terrible conflict between white settlers and native tribes in North America to a simple collection of points, area control conditions and dice rolling (Figure 3.3). Of course this is not at all the case with these two highly documented and informational games, coming each with its own comprehensive and accurate historical booklets, as well as the event description on the game cards . . . and yet, much attention has to be given to the real inclusion of historical dynamics into the functional elements and interactions of the game, and not only to exterior bits of content that sadly can be ignored by non-sensitive players.

An interesting solution has been applied to the famous boardgame *Puerto Rico* (alea), in which the brown cubes actually represent slaves working in the players' plantation, a detail regretfully not adequately explained in the game materials. To correct this, a more historically identifiable version was created, *Puerto Rico 1897*, dedicated to the brief year of independence of the country when slavery was actually abolished . . . but the game did not contain any information about what happened to the country in the following year, as a repercussion of the 1898 Spanish-American War, nor the fact that in many ways the formal abolition of slavery did not stop in any way the actual exploitation of former slaves and their descendants by more "liberal" governments.[18] History has a way of always reasserting itself even against our best and honest intentions.

And yet, we still have to ask ourselves the most sensitive question of all: why do we really need to deal with these events?

For historical knowledge, of course, as well as for increasing our awareness over a more global and interconnected concept of history. But this is also true for games related to much more "traditional" topics like Alexander the Great, Waterloo or the Bulge. In this particular case, there should be something more behind our desire to recreate these events, especially in this particular moment of our collective history,

FIGURE 3.3 *Bleeding Kansas* (Decision Games). Criticized by some players for its assumed too "gamey" approach to such a sensitive issue as the confrontation between pro- and anti-slavery factions just before the American Civil War, this game offered nonetheless a unique and deeply documented rendition of those grievous events.

Source: Photograph by the author.

answering to a very specific sensibility of large quotas of public to such particular topics—a sensibility reflected in the multiplication of titles dedicated these issues in the last few years.

There is no easy answer to that question, of course. But there could be a general, almost universal one: we feel the need for those games, we look for those titles, because events like colonization, exploitation, cultural domination, expropriation, injustice, social inequalities, racism, mass slaughters and the many other "bad things" that happened over the millennia are still portions of our collective conscience that we have not yet entirely dealt with.

An interesting solution could be found in a somewhat alternative direction. In the last years many hybrid simulation/generic boardgames have appeared on the market, each dealing not with a particular history (be it "real" or "fictional") but with the concept of history itself.

Master game designer Cole Wehrle has become somewhat specialized in this topic, with titles like *Root* and *Oath*, dealing in the former with the main dynamics of every insurrectional movement together with the subsequent irregular warfare against "government" authorities, and in the latter with the processes behind the rise and fall of kingdoms (and the following collective memory of those events). Again, in 2020 the relatively small and yet highly innovative publisher Surprised Stare published a highly metaphorical game, aptly called *The March of Progress*, dealing with the general concept of wars and their conduit as seen through five different conflicts (from the Thirty Years War up to World War Two), recreated in their core elements through an only apparently abstracted card game. Finally, as a last example, *Hegemony* (Hegemonic Project Games) adopts a sociologic view on the great events of history, dealing with class struggle and elaborate relationship of the many different bodies composing a nation in times of peace and crisis as well; the game also includes an optional *Historical Events* deck, to give more actual context to the players wishing to apply the game dynamics to recognizable historical periods.[19]

So, when dealing with games more strictly regarding real and identifiable events, one last thing remains to be said: we should not be afraid of their capability of pushing us to face even "unsavoury" moments of global history. We should embrace it, instead, ready to expand our awareness in the hope not only of never seeing those terrible moments, but also of being actively engaged for as little or as much as we can in actively preventing them from happening again.

And we may always be thankful that, after all, every simulation, however accurate and painful in its depiction of contents, still remains "just a game".

3.3 SQUARING THE CIRCLE: ELEMENTS OF NON-LINEAR SIMULATION

Two are the most common critics brought forward against the link between actual history and game simulation in traditional wargaming.

In the first place, the fact that through fixed and easily calculable equations based on force-ratios and CRTs, you obtain a far too accurate and predictable picture of the situation, leaving all that unrealistic knowledge to fall straight into the hands of the commanders in the field (i.e., the players).

Secondly, after all the maneuvering, and strategizing, and planning and counterplanning . . . the final outcome of the actions is determined by a single die roll, however rationalized through the game systems derived from the historical interpretation of the designer.

As we have seen, countless and highly effective mechanics have been found to mitigate the two extremes, and all these have created countless and highly diversified dynamics within the games themselves. This allows us to find an easy answer to the aforementioned critics . . . but there is also room for something more. Something . . . non-linear.

In the world of non-linearity, forget all your 3:1 obsessions, endless card counting and the like. Your attack *may* have a fixed probability of success . . . but not if your opponent plays a special card cancelling it, or even reversing the entire maneuver and putting you on the defence. In fact, that enemy unit might not even be *really there*, it could be a decoy . . . or in most extreme cases your own unit might not have the necessary resources to attack with its full potentials. And after all that, your leadership may prove itself simply not up to the task: in CDGs leaders can have very different proficiencies on the strategic level (overall activation ratings) and the tactical one (specific battle values), of course if you manage to get that order to them on time (the tried and true limited hand of *Commands & Colors* titles). Oh, and by the way, winning that particular engagement on a single point on the map might even actually worsen your strategic position, considering the variable, interconnected and not entirely known nature of victory conditions.

Does all this sound confusing? Well, even real historical situations were not so easy to read for those who lived them: just remember the American War for Independence as seen from the British side, the Vietnam War or the many intricacies and contradictions of global anti-terrorism operations, from its unheard-of logistics problems related to waging war on such a continental scale (*Supply Lines of the American Revolution*, Hollandspiele) to the tight interconnections between military operations outcomes and local popular consent (*Washington's War* and *Liberty or Death*, GMT).

And yet, there non-linearity is, in every single component of the model, even the totally rational CRTs. It lies hidden behind that "1" on the die roll on an apparently trustworthy 3:1 column, which means that by all conventional military standards your "perfect attack" *should* have succeeded . . . but the captain of the enemy unit managed to keep his men together, refused to surrender and held his ground, also inflicting serious losses on your advancing units. It is not rational, it is not predictable, it is not even fair . . . but it happens.

The first thing to understand when we are dealing with non-linear elements in simulation is that we are essentially including other dimensions in the model's fundamental equation. When you think about the most linear kind of wargame, such as a hex and counter system, you will be almost entirely absorbed by the kinetic aspect of a conflict. This mono-dimensional treatment of reality is of course inadequate in representing all the different facets of a historical event, and at the top of that its transparent linearity is also quite an illusion.[20]

Yet, there is another ongoing trend in wargame design. Titles like *The Plot to Assassinate Hitler* (SPI, 1976) and *Nicaragua!* (3W, 1988) may be regarded as just highly experimental designs, but they actually are early attempts at obtaining something new from simulation rather than a simple factor counting hunt or a bundle of die roll modifiers.

Even if more open-minded players would have to wait a couple of decades before this trend became as widespread as it is today, the seeds were planted for a new generation of titles that made "gaming the non-kinetic" really the thing for modern historical simulation, exploring the interconnections between all the different dimensions of not strict military nature operating inside a conflict.[21]

A good approach in describing this tendency would be to differentiate between simulations of different levels: strategic and tactical.

By meaning with the first term all those simulations dealing with entire conflicts, often spanning over decades of time and encompassing vast amounts of land and sea, we can understand that the non-linear elements tend to gather around a dimension conventionally defined as "politics". Of course, this is an improper use of the word, but for the purposes of our study we could use a more open meaning of it by including also those social, economic and cultural events so closely inter-related to the decision-making processes of the political leadership of a competing faction.[22]

The political dimension has been dealt with since the very early days of modern historical simulations by negotiation-based titles such as *Diplomacy* and *Origins of World War Two* (Avalon Hill). Later on, that freeform approach was first subjected to further direct elaboration upon the same systems (*Machiavelli*, Avalon Hill), later completely revised in the context of sophisticated and detailed games (*Kingmaker*, *Empires of the Middle Ages*, Avalon Hill) and more recently totally re-imagined by more streamlined designs integrating even more dimensions (*Europe Divided* and *Coalitions*, Phalanx).

In other cases, political confrontations have been at the very centre of the simulation often through a focus on electoral competitions (*1960: The Making of the President*, *Votes for Women*, *A Corrupt Bargain*, and others). Sometimes that has been subsumed as an ideological premise of truly armed conflicts, finally depicted with a more nuanced and comprehensive historical approach (*Red Flag Over Paris* about the 1871 Paris Commune, *Halls of Montezuma* about the 1846–48 war between the US and Mexico). Finally, politics has also been considered to be just one of many equally relevant dimensions expressed on point tracks and manipulated through special actions (*COIN* series) or, on the opposite, as the primary dimension of it all (*Ideology*, in which the players do not represent single countries but dominant systems to which the single countries have to be pushed and maintained).

Politics is now generally considered such a paramount factor as to impose a limited use of direct military force to decrease tension and keep more options open to the players (the classic *Twilight Struggle*, with nuclear war actually ending the Cold War confrontation with no real winners; *13 Days* and its inspired evolution *Fort Sumter*; or even *Flashpoint: South China Sea*, GMT), or when politics itself is a fragmented element of the equation with frequent factional infightings and unaligned objectives undermining its impact on the events (*Pericles*, GMT, with the different parties in Athens and Sparta; *Prelude to Revolution*, Compass Games, with the competing factions in the months leading to the Russian Revolution; *Churchill*, GMT, with the "Big Three" arguing with each other about the post-World War Two power balances).

The more we narrow the scope of the simulation, however, the more we encounter other families of factors. Here we are dealing with tactical or even man-to-man simulation, in which politics and economics are much less influential than what the poor soldier or guerrilla fighter with his boots in the mud can see, hear, feel and think about the inherent dangers of his or her situation: being stuck in the middle of a live firefight.

At this size of representation, myriad irrational and non-linear things can and do happen, providing an even more vivid and direct image of "unpredictable events". Here, von Clausewitz's Friction is expressed through missed or misinterpreted voice orders, a jammed gun, someone who slips on the ground and spoils the whole ambush maneuver, your advance element that freaks out and runs away at the first sight of the enemy tanks . . . all the things that tend to ruin the day of a junior officer, actually.

For example, let us consider a key non-linear element of tactical games: morale.

Sometimes described as the will to carry on fighting, morale is a much more complex concept. It means maintaining your average efficiency even in the direst situations, staying calm under enemy fire, avoiding unneeded distractions in your decision-making process, controlling emotional responses and being able to "read" the situation around you in a rational and effective way.

It is, in the end, one of the most essential (if not *the* most essential) elements of command, granting or denying the possibility for the orders coming from above to be properly executed. It is not by chance that in a famous passage of his monumental *War and Peace* novel about the Napoleonic Wars, Leo Tolstoy describes morale as the only element of warfare worth any attention from a commander. Again, it is not by chance that in the very same passage Tolstoy is also sceptical about using chess as a good model for warfare: you need a game in which a charging knight can be defeated by a stalwart pawn defending his position to the utmost . . . because things like that happen regularly in battle, and are all dependent on morale.

A game with stalwart pawns possibly defeating charging knights does exist, and naturally it is called a "wargame". Sure, morale is not at all the only factor at work in its combat resolution mechanics, but it is present in all of them, declared or not. Every single die roll on a CRT, every special card, every modifier also includes the morale element in his function and nature.

In many cases, however, this representation is much more direct and evident. We can have simple "morale tracks" by which players lower the resistance of the enemy by destroying their units. Or special units which have better resistance values, fixed or conditionally granted (for example by the proximity to a specific location or to a friendly leader). Or even more sets of CRTs and progressive modifiers to represent the various levels of attrition felt during an entire conflict . . . et cetera.[23]

The morale level of the entire army could also be dependent on the outcome of the single engagements: lose too many units and your men will begin doubting your leadership diminishing their efficiency, as in the *Battles of the American Revolution* series (GMT) which compensates for this by including the concept of positive "momentum" when your actions obtain good results. In *Triomphe à Marengo* (Histogame), morale is not lost in every single engagement but ideally "placed" on the maps in the positions interested by particularly vehement actions.

In the *Napoleonic 20* series (VPG) these variations can be directly managed by the commanders, which "spend" morale points to rally broken formations or order particularly aggressive attacks . . . and interestingly morale itself is the main victory condition in the system, since the game ends when one of the two armies finally disintegrates after losing the last morale point!

This only apparently simple game system also integrates another classical non-linear element such as cards, which are blindly drawn at the beginning of every turn and impose various forms of Friction, most of the time impacting morale in a good or a bad way. A similar situation happens also in the *No Retreat!* series (originally VPG, now GMT); the difference is that the cards including highly differentiated (kinetic and non-kinetic) elements are in the hands of the players themselves who can at least somewhat influence the order of their appearance.

There are other instances in which the loss of control pertains not simply to the men under your command, nor to the command itself with all the well-known "fog of war" issues . . . but to the space itself that should go under your control.

Possibly due to their highly mobile nature (tens, if not hundreds of fragmented counters moving freely on a single fixed map), even traditional hex and counter wargames demonstrated how good they were at showing de-linearized confrontations, with pockets of resistance, flashpoints and sudden "behind the lines" actions happening in every play, or even randomized variations of terrain with hidden maps or hexes that could change their features unpredictably (just think of a ford to be found in a bunch of river hexes, all regulated by a single die roll every time one of those hexes is explored by advance recon units).

This non-linearity, in fact, could be expressed by a combination of different grid dispositions on the map and fragmented activation procedures: aka, "area impulse games". Officially born with *Storm Over Arnhem* (Avalon Hill), a classic wargame about the most advanced spearhead of Operation Market Garden (1944), this system not only dispenses with hexes substituted by broader "areas", but it also de-structures the sequence of activations, with players alternately activating some of their forces, making them "spent" and then leaving to the other player the possibility of responding (directly or indirectly, in the same or another area).

This mechanic has been one of the most successful innovations of early 1980s wargames (possibly second only to the chit pull random activation approach), and has been frequently used to successfully depict the chaos and irregularity of urban warfare, being after that used also to recreate the confusion and command challenges of more linear battles like in *Napoleon's Final Battle* (CWG) or *Not War, but Murder* (ATO), or even entire operations such as the whole Market Garden endeavour itself in *Monty's Gamble* (MMP).[24]

De-linearization in space and unit activation then leads directly to the next level: the strategic approach of *COIN* games. Here terms like "area control" or "front-line" really lose any of their traditional meanings . . . to adopt brand new ones. You begin to understand the fact that control means essentially having a local superiority over your rivals, that (once again) there are so many different dimensions of control beyond the mere space occupied by the physical boots of your soldiers, that the very concept of enemy is much more "liquid" than what you would think, given the presence of underground enemy cells and irregular troops.

An interesting nuance is then provided by non-linear games dealing with the fact that, considering the demographic revolution of the last decades, many insurrectional actions happen in deeply urbanized territories, a trend recognized by many analysts all over the world.

So, we can find plenty of titles presenting the specific features of city confrontations between regular forces and the usual mix of insurrectional troops and/or average civilians (the classic 1980s game *Corteo* (Figure 3.4) and its ideal and more analytical successor *Civil Power*, the duo *Days of Ire* and *Nights of Fire* about the 1956 Budapest revolt, as well as by other more hybrid titles like *Le Barricate di Parma*). Together with them, we can have other games which highlight the different dynamics of insurrection spreading in city as well as in more rural areas: for example, *District Commander* series (Hollandspiele) and the challenges of a unified counter-insurrectional control, or the partisan local aggregations in the mountain towns of *Repubblica Ribelle* (Aleph Game Studio).[25]

An interesting common theme of those games is that they introduce, albeit in an indirect way, a typical feature of non-linear simulations: asymmetries.

With the term we mean all those factors that somehow break too rigidly mechanical dynamics, by providing relevant "imbalances" in a game, reflective of historical realities and capable of making the situation interesting from a simulative standpoint.[26]

Defining not only the nature but also the true extent of these "healthy imbalances", to make them relevant enough but not excessively overwhelming, is not an easy task.

FIGURE 3.4 By using traditional wargame mechanics, coupled with a deeply ironic style and a direct knowledge of the events just a few years after the most violent phase of Cold War-related political terrorism in Italy, *Corteo* (CunSA, Mondadori) managed to create a convincing depiction of urban insurrectional and counter insurrectional tactics. The title is considered still today to be one of the best in this very selective genre.

Source: Photograph by the author.

It is not just a simple matter of giving a +1 or 1 bonus to a unit when fighting a certain type of enemy force equipped in a particularly effective fashion . . . you have to delve deep into topics like different victory conditions, or asymmetric turn sequences full of "exploitation phases" and even alternative CRTs reserved only for one army and not the other, or distinct operational doctrines and the best way to represent them in a game, keeping that system not only fairly balanced overall, but also still playable and not plagued by endless special rules and exceptions.

It is not all so nice and balanced, though. Think about the inevitable Italian defeat at Caporetto as depicted in *Durchbruch* (Acies), in which the Italian player can only "win" by limiting the damages to something less than the historical disaster, by no means a simple task. Here the victory conditions are so out of balance and asymmetrically devised that some players even complained that "victory" for the Italians was a bit too easy to reach in the game.

Other non-linear approaches to the final moment of a game can include interconnected, variable, random-based objectives.[27] Sometimes even objectives not fully known to one of the two sides, the most famous example of which is *Battles for the Ardennes* (SPI) and its optional rules about the possibility for the German player of choosing a specific historical German plan for the entire Bulge operation, unbeknownst to the Allied player, representing the confusion about the true Wehrmacht goals in 1944.

Sometimes, as is the rule for the *COIN* series, the asymmetries work both inside the factions as well as between the factions.

In the first case we have the players counting on very different sets of possible orders and actions, some more direct combat-oriented against the opponents and others operating on the political and social dimensions of the simulation. In the second, we can have complex interaction between different factions belonging to a specific "side" of a conflict. *Liberty or Death* has two pairs of factions (Natives and British, versus American Patriots and French) closely connected on one single victory condition but somewhat opposed on another, while the upcoming *China's War* will see three Chinese players fighting together but for different purposes against the same Japanese invader. And countless discussions have been inspired by the choice of *Fire in the Lake* designers, Herman and Ruhnke, of introducing the Viet Cong as a separate faction in the Vietnam War, with diverging popular consensus goals than the more militaristic North Vietnamese with their Regular Army tactical objectives.

Asymmetry is, of course, a prominent feature of all tactical games, even the most "traditional" ones. Just look at your average *ASL* scenario sheet and you will find no shortage of differences in equipment, training and military doctrine of all the various armies involved in WWII firefights. A similar phenomenon is to be found in the different troops categories represented by "weapon matrixes" of systems like *Simple GBoH* (GMT) or your average Napoleonic game with French columns covered by thick skirmisher screens clashing with British two-rank deep lines, accompanied by the occasional rifle unit.

By pushing this concept a bit further we can arrive at more modern settings, with conventional armies fighting against irregular forces composed of militia, armed civilians and insurgent groups of all kinds. A quick play at *Warfare: Modern Tactical Combat* (WBS) on the tactical level or at *We Are Coming, Nineveh* (Nuts!) on the operational side (all complete with different rules of engagement, political implications and divergent battle behaviours) can be quite enlightening in this respect.

Of course, these models are not always perfect, and every single asymmetry introduced can be the subject of unending (and quite interesting) discussions.[28] One of the greatest tasks for a game designer becomes then not to just include enough non-linear elements in his or her design, but to include not too much of them. The entire game Flow must be kept easily understandable by the players, making everything possible in order to avoid losing their cognitive and experiential focus during the gaming activity in the "labyrinth" of non-linearity.

Unpredictable elements constantly happening on a battlefield are both the boon and the bane of wargamers. They could hate all these variations that defy their beloved total control complex, but they also love the flexibility of simulation games when everything can effectively happen, when you can and must do your best to minimize the impact of fortune's whims, when every single gaming session is different thanks to the continuous mobility of the results and their consequences.

In the end, however, the highest form of Friction remains the human being itself, with simulations always looking for new solutions to represent what we could call "The Grouchy Paradox": how to properly represent bad choices by local or overall commanders highly influential to the final outcome of the events. "Stupidity rules", low command values, temporary losses of control of whole groups of units, unexpected delays in the reinforcement tables . . . all of these are game design tricks devised to include irrational and plain wrong behaviours in a totally rational statistic model.[29]

The end result is a simulation in which all these non-linear pieces combined represent an imponderable and yet highly manipulable element of the player's decisional space, derailing formal statistical calculations and imposing a new, wider and sophisticated concept of strategy: an apparently irrational factor transforming the entire equation in something actually more similar to real history, with the focus not on apparent odds but on practical interpretation of the overall situation in all its many, unpredictable facets.

A good example in this regard is Mark McLaughlin's World War Two in Europe game, *Hitler's Reich* (GMT), in which players compete with the same card-based mechanics not only for the success of direct military operations, but also for scientific research, technological innovations, political coups, reformed social structures, individual leadership and so on, all contributing to the final outcome of the war.

This is a very symbolic way to introduce a new concept of "military history" in wargaming; a broader vision of what a "war" really is, with all its interconnected and reciprocally influenced elements, leading up to a broader concept of what a "wargame" should be.

3.4 THE HYBRID APPROACH, OR HOW I LEARNED TO STOP ASKING IF THIS IS A WARGAME OR NOT . . .

It is hard to define a precise moment in which the drive towards a greater inclusion of non-linear elements and mechanics into simulation games actually began. One could argue that it is a relative novelty for the wargaming world, more or less traceable up to the mid-1990s with game designers pushing for greater "hybridization" between simulation and other forms of generic boardgaming. Those observers often mention mechanics like cards and various forms of manipulation (deck building, card drafting, special cards . . .), resource management, worker or tile placement, abstracted game components and even more refined visual interface solutions as telltale signs of this mixture between different gaming genres in clearly identified titles. As could be expected, for some this hybridization is a good thing, for others just a natural evolution of game design the quality of which should be evaluated title by title . . . and of course, there is no lack of traditionalist voices calling out for the betrayal of the "true principles" of wargaming and the end of the hobby as we know it.

For however moderated and well documented these opinions may be, there are some aspects of the issue that should not be ignored if we want to have a full picture of the problem.

First of all, it is not so easy to adjudicate a game mechanics to a single, unambiguous gaming sub-genre. Are the wooden blocks really so "Euro", considering that they were used (together with special symbol dice!) in some of the earliest versions of *Kriegsspiel*? Should we consider cards an exclusive feature of German-style boardgames when they are present in various forms also in traditional 1970s wargames? In short, are we really affirming that everything that is not rigorously a hex and counter mechanic (you know, hexes . . . and counters . . . and zones of control, CRTs, modifiers etc.) cannot be considered to belong to the inner circle of "true wargames"?

Secondly, broader content has always been a key part in many wargames. Political issues and espionage can be traced back at the very least to *The Plot to Assassinate Hitler* and *Spies!* both published by SPI in 1976 and 1981, respectively. And if someone can justly argue in favour of the exclusion of these titles from the strict category of wargames, how else should we classify titles like *The American Revolution 1775–1783* and *Empires of the Middle Ages*, still by SPI, which include specific treatments for politics, diplomacy, consensus, economy in spades?

Even from this short inventory of "proto-hybrid" titles it is evident that this process existed well before the very term "Eurogame" was even created. Those were just possible game design solutions explored by authors looking for elegant and effective mechanics, capable of achieving the best possible compromise between realism and playability.

A correct way of studying the trend toward hybridization (whatever this term may mean in practical terms) would be to first understand how this operates both on the content as well as on the mechanical side of the game design equation. Nowadays, simulation games are more and more hybridized both for what they bring to the gaming table in themes and events covered, and for how they represent them: in other words, the collective perception of reality itself, the actual subject of these games.

Or, as podcaster and game expert Liz Davidson put it, while dealing with the opportunity of including *Votes for Women* in the "wargame" category of a popular game award:

> But the primary reason for this mismatch in treatment [that is, all the ongoing debates about the "nature" of *Votes for Women* and the failed recognition of it being a wargame], in my opinion, is that our understanding of political/historical/war games is in flux and we are still figuring out what to do about it.[30]

Davidson's emphasis on our vision of what this highly peculiar kind of game is or ought to be, and by extension our idea of what the history that they are attempting to recreate is or ought to be, is very up to the point and thought-provoking.

The core concept to keep always on our minds while dealing with this very insidious and thorny argument should be that wargames and simulation games are *not* to be considered synonyms, contrary to what many hobbyists believe. *Risk!* could technically be considered a "wargame" (since it is a game based on global armed conflict) but it has no pretence whatsoever of being considered a simulation, while even a very statistic-heavy sport game like *Stratis Pro Baseball* (Avalon Hill) has nothing to do with military matters.

But what is this "flux", anyway?

The nature of wargames is in constant transition, and remains highly dependent on the perception of what "war" and "game"—the two "unsavoury terms" to borrow Dunnigan's words—actually are: just ask any recent military analyst about the latest concepts of military strategy and you'll be surprised to see "proper warfare stuff" like tanks, planes and guns getting lost in the background.

Considering that the two terms of "war-game" are so closely related, of course a radical change in the former had many consequences over the latter. And so, with a change of scope of what a war "really is" (better, how it is perceived), even games had to become much broader in their approach to military simulation to keep the pace. This, however created an unforeseen new issue: in order to maintain an acceptable cognitive economy in their rules, wargames dealing with many dimensions (non-kinetic, political, social, cultural factors and even more) had to contain their general complexity.

As early as 1977, highly influential graphic designer and artist Redmond A. Simonsen (to put it shortly, the man that defined most of the visual layout and user interface of modern board-wargames) wrote an article in *Moves* magazine about the difference between "Naturalism" and "Realism" in simulation.[31]

What matters is that the structural essence of the subject is brought into sharp focus and totally explored in a meaningful and enlightening manner. Put another way: naturalism captures the symptoms of truth; realism captures the substance of truth.[32]

Also, according to Simonsen:

Notwithstanding all its numbers and probabilistic tables, a wargame is closer to a work of art than a work of technology—it is an abstraction of an aspect or aspects of the object. Just as in art, the level of abstraction is not directly related to the level of realism (strictly defined) found in a given game. The higher one goes into the levels of abstraction, the less obviously realistic the game will seem; the lower the level, the more apparently realistic the simulation will seem.[33]

Simonsen suspected that many games boasted pretences of "historicity" and "accuracy" only based on "naturalistic" techniques, not so useful in a properly functional and meaningful simulation game. A final result paradoxically less valuable for the educated observer, but oddly more satisfying for some gamers, having the impression of playing better simulations only on the grounds of their higher complexity.

My instincts tell me that, given the choice between a very naturalistic (but basically untrue) "simulation" game and a very realistic (but non-obvious) simulation game, most players would be seduced by the former and be lukewarm to the latter.

Could clever hybridization techniques be instead instrumental into achieving the greater "realism" so sought after by Simonsen? It is hard to say, and one must not consider "hybrid" and lighter simulation games as better designs *per se* . . . but it is also hard to find a better advocate than Redmond A. Simonsen for clever techniques allowing games to be more realistic even if less "naturalistically accurate" than overly sophisticated traditional designs. In cruel materialization of Simonsen's worst fears, over the years and especially during the years of deepest crisis of the hobby (approximately from 1995 to 2010), rules complexity began to be considered to be a trademark for good simulation.

Some designers decided to use a *quantitative* approach: a wargame (or, better, an historical simulation game, since strictly speaking the two definitions are not necessarily synonymous) is defined as such by the level of realism represented by its rules.

So, what exactly is this "quantity of reality" we are speaking about? At first glance, one could conclude that it simply is the mere amount of detail a simulation game represents on the table, through its many diverse mechanics: modifiers, exceptions, turn sub-sequences, special scenario conditions and so on, and so on . . .

The issue with this very characteristic trend of wargame design that became dominating in the mid-late 1980s is that, while all these small bits of rules really give you the idea of a very specific and "highly detailed" simulation, as a trade-off the stratification of exceptions and special rules is a very strong detriment to the game simplicity and, what is even worse, to the narrative value of the entire experience. In other words, if I need to check my rulebook for the specific behaviour of shot detachments compared to pike *tercios* every two minutes while I am playing a wargame about the Thirty Years War or the English Civil War, I will be inevitably drawn out of the narration of the events happening in the battlefield.

In 1991, renowned wargame designer and publisher Dean Essig wrote an article in *Operations* magazine,[34] sketching out an interesting theory: the more stratification of rules you include in a game system, the less simulative that system becomes. In order to simulate the results of a cannon shot coming from a single tank trying to knock another tank out of action, you have two possible routes: describing every single step through different sets of modified die rolls or resolving the action through a single all-comprehensive roll.

The quantitative approach would obviously lend itself towards the first solution, but in so doing it will be faced by the many inevitable statistical distortions of every single die roll. The second path, while *looking* more simplistic and reductive, would be much more accurate in depicting the actual comprehensive probabilities of a specific outcome.

The fact is that complexity is not a synonym for accuracy, nor it is a value *per se*.

Complexity, as are all things in a wargame, is a derivative of the author's interpretation of historical events. But, considering how biased and distorted our own vision of the past is, including more "detail" just risks introducing more biases and distortions in the overall simulation model. Essig described this relation in very effective terms: while in theory I have a better simulation, in practice I will be receiving a much worse overall experience of the historical facts represented by the game itself. That is exactly why I personally like to call this phenomenon the "Essig Paradox", as a tribute to its first theorist.[35]

A possible virtuous compromise between the two approaches would be a definition that considers quality and quantity in simulation not as two discreet factors, but as integral elements of a single organic model.

In simpler terms, by adopting a functional vision, both the nature and the number of historical details in a simulation are put together into a single melting pot, taken in motion and studied for their many possible interactions between them and the players' perceptions and behaviours, with all the attention focused only on their final results and credibility as an historical simulation.

This also opens the way to different titles dedicated to the same event: if you want to reproduce the actual development of a Napoleonic battle a traditional wargame such as *Napoleon at War* or *Napoleon's Last Battles* (SPI) would be great, but other titles such as the hybrid Euro-wargame *Waterloo* (Warfrog), the simple yet genial fixed moves games *W1815* (U&P) or even the card game *1815: Scum of the Earth* (Hall or Nothing) would be as valid or even more capable of depicting different facets of the same event, in a manner not unlike the one represented by different essays about this climactic engagement that are undoubtedly sharing the same bookshelves of countless historical enthusiasts and scholars worldwide.

This open-ended and probably more evolved method of reproducing history through simulation games cuts through the endless debates about "tradition" and "innovation", giving an entirely new perspective to the old dilemma about "simulation" and "game" in wargaming, considering them two different faces of the same thing: an interactive model capable of recreating past events with enough players' decision space, plausible results, narrative value and simplicity of rules management.[36]

At least as many issues as possible advantages are raised by this approach, though.

In general, it is possible that an excessively broad interpretation of what a "historical game" is could lead to uncertainty and approximation, two fatal flaws when we are dealing with a scientific method of dealing with historical reconstruction. The shift from the *jeux de guerre* to the *jeux d'histoire*, for example, has been a staple of the French game design school since the days of the very influential *Jeux et Stratégie* game magazine which in the early 1980s formed the future generations of game authors, with even more conventional wargames often including elaborate forms of command and control, fog of war, non-kinetic factors in their systems. Most of these games represent some of the highest forms of modern "neo-classic" wargames, such as the *Jours de Gloire* or *Les Maréchaux* series (and the latter's offspring, the *Napoléon* hybrid block and CDG titles by Shako); others were not so successful trying to represent too many things at once or ending up as too bland and generic reproductions of historical "flavour" rather than actual facts and dynamics.

This approach, however, reaches its best results on a conceptual level, with the possibility of defining a comprehensive theory capable of giving a fairly precise understanding of a historical game nature. In 2019, French designer and game expert Fred Serval published a video on his YouTube channel, *Homo Ludens*, as part of a series of analysis on simulation games aptly called *Wargamology*.[37] While still remaining respectful of the traditional equation "wargame = simulation", Serval proposes an interesting evaluation of historical simulations based both on the level of detail included and of general abstraction of its treatment. Those two elements are presented as polar opposites, yet interconnected inside the same system, in order to categorize a game and obtain a broadly accurate representation on a line traced between "simulation" and "abstraction". This line could be thus called a "Serval spectrum".

Part of the issue lies then in what we consider to actually be a "simulation", and this is possibly the highest and most useful point of the entire debate. By trying to define what a true wargame is, we are expressing a personal judgement on the value of the mechanics used to reproduce the reference reality, that is the subject of the game be it a battle, a war or a political confrontation. Having said that, of course, it will appear evident how untenable is the position of traditionalist players that consider only hex and counter games the "true wargames", and refrain from attributing this almost mythical definition to simulation games with cards, special dice, highly accessible rulebooks or wooden blocks depicting generic units instead of "proper" paper counters with highly detailed IDs for this or that regiment.[38]

A very simple game such as *300: Earth and Water* (Figure 3.5), for example, still includes the representation of the many factors at work during the wars between the Persian Empire and the Greek city-states, even if the designer Yasushi Nakaguro did all his best to do so in the most streamlined and weight-effective way. In order to do so, he relied on abstractions, hidden complexity solutions, diversity of game elements such as cards and modified die-rolls, hybrid mechanics such as resource management and so on.

300 then represents all the different historical elements such as asymmetrical military doctrines, logistic challenges, important characters, even cultural and religious factors in its simulation, summarizing them all into "game functions" relying on their *indirect* representation. All those factors are included "inside" the game mechanics and not overly present, not immediately manipulable by the players: they are opportunities presented by specific cards as drawn, or by the decisions of the opponent, or by the distribution of the game components, or by the features of the map et cetera.

Even if another designer took a much more traditional (and elaborate) route, the end result would be the same: an interactive reconstruction of historical events and dynamics, in which the open-ended decisions by the players would lead to plausible results regulated by the game mechanics—only in a very different way, with different experiences, not necessarily opposed to each other and all perfectly capable of coexisting as valuable historical simulation games.

Yet the discussion remains and with all probability will stand also for the future.

FIGURE 3.5 Even with its very simple mechanics (or possibly, also because of them), *300: Earth and Water* (Bonsai Games, Nuts!) is regarded as a highly innovative and effective hybrid wargame, delivering a believable rendition of the wars between the Persian Empire and the Greek city-states.

Source: Photograph by the author.

This is very effectively represented by an open debate in the pages of the prestigious *C3i* game magazine, in the regular column *Snakes & Ladders* held by game designer and podcaster Harold Buchanan.[39] In his article, Buchanan justly argues that the definition of what a true wargame should be is actually much broader than many wargamers think, considering how wide and diversified all the different approaches to military and in general world history are. To these very convincing remarks, another very influential game designer and expert, Volko Ruhnke, replies by stressing an element that we have not yet fully covered in our study: the perception of the wargamers themselves.

While it is true that many different approaches and elements and factors and dynamics all contribute to defining the actual nature of a game and its relative position on the Serval spectrum, in the end it is only the players and their opinion that really matters. Thus it is up to them, concludes Ruhnke, to decide if a game is a "true wargame" or not.

With a final mention to the definition of wargames as "paper time machines" by Dunnigan himself this looks like a very fitting (and yet inevitably provisional) conclusion to the debate. By adopting a very *subjective* approach, as we will during the course of this book, we will consider wargames as intellectual objects that can be seen and considered in very diverse ways by every single person that comes into contact with them.

In this context, no single game mechanic such as hexes, counters, CRTs and the like can be considered an essential and "not negotiable" for a game to be considered to belong to the "true tradition of wargaming". This is firstly because that tradition has often been carried on by titles based on alternative design solutions (should we really consider a classic game like *Storm Over Arnhem*, the very first area impulse title, not a "true wargame" for not having hexes on its map?); secondly because there is no single tradition in simulation gaming, but many diverse, ever evolving and always increasing in number traditions, often times interconnected by experimental combinations, aka "hybridizations".

This realization should also reassure the veterans of the hobby: the emergence of diverse and innovative titles not only means that more traditional titles will cease to be published and played, but also does not imply the death of the classical wargaming reference frame. Rather, it is just the birth of many new classical wargaming reference frames.

Anyway, once again the best solution is to resort to ancient philosophy and conclude that no theoretical description of an object can change its inner nature, only its perception by the observers.

In the end, we can just assume that true wargaming really is in the eyes of the wargamer.

NOTES

1 Once again, Dunnigan's words are enlightening: "I, and many others, wanted to do more than read about history, we wanted to see a convincing model of how historical events worked, and have the ability to explore "what ifs" in a believable fashion. Most importantly, we were creating historical games that convincingly allowed the players to make the same

historical decisions, and get the same results. But, most importantly, you could make other decisions, and see an accurate alternative result." Dunnigan, J., *Simulation games design*, https://dl.acm.org/doi/10.5555/2031882.2031885 (2011).

2   In other, more pragmatic words: Seek Out and Play, *Wargaming: The reverse engineering of history*, https://youtu.be/Sjy7YlWgXfM?si=i-zzNYknPiF4tANX.

3   For a revealing example of one such author, see Ardwulf's Lair, *The chit show, designing across many eras with Joseph Miranda*, https://www.youtube.com/live/qgZmxcvt3aE?si=Z49tIDwJPu2LWGWo.

4   This flexibility in game design should not be taken for granted, though: let us not forget that the never-changing composition of CRTs on games related to different eras was one of the main criticisms behind Dunnigan's original letter sent to Avalon Hill in the 1960s, which prompted a small revolution in wargame design history as well as the conceptual birth of SPI.

5   So great and strong is this diversity, that it can be found also among the work of the very same author, sometimes even regarding the very same title. A good example in this is Sergio Schiavi's *Radetzky's March* about the 1849 Battle of Novara: a first 2018 edition has been recently updated in a second edition with several revisions and further historical research by two academic historians, Alessandro Barbero and Marco Scardigli.

6   Consider the combined rules allowing operational decisions taken in the Battle of Britain scenarios proposed by *RAF* (Decision Games) to have a direct effect on the tactical dog-fights and interceptions represented by *Skies Above Britain* (GMT).

7   Similarly, even a lower-level Napoleonic simulation like *Napoleon's Battles* (Avalon Hill) decided to avoid complex sub-systems to deal with light infantry screens or company-level formation nuances, mentioning modern-era military studies affirming that actual battle-field leadership cannot be exerted more than two levels deep by engaged commanders. These details are best left to more tactical-oriented games like *Voltigeur* (SPI), a system re-implemented by Peter Perla in *The Pratzen* (CTP). However, Bowen Simmons's *Triomphe à Marengo* (Histogame) dispenses entirely with formations, introducing abstract concepts like "blocked approaches" and "reserve positions" to the tactical areas depicted on the game map.

8   Something similar happens also with the great "rival" to *Commands & Colors*, that is the action-point based series *Horse & Musket* (Hollandspiele), initially designed and curated by Sean Chick, and dedicated to conflicts ranging from the seventeenth century up to the American Civil War. Here the differences are even more evidently exposed by the use of special rules depicted on single cards, specific scenario rules and some minor yet very significant changes in the overall system.

9   As further proof of this, the GMT Games website includes a special filter enabling visitors to classify the titles in the publisher's catalogue and pre-order P500 programs by the name of their game designer.

10 An explicit interpretation of *PRESTAGS* as a form of "simulative military history" can be found in Thomas, J., Ancient and medieval armies, in *Moves*, issue not identified, http://www.spigames.net/MovesScans/Prestags_Article.pdf.

11 It is not even necessary to have all the games bundled together in a single explicit collection. Burden, David, J. H., The battles of Hue: Understanding urban conflicts through wargaming, in *Journal of Strategic Security* 16, no. 3, https://digitalcommons.usf.edu/jss/vol16/iss3/9/ (2023) compares five different wargames regarding the same military event, their respective design features and analytical approaches.

12 As reported in Angiolino, A., *Che cos'è un gioco da tavolo* (*What is a boardgame?*), Carocci Editore (2022).

13 Ellis-Gorman, S., But why Pickett's charge? Or, how I liked the game but not the slaver, in *BoardGameGeek*, https://boardgamegeek.com/thread/3154585/why-picketts-charge-or-how-i-liked-game-not-slaver (2023).

14   @jrg262, A subversive dice chucker and welcome addition to the ACW genre, in *Board-GameGeek*, https://boardgamegeek.com/thread/3166201/subversive-dice-chucker-and-welcome-addition-acw-g (2023).

15   For brevity, we will be primarily dealing with strategic-level titles, but it should be mentioned that also the many wars derived from colonialist enterprises have inspired countless wargames such as *Victoria Cross II* and *Custer's Last Stand* (Worthington), or *55 Days at Peking* (The Historical Game Company).

16   For a much deeper exposition of colonialism in historical-themed games and its ideological repercussions even in fantasy and sci-fi boardgames, see Suckling, M., *The postcolonial turn in commercial historical board wargames*, Georgetown University Wargaming Society, https://youtu.be/RxETwdPNYCo?si=ylgHqYsTjY_iqWXp (2023).

17   That is exactly the function of the rules combining the four scenarios of *The British Way* into a great "campaign" game.

18   A good depiction of this particular historical process can be found in the 1969 movie *Queimada! (Burn!)*, featuring Marlon Brando and directed by Gillo Pontecorvo.

19   One could argue that also games standing at the crossroads between abstraction and simulation could be included in the very peculiar category of "games about history itself": *Antike* (PD-Verlag), *Roads & Boats* and *Food Chain Magnate* (both Splotter Spellen) are good examples in that sense.

20   Once again, see Sabin (*Simulating Wars*) and his criticism of too rigid and mechanical "Lanchestrian equations" depicting optimal combat odds and force ratios with an almost ideological quantitative stance.

21   The title refers to a comprehensive exposition of these elements to be found in Brynen, R., *Gaming the non-kinetic*, GUWS, https://youtu.be/Lv4cWw7kMM8?si=KKsuKMxleBm-wCYeY (2020).

22   See also Matthews, J., *Politics in wargaming and wargaming politics*, GUWS, https://youtu.be/ub2Nj6iKBbM?si=RitL2osZ5ToXC-nq (2021).

23   This need for a better morale representation was felt since the earliest days of modern simulation games, as testified by the attempts at devising a universal system proposed in Sayre, C. L. Jr., Simulation of morale, in *Moves*, n. 9 (1973).

24   Designer Joe Miranda somewhat adopted the alternate activation approach to the extreme, marrying it with the granularity of hex and counters, in *First Blood in Crimea* (Compass Games).

25   Urban insurrection brings to the forefront the role of civilian populations in modern conflicts. Surprisingly, apart from highly effective existential treatments in titles like *This War of Mine* (Awaken Realms), this particular topic and its influence over the conduit of conflicts has seldom been given enough attention by traditional wargames.

26   Interestingly, this solution was used in the cruellest games of them all: gladiatorial games, in which pre-set couples of fighter types were established, combining the strengths and weaknesses of the respective weaponry and defensive weaknesses.

27   About interconnected objectives in game design, see Starkweather, A., On to victory—victory condition considerations in bravery in the sand, in *Operations Special Issue*, n. 2 (2009).

28   Even on this aspect, see the live chat between Serval, F., Rangazas, S., The guerrilla generation: COIN beyond COIN, in *Homo Ludens YouTube Channel*, https://youtu.be/keUR15gYwSM?si=w_DO3wy1Ldz0pgoo.

29   Ironically, in the world of simulation, we also have to include the possibility that Grouchy could be "right": in a game of *Band of Brothers* (Worthington), a WWII tactical simulation heavily dependent on units' morale, I spent three turns trying to convince two squads of US paratroopers to exit from behind their piece of Normandy *bocage . . .* only to discover that there was a hidden German MG waiting for them hidden in a nearby house, losing both units in a single enemy attack.

30 Davidson, L., *What is a wargame? A case study*, https://www.beyondsolitaire.net/blog/what-is-a-wargame-a-case-study (2023). Also see the following debate on the nature of wargames continued on Davidson's Twitter account.

31 Simonsen, R. A., Naturalism vs realism in simulation games, in *Moves*, n. 31 (1977). At the time of his writing, Simonsen was editor and executive art director for the magazine. The idea that simpler and more streamlined games can be more "realistic" than complex and sophisticated ones is at the basis of Philip Sabin's theories, but also often linked to the concept of "playability" that is an easier management of game systems by the players. For this, see also Hill, J., Designing for playability, in *Moves*, n. 14 (1974).

32 Simonsen, R. A., Naturalism vs realism.

33 Simonsen, R. A., Naturalism vs realism.

34 Essig, D., In brief: The simulation of what? in *Operations*, n. 2 (1991).

35 It could be argued that Andrea Angiolino's hidden complexity theory is complimentary to the Essig Paradox.

36 "Let a hundred flowers bloom!" is the slogan used by game designer and military analyst Brian Train in the insightful conversation with Fred Serval in The future of wargaming, in *Homo Ludens YouTube Channel*, https://www.youtube.com/watch?v=vyyxGy_xF7I.

37 Serval, F., Wargamology—what is a wargame—part 2 (Game design, families of wargames), in *Homo Ludens YouTube Channel*, https://youtu.be/OnD24unVVCc.

38 And yet, games like *Fire in the Lake* (GMT Games) or *Verdun 1916: Steel Inferno* (Fellowship of Simulations) reproduce quite effectively the historical sense of detachment from the identity of the single soldiers felt by higher-level decision makers, exactly by having the players move nameless wooden blocks on a map.

39 Buchanan, H., *That's not a wargame!* and Ruhnke, V., *What is a wargame?* in *C3i*, n. 35 (2021).

4 The Real "Engine"
Game Designers and Gamers

(The Flow is) "a state in which people
are so involved in an activity
that nothing else seems to matter;
the experience is so enjoyable
that people will continue to do it even at great cost,
for the sheer sake of doing it."

Mihály Csíkszentmihályi

It could come as a surprise, but with all the words spent since the beginning of this study, we still haven't touched more than superficially one of the most fundamental elements of games: the subjective and psychological aspect of those who create them and, even more, of those who play them.

The issue when approaching this element based on evocative techniques as well as functional renditions of historical dynamic, however, is that it is much easier to understand, describe and apply all the intricacies of the entire *Advanced Squad Leader* manual than to obtain useful results from the study of the experience of a player engaged in the simplest wargame ever created (and much less those of the original designer of the game). The drive behind the mere idea of creating a game, the conceptual premises and the expectations involved in the work of an author and also the behaviours, perceptions and different stages of the inner decisional process enacted by the players—these are the prime forces of the entire universe of simulation, and as such some caution when speaking about them is required.

So, much more than "games" in this chapter, the focus will switch to a deeper analysis of "gaming". The result would not be just another perspective on the subject of our study or an additional layer of knowledge about its practical features . . . but also a fundamentally more complete awareness of what simulation is, does and—most of all—*means* for those who create and regularly practice it.

4.1 POINT OF DEPARTURE: THE GAME DESIGNERS

Creating something is not an easy task. Creating something that has to intelligently react to the inputs of someone in a continuous interaction is an engaging task. Creating something that interacts with unpredicted inputs while remaining at least ideally faithful to a pre-determined reference reality actually borders on a daunting and almost impossible task.

Yet, this is the essential definition of what designing a simulation game requires, and so many people have taken on this mission in the past decades, considering the

DOI: 10.1201/9781003429098-5

amazing number of titles available on the public market. In fact, the motivation for becoming an author might look like something of a weird puzzle for external observers, much less for remaining one over the years with multiple titles published and such a relatively scarce economic return.

Sure, one might mention the satisfaction for being repeatedly mentioned by fellow players and reviewers. Or the pride for having been able to translate historical studies in a statistically sound and functional model. Or even the emotion of seeing that model recreating in tangible form, if not history itself, at the very least your own impression of it.

It presents many peculiar challenges, too. As a game designer, it is not enough to formulate your own interpretation of the reference past events and translate them in a model. That creation and its many intricacies have to be both mathematically coherent and sufficiently evocative of those events, as well.

Modern game design processes include extensive playtesting (even if not as much as in the past, given the frantic release schedule even for major publishers) and the intervention of several game developers (that is, people that transform your wonderful and genial ideas into something that can be printed, manufactured and, most of all, played). Yet, the starting challenges remain and have a deep influence on many of the author's later choices.

How many points in combat value should I give to this particular regiment, starting from their historical performance in the simulated campaign? Did this class of ships already have torpedo tubes on board in 1940, or should I wait for 1941 to include that capability in my scenarios? Which were the timing and extent of the actual impact of this specific event on the 1960 presidential campaign? And so on, adjusting and readjusting numbers, symbols, counters, terrain hexes, map connections, card distribution and even more general procedures, rules and exceptions *ad libitum*.

In fact, even component creation can (and usually does) represent a major conditioning factor in the design process.[1] Game authors have to contend with limited numbers of counters or map sizes just like writers have to face constraints in the number of pages or in the presence of pictures in their books, or still like movie directors being forced to cut some scenes in order to maintain the narrative rhythm and remain inside the duration limits for their films.

Any way you want to put the problem of why someone should put him- or herself on the task of creating a historical simulation game, a general definition of what a game designer does in relative perspective could be to formulate and calibrate general systems, capable of dealing with both predicted and unforeseen particular situations created by players in later and separate moments, in a roughly predefined but ultimately freely modifiable scenario.

If that looks complicated, it is because it actually is, and not few systems have failed in some extent or the other in the mission.

Every author in every chosen medium—be it a book, a poem, a movie, a painting, an essay or whatever you prefer—not only makes unwilling mistakes (sometimes derived from lack of study, other times from lack of historical knowledge at the time of the creation[2]), not only willingly accepts to introduce distortions imposed by the nature of the chosen medium itself, but also honestly decides to focus on different aspects in his or her re-telling of the facts.

The same goes for games, which explains the existence of countless simulations over the same subject (yes, Waterloo, Barbarossa and the Bulge: this means you) but all of them, with varied value of course, dealing with different peculiar aspects. These design choices could come from both an "artistic" and a creative point of origin (card-driven games and *COIN* series), from minor yet highly impacting variations of already established classic mechanics like diversified CRTs or untried units of uncertain value in hex and counter systems (respectively: *The World Undone* series, CSL, and *Panzergruppe Guderian*, SPI), as well as descend from an easily identifiable level of historical awareness in the chronological moment of the creation of the game itself (in the process giving us precious insights into the societies producing games in that specific moment of their development).

So, when designing wargames and similar titles, game authors translate their personal interpretation of past events in a sort of "ludic historiography".

A game component particularly suited to that literally singular purpose is, once again, cards. Their versatility lends itself very well to support various expressions of originality by the authors: after all, this has been true since the actual introduction of cards as a fully functional element in game engines with the invention of card-driven games by Mark Herman and his *We the People* title.

Later authors have gone even further down the road of including their personal views on the simulated events thanks to these small bits of paper. Volko Ruhnke focused on the exploit timing of common opportunities by the different factions by putting universally available event cards in the middle of the table of *COIN* series titles, while Mark Walker reproduced the high variability of tactical proficiencies by the troops engaged in the unpredictable Vietnam environment with his card-driven combat system in *'65* (Flying Pig Games). Regarding direct engagements, in *Dawn of Battle* (Worthington) Mike Nagel put variable CRTs on every single card to better portray their highly individualized and random nature in ancient linear battles. Also command structures can be the subject of different interpretation, both in modern warfare as seen by David Thompson's *Undaunted* (deckbuilding mechanics used to recreate the challenge of keeping control of your unit under enemy fire), as well as medieval operational campaigns as described in the *Levy & Campaign* series (the pre-determined activation sequence decided at the start of the campaign turn) once again by Ruhnke.

Of course, not only cards are susceptible to frequent and dramatic variations inspired by the personal historical visions of the game designer. Every single choice in every single title regarding different map structures (hex-based, point-to-point, area . . .), turn sequences (symmetrical or asymmetrical, variable or fixed, linear or impulse-based . . .), combat resolution systems (force-ratio, differential, bucket of dice . . .) and so on has a specific meaning in the general order of the simulation.

This is just as or even more relevant in "traditional" wargames in which even a small variation like a different type of zone of control, or a specific stacking limit, has very significant effects on the proceedings of the entire game . . . and this is actually why it was so important to understand the *functional* differences between all those game mechanics as we have done until now, before carrying on the study and get to the next level in our analysis of simulation games: dissecting their *historiographic* features and why a game designer chose one over another.

If we adopt this more comprehensive approach, other things appear before our eyes when looking at a specific ruleset, the most significant of which is the actual purpose of the game designer: the core elements of history on which the author has decided to focus in the treatment of certain events.

Naturally, in some cases the end results of an author's effort might not reach the intended objectives, even if this does not necessarily detract from the overall quality of a ruleset.

The much-appreciated game designer Bowen Simmons declared in the notes to the latest title *Triomphe à Marengo* (Histogames) that she wanted to dispense with CRTs, dice rolls and counter values in order to reobtain the original "look" and feel of classic *Kriegsspiel*, eliminating the obsession for accurate statistical predictions of outcomes (Figure 4.1). Putting apart the fact that in most of its incarnations, the Prussian ancestor wargame used dice of various natures, the elaborate *Chess*-like system devised by Simmons excluded random elements and statistical variations . . . to introduce another kind of *alea*, in the form of the deterministic resolution mechanics used by Simmons herself governing the entire combat element of the game. Even if the same could be said also for more traditional dice-based wargames and for all the very convincing and original internal balance of the system, with *Marengo* you get the strong impression of simulating not Napoleonic warfare *per se*, but the idea of how Napoleonic warfare worked . . . as seen by Bowen Simmons.

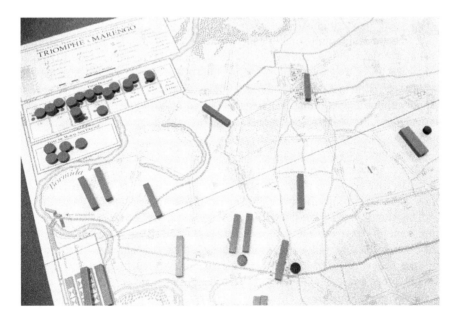

FIGURE 4.1   The last incarnation of her very characteristic system, *Triomphe à Marengo* (Histogame) puts into reality the personal beliefs of its creator, Bowen Simmons, not only about the nature of Napoleonic warfare but also about the general features of Napoleonic wargames.

Source: Photograph by the author.

There are other instances in which, however, opinions, experiences and even personal biases might play an undeniably positive role in game design. Authors like Herman, Ruhnke, Train, Thompson and many others have put in their work on simulation games not only the results of deep and well documented historical research, but also their professional competence as strategic studies and political analysts with dedicated approaches, simulation models and real-life experiences, as well as their individual beliefs.[3]

What should be considered with at least similar if not even more pressing attention is also another influencing factor in game design: players' expectations.

It cannot be overstated how much the consideration of that aspect can be a significant factor in the production of objects aimed at such a small and specialized public, even more considering that the two populations frequently overlap with people being at the same time game designers and players themselves. Expectations do not regard exclusively the quantity of the rules, yet also their quality, that is which historical approach to follow, on which issue to focus the experience, which elements of the historical narration consider high priority and which ultimately negligible.

To fully understand this aspect, we need to keep in mind the fact that commercial simulation games and wargames, being published products aimed at maximizing their diffusion among the public of prospective buyers, are a popular culture product. So strong is this reality, that the general dynamic remains true even when some of the more elaborate forms of simulation games are aimed at an already specialized public . . . but public, nonetheless.

As such, they cannot be but deeply influenced by other forms of popular culture, like music, literature and of course movies. For all Jim Dunnigan's efforts, and including titles published by SPI itself, we can't have a wargame about British colonial war without images taken from *Zulu* (1964), or about the naval war in the Pacific without referring to *Tora! Tora! Tora!* (1970) or *Midway* (1976), or even a Napoleonic game without us imagining Napoleon as played by Rod Steiger and Wellington as brought back to life by Christopher Plummer in Sergei Bondarchuck's *Waterloo* 1970 movie.

Those mentions are scattered and yet constantly present in the rulebook, on the counters, on the map and even on the game box lid graphic art.[4] This happens to provide narrative reference points to the players, as well as to satisfy their expectations for a game set in a specific and highly recognizable historical period.

This should not be considered in a totally negative fashion, as a simple deviation from proper treatment of past events. With all the critics we can move against their stereotypes, by following Georges Duby's teachings about the historical value of false beliefs diffused in a certain time, the study of such deviations gives much insight about how some events were considered in a specific time in which games about them were designed. This "how" does not include only single elements of the simulation, but also a general approach.

A very good example in this regard might be represented by the pivotal event of the Western theatre of operations in World War Two. Considering its image in cinema history we pass from celebration and eminently kinetic description (*The Longest Day*, 1962), to well-documented critics (*A Bridge Too Far*, 1977), to stories focused on individual experiences (*Saving Private Ryan*, 1998, and *Band of Brothers*, 2001).

Interestingly, and not at all by chance, one might find the exact same evolution in wargames dedicated to these same events published in the respective years, up to this day: *D-Day* (Avalon Hill, 1961), *Highway to the Reich* (SPI, 1977), *Combat Commander* (GMT, 2006). A poignant testimony of the close relationship between the ongoing and almost parallel evolution of game designers' approaches, players' expectations and artistic renditions of historical events.

Of course, there are instances in which historical interpretations later to be revealed as partial, distorted or just plain wrong are due not to players' expectations and the popular image of the event prevalent at time of publication . . . but much more simply to insufficient work on part of the game designers.

Sometimes this is due to material errors in reading an order of battle, unreliable or wrongly read sources, personal or cultural biases and so on. Other times, those deviations are unavoidable, being caused by the inadequate information basis available at the time of the design.

This is especially true when we are dealing with simulations designed almost at the same time that the events are unfolding, the so-called "instant games". One famous example is *Sinai* (SPI), a game about the Arab-Israeli Wars whose design was still underway when the Yom Kippur conflict broke out, pushing Jim Dunnigan and the SPI developers into creating an *ad hoc* scenario about the new war. This was not originally foreseen, so the designers had to spend entire days in front of TVs and newspapers absorbing every bit of information filtering from the front in the pre-Internet era, re-elaborate them in game form and playtest them literally "on the fly".

Naturally this entire process was prone to mistakes, constant corrections and inaccuracies of all kinds (some of which would not be known and understood until years or even decades after the end of the conflict), undeniably reducing the practical value of the simulation. Yet, by examining the 1973 scenarios as designed and trusting the proverbial strive for accuracy of SPI authors, we can have a fairly good idea of the image of the conflict enjoyed by the foreign public in those days, how much info was revealed and of which general quality, the impressions made by the events and even the documents available at the time for those who were studying and even planning portions of the conflict itself.

The same can be said about games designed by people who are in an active part of a conflict during the conflict itself, with a very interesting case represented by the cooperative game *Armed Forces of Ukraine* (3CY), designed in 2022 by Ukrainian authors to show the nature and driving purposes of the first phase of their struggle against the Russian Federation forces invading the country. One could only imagine how precious a wargame designed by Roman authors about Hannibal's invasion of Italy in the years between Cannae and Zama could be for any historian, notwithstanding all its inevitable distortions and inaccuracies—sometimes, even more valuable because of them.

Another advantage of a practical study of game design deviations has a more conceptual nature. It shows how the traditionally celebrated connection between the amount of "historical detail" included in a game and its overall "realism" cannot be taken for granted: actually, what a game designer could honestly believe to be "historical" could be not historical at all, and so the end result will be an objectively non-realistic game.

In this regard, Sabin's penchant for simpler systems appears to be somewhat of a safeguard against those issues, since their apparent simplicity avoids any entanglement with excessive direct simulation of information based on less-than-reliable sources. More essential systems have thus repeatedly shown their capability of producing more useful and comprehensively more "accurate" (even if less "precise" and "detailed") descriptions of the events treated. This in conjunction with having a much more effective "cognitive load balance", providing much more flexibility in outcomes management as well as allowing the players to stay focused on the situation rather than on the rules used to represent the situation . . . and fill in the gaps much more easily through later research and, if the need arises, simple house rules and corrections.

In conclusion, game designers have always been by nature the real point of origin of all the objects that we call "simulation games", sometimes showing great originality in their approaches, sometimes re-adapting the works of other authors, sometimes standing right in the middle of the old and new trends in their job.

Their creative activity can sometimes take the semblance of an almost magical discipline, other times of a scientific application of mathematical and statistical procedures. These two impressions combined form what can only be described as an "artform unlike any other", to borrow the words of renowned game designer and expert Greg Costikyan.[5]

In that sense, unsurprisingly, their personal status has steadily increased over the last years, and deservedly so. Having considered this and all the other concepts regarding game design until now described, this could be a very good time for game critics to start working on a veritable "*auteur* theory" in game design, not dissimilar to the one adopted in the study of movie directors and screenwriters.

After all, they are all cultural products with many more similarities than differences between them.

4.2 DESTINATION: THE GAMERS

There is one element in analog boardgaming that is so fundamental to its core nature to be so often taken for granted that it seldom receives proper attention: the fact that, for all the sophistication of the genial game mechanics and extensive research made by the designer, that game would still remain just a senseless heap of paper (sometimes, plastic) without its proper material "engine" . . . the players themselves.

Given the assumption that, in order to speak of analog simulation games, you always need to have at least a human player standing around and dedicating his or her attention to the proceedings of the gaming session, it is clear that no study of simulation games could be considered complete without even a summary description of its psychological and behavioural aspects.

A good reference in this is, of course, Mihály Csíkszentmihályi's and Jeanne Nakamura's "Flow theory", about the strongest states of absorption by an individual engaged in a specific activity. Without going too deep into psychological details, Flow can be described as a total concentration of focus, knowledge and skill application by a subject while enjoying an involving creative activity. In this peculiar state, a person is so absorbed in what he or she is doing to be essentially "taken away" from our world in another universe, populated by mental projections and constant challenges.

While being in the Flow you just want to stay in the Flow as long as possible, finding in it the truest expression of your intelligence, competence and capabilities. So much do you desire it that in many instances the Flow begins even before the start of the experience, in its preparations, and remains also in the long-lasting memories of the experience, to be shared with others. Thus, it can be said that the Flow exists before, during and after the experience itself.

Csíkszentmihályi and Nakamura originally formulated their theory while observing artists and athletes, but its features can easily be found also in the experience of boardgamers, and in particular of wargames and simulation games *habitués*. In the latter, we find what could be described as a "double Flow": the one created just by playing a game, and the other derived from playing a game that is in itself declaredly creating another world during the session.

By taking another step backward, however, we might ask ourselves actually why someone should choose to dedicate precious time, considerable effort and not the least of all even some economic investment to such a curious hobby as playing games with the goal of recreating past (and very often quite dramatic) historical events.

Several studies have been conducted on this specific subject, unsurprisingly leading with very diverse results.[6] There are, in fact, some players dedicated to the hobby by reason of its highly narrative nature, others attracted by the possibility of watching their historical research take life during the game moves, others still drawn mainly by the confrontational aspect and by the challenges provided by a typical game sessions, and even those simply fascinated by the dance of the mathematical procedures composing the game's openly readable (and even freely modifiable) algorithm.[7]

Now, those expectations may vary both in their nature and in their actual historical accuracy, but it is undeniable that almost all historical events that form the basis for simulation games enjoy a specific semblance deeply engrained in our collective imagination. And those so exotic to not have such luxury are quickly researched by wargames in search of at least approximate starting reference points for their experience.

Naturally, when dealing with history and popular imagination, the importance of cinema, literature and other artistic sources that we have already met in our study cannot be overstated enough. They will accompany the choice of a title to play with their friends, the reading of rulebooks, the desire to enjoy that particular experience in that particular moment of their life. Those voices and images, in other words, will be an integral part of the gaming Flow.

So strong is this projective imagination element that it could cover historical inaccuracies, as well as practical distortions of the experience itself. It won't matter, though, since players will be frequently so absorbed in the moment to realize those issues only in later moments after the conclusion of the session . . . or even be actually aware of them *during* the experience itself, but carry on anyway![8]

Another possible approach at the issue would be to focus not on the subjective vision held by a player about a game even before its start, but rather on the psychological attitude followed by that player during the gaming session. Here many other factors come into play and the Flow becomes, if not more difficult to trace, at least more perturbed and subject to abrupt changes.

In order to proceed along this oblique path, one should always take as reference the very close proximity of wargames and role-playing games. Those two categories, apparently so different from each other and prone to open contrasts in past ludic history, are in fact not just "close cousins", but direct derivatives. Both can be categorized as simulation games, both use sophisticated mathematical procedures to represent different states of reality, both have the creation of a different world and the rationalized description of players' interactions with it (be that world "real" or not) as their primary purpose. In essence, role-playing games are just wargames that began to pay much more attention on individual storytelling rather than on collective storytelling, shifting the attention from an entire army to a single warrior . . . but their core dynamics still remain, if not outright identical, at least closely similar.

The question then would become: in a wargame, who actually is the player?

Instinctively, when taking a game about Waterloo as a classic example, one could say Napoleon Bonaparte or Wellington. Yet, already at this primary grand tactical scale, the poor Blücher would remain ignored if the game is played by just two people. Still, if we study even a very simple game like *Napoleon at Waterloo* (SPI), we would find a myriad of small-scale tactical decisions: Which artillery batteries to use in a bombardment? How to distribute my attacks? Where to direct my advances and retreats?

In a real-world situation, all of these choices would be delegated to local subordinate commanders, but in a typical wargame they are all entitled to one single player, literally putting so many different hats on his or her head (Figure 4.2). Also adding to this the fact that even when playing the role of the overall commander, average wargamers constantly have to shift their attention to unforeseen events, once again taking different roles and losing much of their illusion of absolute control.[9]

In simulation games, differently than what happens with generic boardgaming in which individual imaginative and creative speculations about the various game elements phases are not so relevant for its operation, everything still revolves around the players' creative imagination and projection activity, not around management skills or purely efficiency-focused decisions. So, the question of the players' role is as relevant as the game itself, effectively shaping the whole experience around it.

Take for example a sophisticated and highly detailed wargame as *RAF* (Decision Games). Both in solitaire and in competitive mode, the German player would think of being in charge of the whole air campaign against the British, in preparation for Operation Sealion . . . the game, however, gives to that player high responsibilities, yet limited by the general framework decided by higher military and even political decision-makers above his or her head. Those superior levels decide when to focus on manufacturing or civilian targets, when to concentrate the raids against British air assets or radar structures, and so on, even when the player would clearly realize that those changes in strategy are just plain wrong.

Yet, savvy wargamers would happily accept those limitations and even celebrate them as perfect solutions to depict the reference historical reality, at least as considered through the lens of their expectations: when I play a game about Caporetto I expect Italian troops to be much weaker than their Central Power counterparts, and

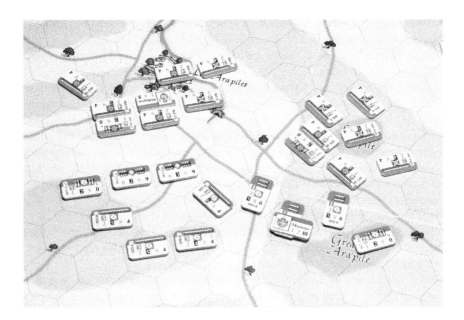

FIGURE 4.2   A typical dilemma of Napoleonic wargames is whether to leave the choice of tactical formations to automated subordinate commanders or, like in the *Vive l'Empereur* series (depicted title: *Quatre Batailles en Espagne*, Legion Wargames), give also that deeper level of control to the human players.

Source: Photograph by the author.

would denounce any attempt at rebalancing the situation as negative elements of the game, to be corrected as soon as possible.

This speaks volumes about the psychological attitude of a wargamer, ready to accept both sudden shifts in their role during a gaming session to always be at the centre of the action (in contrast with the much more individually-focused role-playing games), and amazing limitations to their decisional space: the apparent contradiction is quickly solved by the historiographic value of those different game design solutions, making any game feature potentially acceptable if it serves as a better tool for a more accurate historical depiction.[10]

Of course, different game designers follow different paths.

Thanks to these varied styles, wargamers can then enjoy a somewhat middle-point compromise between the dry resource management approach of German-type games and the exciting but sometimes confusing point of view provided by role-playing games. Their peculiar Flow will let them see personal stories of this or that unit, of this or that soldier, in the face of the consequences deriving from their own decisions. You don't just "lose a point", you see people live or die under your command.

Taken to the extreme, these highly formative experiences can lead the more sensitive wargamers to some very important "epiphanies" during their gaming sessions. By looking at the pile of enemy counters eliminated and referring to how many soldiers each of those small bits of paper represents, you can have a sudden and very tangible proof of the horrors of war's extent, as well as their tragic paradoxes such as when you realize how many of your soldiers have you saved by using poison gas attacks against the enemy in a typical World War One simulation. It is cruel, of course, but not being aware of the nature of those facts is much worse than "cruel": it is dangerous.

Session after session, repeated playing of wargames might even lead to more universal conclusions: some "Joshua moments", such as the one experienced by the NORAD computer going by that name depicted in the movie *Wargames*.

Of course, not all wargamers would be sensitive to these reflections, not all would end up creating a personal philosophy about personal relationships and the sense of the entire human history out of their passion for simulation games, as the protagonist of Roberto Bolaño's *Third Reich* did . . . but for those who do, maybe wargaming reaches a higher cultural value of many other leisure activities.

While reaching those high points of awareness sounds a bit idealistic, a much simpler (but by no means less important) recognition might be found in the temperance of competitive and even aggressive attitudes by those who regularly practice wargames.

It might seem a bit contradictory, but every expert player would tell you that the very first thing to read in a rulebook is the victory conditions chapter, delineating exactly what the game (that is, the system devised by the game designer to recreate his or her personal vision of the simulated historical events) expects from you.

Now, many simulation games include victory conditions based on direct elimination of enemy assets, but in at least an equal number of cases parallel, if not altogether alternative, victory conditions are regularly given: obtain control of a certain location, prevent the opponent forces from getting out of the map or, vice versa, evacuate an entire formations while suffering minimal losses, even winning indirect competitions on different political or economic tracks, rendering direct aggression more than useless—actually counterproductive. If an aggressiveness element is present in wargames, it cannot be anything else but a very selective and goal-oriented kind, an instrument for reaching higher and more important goals, not a drive towards wanton and useless destruction just for the sake of razing enemy cities to the ground or "watch the world burn" à la Joker.

First of all, it is all a fake aggression, with no physical harm whatsoever and no more socially dangerous than the one we find in actors playing on stage or in athletes engaged in direct confrontational sports like boxing or martial arts (and even less than that!). In other words, it is really just a game, and already the simple practice of re-playing the same game switching sides represents a significant lesson in empathy, critical historical analysis and sportsmanship.

Secondly, the competition, whenever present, is limited to the single playing moment. Remembering Huizinga's words, the "magic circle" exists only as long as the game that created it is in action. The moment after we put the game pieces back in the box and close its lid, even the attitudes of the most competitive wargamers disappear at once, leaving only a handful of friends sharing their passion for history and those games that are based upon it. Sure, the experience would carry on in their discussions, after action reports, social media posts, reflections upon this or that strategic decision . . . but all the former "aggressiveness" would be just gone. Or it should be.

And finally, there are few things that tie people together like shared experiences of well-liked occupations. Long-lasting friendships, working collaborations and even sentimental relationships have flourished around the gaming tables among "fierce and irreducible enemies". Wargames are by no means an exception to this.

So, all these considerations lead us towards a re-consideration of the meaning of "competition" in the wargaming environment.

"Competition" in simulation game practices is much closer to another term, "competence". Taken by its Latin roots, the word means essentially "to be capable in something" and is often linked with the concept of "teaching" and "learning" an ability.

In this scenario, the two (or more) participants in a wargame are actually trying to reciprocally augment their own knowledge and tactical senses, without any particular need of showing their own greater ability. External "competitivity" linked with gratuitous "superiority" is quite another thing and is rarely seen (and much more frequently frowned upon) among wargamers, because such a destructive and egotistical attitude would greatly damage the aggregative basis of play.

A great teaching in containing one's own aggressive behaviour, indeed, compounded by other more rational calculations about asset conservation, passive or active decision-making, unbalancing tactics aimed at retorting back the opponent's attacks against those same enemy forces, and so on. More formal descriptions of these phenomena might entail famous logical problems like the "prisoner's dilemma" or the "hawk-dove theory", all of which revolve around a limited and very focused use of force to reach (or even re-define on the run) the true objectives of one's actions.

The final judgement of the nature of a gamer's experience is, however, very dependent on something many wargame enthusiasts (and game designers, too) sometimes tend to overlook: actual player reception of game-generated information.

With this complicated term, we can describe what players get from their simulation in terms of data, situational awareness and historical content. Rules are not the reference point for the entire experience, but just an instrument to vehiculate a greater quantity and better quality of data from the game itself to the players' intuition and memory, losing some of their sacrality in the process but gaining much more practical utility.

It is here that the Flow encounters one of its greatest obstacles, that is a delicate and functional balance between direct representation and comprehensible insight gathering for those who actually run the whole thing and make their decision based on a broad perception of what is happening on the game board, rather than losing precious time and energy in finding this or that paragraph in the rulebook.

This is in effect the core of Philip Sabin's simulation theory valuing simplicity over hyper-sophistication, not just for the sake of some condescending "playability" issues, but as an actual path towards a better understanding of content.

Sabin's revolution of terms on the objective side of the issue really redefined the entire framework of simulation games analysis and, while originally focused on a re-evaluation of more essential classic games of the 1970s, it could easily be applied also to new hybrid designs adopting equally simpler approaches to historical interactive representation, as the original author of the theory himself quickly and repeatedly recognized.

In this context, for example, letting players practically understand why the occupation of an enemy airfield to increase their air cover range, rather than just adding some abstract points on a separate "air support" track, is much better not only from a playability standpoint but also for a more effective and complete reproduction of historical detail inside the complex simulative equations. An apparently simple game like *Freezing Inferno* (Princeps Games) showed that beautifully.

A good comparison might be the one between simulation games and photography, both being activities aimed at representing reality in emotionally engaging and intellectually significant ways, by using specific machinery and reproduction techniques, among which one could find elements such as diaphragm aperture and shutter speed: by carefully balancing those elements, a good photographer can choose between obtaining a highly impactful or highly definite image of the subject, but not both at the same time and always being forced to choose between one solution or the other. Other photographers shooting the same subject at the same moment could and would use other settings to obtain other results.

It is not by chance that the famous SPI hexagon logo so closely resembles a photographic lens shutter system, also considering Redmond A. Simonsen's passion for this art form. Nor the fact that professional simulations used in practical military operations and strategic studies tend to be much simpler in their core mechanics and at the same time much elaborated in their components and final dynamics than commercial games: their simplicity is much more than a stylistic choice, it is a *functional* and *necessary* decision, dictated by the need of providing a clear and easily manipulable depiction of the events in a relatively short time and with the greatest possible efficiency.

But what about the subjective side of the issue? Can the emotional management of such a great information and experience Flow stay calm, balanced and inspired by the utmost rationality?

Already in a normal condition the average intellect can process only a limited quantity of information, juggling among countless deviations, distractions and cognitive distortion deeply influencing the final judgement of "what's best for me" among all the possible alternative choices; and this by postulating that the "average intellect" is able to see all of them, by the way.

In a challenging, even if pleasantly so, environment such as games, other factors enter the equation further complicating the scenario: competition, expectations, individual visions of the simulated historical events, personal relationships with the other players, mere rules knowledge and so on.

On top of all this, games (and simulation games with a special degree of sophistication, sometimes bordering on intellectual cruelty) regularly include many mechanics with the declared purpose of introducing active distortion elements of the players' rational decision processes, such as deception, bluff, fog of war, planned diversions, limited information and so on. There are instances in which these elusive elements are totally out of control of both players (such as random initial setups such as the scattered paradrops of *Highway to the Reich*, SPI), only partially manipulable by them (maneuvering to obtain a certain force-ratio or even limiting the strength of an attack to minimize the chance of getting highly negative results such as the "secondary" CRT of *Bulge*, Decision Games), totally resting on the shoulders of a single player.

Hidden units in block games such as the typical Columbia Games titles, double blind games like *Chancellorsville*, Worthington Games, or even untried units in *Panzergruppe Guderian*, SPI, whose values are unknown also to their own commanders!

This shaky cognitive ground creates a very peculiar tension in wargames, totally unknown to (relatively) predictable and deterministic games as *Chess*: a psychological "game within a game" which is one of the secrets behind the strong fascination these games exert on their players.[11]

Bluffing occupies a first-rank place in this comedy, since almost every single decision in a wargame is permeated by this very peculiar diversion. Even in the most essential hex and counter game, by launching an attack from my right flank, I am actually hiding the weaknesses lying on my left sector, hoping to occupy so much of my opponent's attention to avoid a dangerous counterattack in that sensible area.

Since ludic activity presents such a golden opportunity for observing human psychology at work in a challenging environment, it is natural that several mathematicians, philosophers and economists began focusing on games-related experiences with the same dedication of military leaders engaged in their pre-planning or exercising simulations.

The results of course varied, ranging from the already mentioned "prisoner's dilemma" and other related situations, to complex and flexible systems describing the possible vagaries of human decisions. "Game theory", as the specific branch of applied mathematics, has been designed exactly to understand and possibly predict human decisions based on a quantifiable description of events and unsurprisingly we would find two of its greatest authors, John von Neumann and John Nash, among the pioneers of modern professional wargaming in the RAND Corporation rooms.[12]

Yet, the omnipresent deceptive element of simulation made its influence felt even here. As we have seen in the description of the three "Realms" of games, the overabundance of non-linear elements in wargames imposes a deviation from the too formal calculations working in the idealized "dilemmas" of game theory.

There, every single player is either non-communicating with the other(s) or, even in the most complex and interesting problems, in possession of a perfect knowledge base of the situation. The decision-maker could thus easily calculate the alternative possibilities of success and failure, in order to choose the more favourable expense-outcome option, min-maxing the losses and gains, obtaining a perfect compromise path considering the general traits of the strategic situation.

Too bad that this never happens in the real world these games strive to simulate, and not even so frequently in those same games wherein, as we have seen, many fundamental elements to form rational judgements are actually hidden from the players, while at the same time the psychological tension obfuscates the vision, encourages emotional responses and leads to the inclusion of expected behaviours derived from the pre-eminent historical interpretation or even from personal feelings among the players. Whoever played a game of *Diplomacy* with some family member or loved ones (and has managed to maintain a decent relationship with them after the end of the experience) might easily understand the meaning of those words.

It is here that an entirely different discipline literally enters the playing field: behavioural sciences.

With this term we indicate all those studies related to the quantity and quality of human perception of the outside world, decision-making processes and in general the constitution of the very same knowledge base to be used as the foundation for the later rational choices of people engaged in intellectually challenging activities. Sadly, the conclusion of those studies is that human perception is deeply incomplete, what we called "knowledge base" should be better called "ignorance extension" and that the choices of people are all but rational, especially in challenging situations.

This does not mean that people make their choices at random or in a totally unpredictable way. At the opposite, their cognitive processes still follow very stable procedures and steps . . . only, those are very frequently inaccurate, partial and distorted by biases (or deviations) which can be summarily listed in typified categories. And that's even before the other player begins "muddling the waters" through active moves in order to deceive us.

Behavioural sciences and their applications, as delineated in the works of Kahneman, Gigerenzer and many others, have given us valuable tools explaining the infinite contradictions of our world and our own, both in the past as well as in the present, opening the way for a much more extensive awareness of reality and its internal relation.

Considering the fact that they exist to represent and recreate reality in interactive yet plausible mathematical models, simulation games then represent an ideal field of application for these disciplines. On the other side, simulation games, being conceived as smaller scale experimental tools for the observation of reality, provide an ideal ground in which one can test human reactions faced not with excessively formal and unrealistic choices such as the prisoner's dilemma, but with complex and multi-faceted challenges inspired by real world situations.

Typical cognitive biases such as loss aversion ("I am risking too many forces for this attack"), narrative fallacies ("My Old Guard units will surely hold their ground!"), confirmation ("I studied my deck well, and surely I will get this important card sooner or later . . .") and the like are all common encounters for wargames and simulation enthusiasts. Much more than stylized and allegoric games like *Chess* (and here Poe is thoroughly vindicated), wargames and simulation in general provide eminently more complete and efficient observation and exercising assets for the formation of future decision-makers.[13]

In other words, *Twilight Struggle* is a very convincing representation of Cold War dynamics and perceptions, with great didactic value considering the amazing number of events included in its cards, but also a highly effective framework for testing and developing the individual players' lateral thinking and indirect confrontation capabilities.

Also, another fundamental aspect of behavioural sciences, the so-called "nudging techniques" aimed at influencing the decisional processes towards positive ends, are extensively found in simulation. They can appear in the form of streamlined interfaces highlighting unit values or procedural steps just when and where you need them in your gaming experience (a part of the "hidden complexity" solutions speculated by Andrea Angiolino), or through internal game functions encouraging you to follow historical paths (fixed and highly lucrative card combinations in CDGs like *Shifting Sands* or *Paths of Glory*). So much that sometimes those "nudges", as in real life, can become too powerful, introducing a phenomenon known by players as "scripting": an excessive intrusion in the decisional process, undermining the fundamental aspect of freedom of choice (and even of "error") which is at the objective basis of every game . . . and of its subjective experiential Flow, of course (Figure 4.3).

As Caffrey notes in his studies on professional simulations, the cost of a well-designed and conducted wargame is almost non-existent both in economic as in real life costs, when considered in relation to the value of its potential results in knowledge, efficiency and awareness. This would theoretically also constitute a great limit to their plausibility: since no player is ever risking anything while "fighting" the Battle of Waterloo on a map with paper counters, his or her decisional process will never be comparable to those of Napoleon or Wellington, whose later careers or even physical life were actually depending on the final outcome of the day.

There is another primary drive which is even more deeply felt by those who dedicate themselves to this kind of game: tension between freedom of action and the range of decisions allowed inside the context formed by the rules.

Games, however detailed they might be, are not alternate realities by themselves and thus cannot have the same internal diversity in the dynamics of the events they represent. They always remain mathematical models, ruled by accurate algorithms, working on precise and predefined sets of operations and procedures. Those fixed elements can be freely modified, of course, but also the new variations will be just as limited and dominating over the players' decisional space as the old ones substituted by them.

FIGURE 4.3 The "hidden complexity" approach followed by Andrea Angiolino in his *Wings of Glory* design is based on a streamlined interface and on the gradual distribution of useful information to the players during their actual gaming experience.

Source: Photograph by the author.

This, as we said, creates a tension between what a player *would like* to do in a game and what he or she *can actually* do, even more than what they *ought* to do in order to satisfy the victory condition and close the gaming Flow with a final success. In fact, the possibility of doing something crazy or never experimented before is a much stronger sensation than the constant research for the right strategy to adopt to maximize the possibilities of success, because it leaves the player with a much stronger feeling of self-determination and personal independence, going even further than the original intentions and historical vision of the game designer.

It should be noted that more modern designs are paradoxically much more restrictive in conceding freedom of action to their players than classic hex and counters wargame were. One just has to compare the multitude of hexes (and thus of possible alternatives for movement paths and combat determination) present in *Napoleon at Waterloo* (1971) in respect to the fixed options provided by the cards of *W1815* (2015).

One thing is for certain, however: no historical gamer worth his or her name will ever ask a game to be any easier and less challenging than the simulated situation itself. This happens because for such gamers the original intent in approaching these titles is not just the game experience by itself, but the possibility of "feeling" the historical events on their skin and the sensation of being able to shape them with their intellectual capabilities.

So, since the historical situation is the beginning and the end of the Flow in wargaming, wargamers accept amazing levels of asymmetry and even imbalances in all the game elements, including the crucial aspect of victory probabilities, if those are necessary to obtain a better depiction of the simulated events. Even in solitaire gaming, it is not uncommon to see solitaire players deliberately choose the higher levels of difficulty conceived by the designers.

There are two main reasons behind such a counterintuitive choice.

First of all, to maintain an adequate challenge value of the experience: if I have no one else to beat on the other side of the table, I have to beat the game itself . . . and in order for this to be at all interesting, I have to provide a suitable opponent in a sufficiently competitive "automated" opponent.

Secondly, since in general solitaire games tend to have a stronger narrative focus than multiplayer titles (being actually closer to reading a book than playing a game with other humans), the decision to keep the level of difficulty high enough is taken in order to respect the situation as complicated and difficult as it was for their historical counterparts, without introducing improper simplifications. To put it more simply, to "tell the tale" in the right way.

A certain freedom of choice among optional rules and also independent modifications to an existing ruleset is a byproduct of one of the most important features of analog boardgaming: since the player is the actual engine of a game whose procedures and algorithms are all readily available and openly known, he or she can easily modify those functions with nothing more than a simple stroke of a pen. Also in digital boardgaming, it could be argued, something similar is feasible, by choosing from among the various pre-set options available at startup; yet, those options are, indeed, pre-set—that is, pre-defined by the game designer—constituting a closed group outside which the average player cannot venture.[14]

Simulation games with their sandbox nature, free of any existential need for perfect balances which are a fundamental element of Eurogames, represent a perfect playground in which to experiment with variations, adjustments and additional content definition. Their mathematical functions are quite easy; even a small rule change can have a pervasive cascading effect over the entire experience, competing historical visions usually encourage modifications of the most diverse kinds and even more, remembering Dunnigan's observations, every wargame player has the dream (and actual possibility!) of becoming a game designer someday.

So, game mechanics can be varied or even removed, mixed among different titles or defined from scratch, adapted or repeated . . . in an endless tinkering which keeps the hobby varied, vibrant and always prone to creating new proposals starting from all this activity in which the borders between roles of player and game designer are often shifting.

We could thus define this constant creative effort as "secondary game design", something that makes boardgamers in general and simulation gamers in particular not just passive spectators or users of a cultural product, but also active "players" in the entire design process of a game even after its final release.

This flexibility takes many forms. We go from the simplest changes of a single counter value, setup position or table modifier, to more extensive "house rules" varying core procedures of the games such as movement, stacking, combat, command, supply, victory conditions . . . to the addition of entire optional chapters of rules or brand new scenarios (sometimes following guidelines already present in the rulebook such as in *Tank on Tank*, LnL, or dedicated systems like in the *Combat Commander* series, Figure 4.4).

To the extreme, we can find even full-fledged "reskins" in which the system is overhauled and transported in an entirely new environment or historical period. This has happened, for example, with the narrative card game *Legion of Honor* (Clash of Arms), describing the life and adventures of a French Napoleonic-era officer, and its "mod" *Civic Crown* designed by a fan of the system taking the players back to the Second Punic War.

But what game designers think of all this activity, subjecting the results of their meticulous historical research to open criticism with the simple change from a +1 bonus to a 1 malus for a specific unit firing out of woods?

Usually they are quite content with it, something that should come as no surprise if we remember how many of those authors started their career just by modifying existing games to their tastes. Some of those game designers effectively already include possible variations in their own handbooks mentioning historical interpretations that might differ from their own (for example, what Volko Ruhnke did in his *Nevsky*, regarding the representation of Mongol light cavalry fighting alongside the Rus). Others, like Mark Simonitch, actually encourage players to try different solutions in playing their games, even outright ignoring systems or scenarios that they might find too complicated or imbalanced. Some even add commonly accepted house rules in later editions of the same title, accepting the fact that they might be better solutions than those found by themselves in the first version of the rules manual or that they could correct historical inaccuracies emerging after the original publication.

FIGURE 4.4 Some simulation games like *Combat Commander* (GMT) include rules systems dedicated to the creation of original scenarios by the players through specific procedures such as random troops generation or points-based unit selection.

Source: Photograph by the author.

Finally, this open approach to rule changes and secondary game design finds its greatest expression in specific events, the so-called "Consim-Jams", in which players and game designers are encouraged to mix and match existing systems, find new environments to set them in and create new original titles that will later be developed and published: GMT's *Vijayanagara*, a game about the conflicts in medieval India, is one of the most prominent results.

Of course, not all that glitters is gold and even the secondary game design can find its limits. After all, the final players usually lack the research assets and playtesting support needed to fully explore the consequences of their variations and, if the game designer chose a specific path maybe there was a good reason to do so. The trend, however, remains and is a consolidated part of wargame history since the earliest days, as proved by the extensive space dedicated to house rules and original content hosted also among the pages of professional magazines from *Moves* onward.

Sure, other wargamers prefer the stability of "rules as written" and wait for the game designers to give their own approval to such variations.[15] They do so out of respect for their beloved author's work and also to maintain a firm common ground in regulations and content when proposing their preferred games to other members of the hobby outside their regular playing group, the next big factor in a player's life and Flow experience: all the other players and the broader "community" that they form.

Our average gamer might be amazed and fascinated by the prospect of entering in a semi-ideal world of easy-to-find opponents, frequently organized tournaments, diversified access to many information sources, constant agreements to share the financial burden of buying this or that title . . . and yet, misunderstandings, factionalism and selfish behaviours lie in wait to spoil this incredibly positive reality. This continuous swing between the two poles (aggregation and isolation) explains the ebbs and flows of the various states of the wargaming community over the decades.

We can thus define first a "classical" period ranging from the 1960s to the early 1980s. This was the period in which gaming clubs made their appearance in schools, universities, local communities and the like, and they made it in numbers, essentially being the prime form of gaming aggregation for those two decades, with a tendency towards lighter and more readily accessible titles.

After that came the late 1980s up to (more or less) 2010, a period also known as "the Dark Age" of wargaming. Here the combined competition with role-playing games, computer games and, later, collectible card games, greatly reduced the mass of wargamers, prompting the fledging community to gather all the remaining forces, put up the equivalent of castles and fortified positions, and thus abdicating to the fundamental task of recruiting new members. Unsurprisingly, much more closed communities fostered the domination of super-heavy titles, which were retroactively considered the only "real wargames" not on behalf of their historical value, but of their actual complexity and apparent highly detailed representations. Those were the so-called "gatekeepers".

And what about today? In a gaming world still coping with the consequences of the explosion of Eurogames, wargaming is living some sort of Renaissance in the wake of their "cousins'" indubitable success. Many old wargamers came back to the fold after decades of absence, a multitude of small to medium-size publishers appeared on the market proposing new titles or revised editions of old classics, and even some relatively young individuals did pop up and asked for admittance into the "serious club" of people playing with history.

And it is also here that the new communication of social media platforms of all kinds made their impact felt also (if not especially) on those very specialized portions of "geekdom". New Facebook groups were born, new YouTube channels began to promote reviews and unboxings of new titles, new specialized conventions began to appear on the calendar.[16]

The end result has been a very tight community in which, thanks to the still very limited number of members, everyone knows each other after a while, a greater sense of comradeship and inclusion is felt (notwithstanding the few, but very "noisy" gatekeepers still in activity) and expert gamers are always ready to help newcomers in making their first steps in such a greater world.

Social media also had another fundamental importance in modern-day evolution of the wargaming hobby, by cancelling all the distances in space and time between players and designers, but also among gamers scattered all over the globe. In an unthinkably short time interval of just a few seconds, an average wargamer can get immediately in direct contact with his or her preferred game designers for solving rules ambiguities *during the actual playing session* (and thus keeping from interrupting the greater Flow), while other players in several continents and time zones can easily discuss among themselves about the latest production news or exchange their respective gaming experiences on the actual "battlefield".

Never has such a tight contact been possible in wargaming history, not requiring two to three weeks for a conventional letter to reach its destination and get back with an answer. And it shows.

It shows also in the other ancillary system of the newer communication technology applied to gaming: remote gaming. On platforms like *Vassal*, *TableTop-Simulator* or rules-enforcing *Rally the Troops*, gamers from all over the world can communicate, arrange for gaming meetings, organize tournaments and actually play a "virtualized" copy of a title, oftentimes immediately playable right from the very short download of the game module. The very same platforms are also used as development tools for new designs, letting authors create, share and compare in real time their prototype games with dedicated groups of playtesters scattered all over the globe: and to change all those proto-versions, you just need the click of a mouse to change the respective *Vassal* or *TTS* module.[17]

While the actual impact of such a diffused and ever-present revolution in the gaming world still needs time to be properly studied, it is clear that social media and information technology gave a very significant contribution to modern-day wargaming.[18] Yet, they also changed some parts of its nature, for example by proposing very aggressive forms of consumerism, superficial (if not, in some cases, partial) information or by vilifying the critical spirit of the average wargamer, by proposing with a weekly schedule always "bigger and more important" titles, each of which is presented with ambitious goals . . . but all too often without the necessary means to reach those objectives, in terms of rules or dynamics.

The sector is in turmoil, however, and now more than ever a gamer curious about simulation can easily find a nearby club, show up some evening on a regular date or also during a dedicated "open-to-all" convention where some players double as impromptu demonstrators and veritable recruiters for new gamers. This does not always go in such a smooth way (it never does, actually), but the trend is there; it is also strengthening thanks to much more accessible titles, and it shows no sign of receding in the near future.[19]

In the end, a gamer's subjective psychology is like a great sea, at least as deep as the objective potential of simulation games. What has been presented so far is thus a very superficial and introductory exposition of the greatest mystery of the gaming world: the gamers themselves. They and their very personal approach to gaming, their highest expectations and their individual image of the Flow: what could be described as their "intention of playing" . . . or, to put it in Latin, their *animus ludendi*.

4.3 THE JOURNEY ITSELF: GAMES

Until now, in our exploration of the subjective side of gaming, in other words of the "Flow" and its many expressions in playing activity and with a special regard upon the world of simulation, we have dealt with two primary agents: game designers and players. Yet, what about the actual object of their relationship, of those objects who put each of these two groups in contact with one another, that actually constitute the bulk of the topics covered by this very book? What about . . . the games?

They are designed, produced, distributed, sold. And then they are studied, played, reviewed, criticized and then played again. Which is all fine, but when leaving the mere practical elements of the gaming activity and getting to know their more existential and psychological aspect, one question stands out, still unanswered: how are they perceived?

Starting at the very beginning, as games they uphold the general principles of this ancient human activity, as perfectly delineated by Johan Huizinga in *Homo Ludens*. And as such, they stand very close to other cultural products of imagination, if not at the actual roots of them, since for the Dutch scholar, father of modern ludology, games and storytelling are two very close relatives, if not the very same thing.

Now, of course, storytelling and gaming are two very different things, with many ideal similarities but also many practical differences. Stories have no pre-set rules and, while structured, have much less formal approaches in their development; they also tend to be unidirectional, with an author describing the actions to his or her readers, not engaging them in interactive decisions along the way as games do with their players. Also, stories do not change with every reading or listening, while games are open-ended affairs and in fact one of their most desired is replayability, that is the fact of shifting their shape every single time they are used.

Simulation games add something more to the equation: their close relationship with their reference realities they are trying to reproduce, even if in the interactive, plausible and open-ended form that we have mentioned so many times before. In their internal equilibrium they appear to be even more formal than "generic" games, since their rules and regulations are themselves subjected to the individual historiographic vision of the events upheld by the designer, introducing distortions, anticlimaxes and deep imbalances in their narration.

Yet, this constant referral to the simulated events may also constitute an obstacle for a unanimous recognition of their narrative value.

It could actually be argued that the faithful representation of events which forms the basis of simulation games is a serious limitation in the freedom of action which is so typical of good storytelling both from the point of view of the author and from that of the readers.

For some, simulation games and wargames are just reasonably accurate reconstructions of historical events, with a certain succession of decision points left up to the players and leading to a set of plausible end results. They do not "tell" stories, but instead describe "history", or at least your own version of it, defined by the final relationship between your strategic choices and the internal parameters of the simulation model.

For all those who wish to go "one step beyond" the numbers written on the counters or the colours printed on the map, however, the answer to such criticism is quite simple.

Simulation is not just a +2 or a +3, one symbol or the other, one exception to a certain general rule or one special procedure present only in a specific title of a series. Of course, those elements are there, and have to be studied well as preconditions for a good gaming experience, but they are not at all the sole purpose for the entire process.

Those representative elements are instrumental in maintaining the not renounce-able bond between the fixed historical facts and the variable gaming elements (also known as "simulation" itself), but also to the expression of a much more dialectic relationship between what has really happened in actual history, as determined by academic research, and what will happen in game history, as defined by the players' different choices.

What all this leads us into is that a simulation is something more than the mere representation of past events, and to become that "something more" it needs another element: narration. Only through the infinite variations of storytelling the very same fixed initial elements can produce the infinitely varied results, however remaining always plausible and thus deeply bonded to the reference reality.

There can be other, more technical objections, though. It could be accepted that in wargames there are possibly some "narrative" elements, but they are not arranged in a traditional sense and do not follow recognized storytelling dynamics. Even more, wargames with their broad spectrum of representation are often based on large-scale events, put the players in so many shoes of so many different decision-makers, con-stantly change their perspective and severely limit the number of choices left open to the players. So, once again, they cannot have a "storytelling" element, or at least not as we usually mean it, mostly because the events and their evolution are not seen through a "ludic lens" based on an individual subject self-relatable to the player.

Such is Marco Arnaudo's position, exposed in the first segments of his study *Sto-rytelling in the Modern Board Game*,[20] declaredly excluding wargames from the rest of the work.

While this take on the topic is perfectly understandable if we use the interpreta-tive tools conventionally used in art critique, there is an issue in the entire reasoning: even if they don't know that they shouldn't, wargames *do* tell stories to their players, constantly, and still use the traditional tenets later mentioned by Arnaudo in his fun-damental work. They just do it in a very different and peculiar way.

This is the main critique posed by game designer and ludologist Maurice Suckling: wargames and simulation games actually do not care about the individual ludic lenses which are so common in traditional storytelling, because they use other approaches.[21]

So, even outside 1:1 skirmish rulesets so common in miniature wargaming, while there is no single common personal perspective in a simulative narration, the focus shift from one decision-maker to the other always follows the same rules, is con-stant in its application and thus does not generate any confusion in the players' view. A single narrative stream is preserved, even if in a profoundly non-linear manner as Jim Dunnigan would point out, but it is there for everyone to read and immerse themselves into.

Also, if a wargame about the Battle of Waterloo does not put you straight into Napoleon's shoes from the beginning to the end, and thus does not trigger self-relating dynamics in your experience, the entire story unfolding before your eyes will be dra-matic enough to feel sympathy or compassion or other strong emotions towards all those involved: the same psychological response one might get from reading literary masterpieces like Xenophon's *Anabasis* or Tolstoy's *War and Peace* (only, this time, *you* are the writer as well as the reader[22]).

As in Greek tragedy, conflict is the key to the action . . . and conflict is one of the main features, if not *the* core feature of wargames, to the point that its management (and the limitation to its undue excesses) is the essence of the experience itself. Everything in a wargame revolves around conflict, is conceived to generate other conflict, is determined by previous conflict; and the end of all conflict simply means that the game itself is over.

Again, the apparent disconnection of event perception in reality is dealt primarily with the time and space distortions in simulation gaming representation, as described by Amabel Holland and Kevin Zucker in their fundamental articles on the subject, as well as with the fact that all simulation games still follow in their turns the very traditional Aristotelian structure of introduction of the general scenario, complication of events, their final resolution under formally recognized terms such as "early game" (or setup), "midgame" and "endgame". Reinforcements coming in have the same narrative function of characters appearing in the middle of the story, eliminated counters are perished figures all gone with their personal history of glory or ignominy, victory conditions are the core motivations of the protagonists and the turn track is an almost perfect embodiment of the implacable running of time which binds all mortals (aka, "players") to their fate: all waiting the ultimate "last turn and score check of the game".

As *ASL* designer John Hill was fond of remembering, there is not a great difference between facing a fire-spitting dragon in a treasure cave or a German MG42 in the streets of Stalingrad.

Of course, things are a bit more complicated than these simplistic comparisons, but in great synthesis it is difficult not to find the familiar trappings of a good story behind these core features of a good wargame. At least, game designers are well accustomed to using them as explicit narrative techniques, and even more importantly players expect to be subjected to them: in effect, the emotional response that they hope to get from a good gaming session is one of the main elements upon which their passion for such an exhausting and engaging hobby is based.

"Engaging" is the essential term here, since *engagement* appears to be the very first ring in the "chain" of wargaming, a progression of mental states experienced by all those who practice simulation on a regular basis.

The second step of the relationship between players and their simulation games is constituted by *knowledge*, that is the pleasure and fascination for discovering in an interactive and enticing fashion new information, broadening your cultural baggage and enriching your personal background with new competencies, especially focused on history and strategic matters.

Yet, knowledge is useless if not applied and so every human being has the tendency to use his or her theoretical competencies as intellectual or practical tools to better understand or even modify outside reality in a way that satisfies the personal inclinations or even actual life objectives. That is the ultimate psychological step, the one that might be defined as *awareness*, a more comprehensive vision of present-day events based on the example of past events as re-lived and effectively "manipulated" in first person through the active gaming experience, and so much more vividly than just a passive book reading.

Engagement, knowledge and awareness thus represent the three primary forms through which the gaming Flow expresses itself in the gamers' consciousness through the games themselves, defining many intermediate psychological states and single episodes along the players' "career".

As a testament to the indomitable freedom-oriented aspect of gaming, not all players give so much attention to storytelling elements, however, and many enjoy a perfectly valid wargaming experience while at the same time totally forgoing any narrative perception of any kind.

David Isby, author of SPI classic titles like *Marengo: Napoleon in Italy*, *Soldiers* and *Air War: Modern Tactical Air Combat*, effectively summarizes this in an interview of the in-house *Moves* magazine:

> The average gamer does not think like a British soldier of the Great War or a US fighter pilot of the Vietnam War, but I have tried to design games that lead him in that direction. But the games are only the tools. To use them requires the player's imagination. He can see either carboard counters being moved over oddly coloured hexagons, or he can see and be part of history. That choice is the gamer's, not mine.[23]

Other authors were less impartial in their preference towards players indulging in the narrative side of simulation, such as (once again) Redmond A. Simonsen:

> The critical difference (I believe) is the level of *imagination* the players bring to games. More than any other factor, the player's willingness to accept the game environment and totally immerse in it, provides the key to understanding the depth and intensity of the gaming world. Those who don't fire up their imaginations, regardless of intelligence, never get a real handle on what gaming is about.[24]

The subjective factor in the game equation, how a game interacts with its players and how it manages interactions between them, has always reserved many elements of surprise, and the very first field of observation can be found by looking at the simplest form of game: solitaire.

Traditionally, many have considered wargames as the quintessential competitive games (a notion not so valid even for those directly confrontational titles, as we shall see), but since the very first days of simulation games history many titles have defied that concept, being designed from the start as solitaire, cooperative or hybrid.

Solitaire games, for example, have clearly shown how a very powerful historical reconstruction of conflicts, battles and various kinds of engagements can easily be obtained even when the player has to contend with the game system itself. Classic titles like *Raid on St. Nazaire*, *B-17 Queen of the Skies* and *Patton's Best* (Avalon Hill), or *Ambush!* (Victory Games) have been succeeded by other equally sophisticated direct or indirect successors for every simulation level: strategic (*States of Siege* series, VPG), operational (*Field Commander* series, DVG), grand tactical (*Vive l'Empereur*, White Dog Games), tactical (*Rifles in the Peninsula*, Tiny Battle Publishing) and even skirmish (*Combat!*, Compass Games), just to name a single instance for every dimension.

Some of these titles have resorted to elaborated forms of campaign management (*Leader* series, DVG), others have relied more on the narrative aspects (*The Hunters*,

GMT, and the many other derivate titles from the same system) even bordering on the role-playing genre (*Legion of Honor*, Clash of Arms), others still have presented quite detailed tactical models to capture the players' interest and imagination (*Skies Above Britain*, GMT). Partisan and irregular warfare are also topics that look particularly adept at being simulated by solitaire titles, judging from the very good results of titles like *Resist!* (Salt & Pepper Games) and *Maquis* (Side Room Games).

Very often, these systems have relied quite strongly on storytelling elements to create the necessary engagement for their players, involving them in daring missions, unpleasant surprises and constant challenges.

A very simple narrative structure, of course, but also highly effective and captivating, especially when coupled with good historical research upon the involved military campaigns, evocative details such as plane models to fly or enemy commanders to face, and maybe also some role-playing elements such as squad management, improvements, additional equipment, abilities to unlock, random events . . .

One step up from solitaire we find games that head-on defy the conventions about the strictly competitive nature of wargames: cooperative games. In these titles, the game generally controls the "enemy" presenting several dilemmas and priority challenges to the team of players. By coordinating their diverse assets and opportunities, our heroes will have to respond to the various crises erupting on the mapboard and obtain a final collective victory.

Once again, irregular warfare topics have demonstrated their flexibility for the various ways in which they can be modelled in simulations, with the couple of linked titles by Dávid Turczi and Brian Train *Days of Ire* and *Nights of Fire* (Mighty Boards), dedicated to the 1956 Budapest uprising. But, considering the conceptual vicinity to many Eurogames' typical principles, it is in the realm of hybridized simulations that cooperative historical games have found their best expressions: the new classic *Pandemic: The Fall of Rome* (Z-Man Games), the claustrophobic and conspiratorial *Black Orchestra* (Asmodee) about the last days of the Third Reich, the logistic-oriented *Race to the Rhine* (Phalanx) or even the highly narrative *The Grizzled* (Cool Mini Or Not).

In some instances, the game system will not be the "enemy", or it won't be alone in its confrontational play against the humans. Cooperative games may in fact also provide for declared team play between subgroups of players cooperating together (*1775: Rebellion*, Academy Games) with highly asymmetrical factions (*Quartermaster General*, Griggling Games). In other cases, both to represent very peculiar historical events as well as to spice up things a bit, cooperative games also include a hidden "traitor" player, that is someone (whose identity is not known at least for the most part of the session) with the personal victory condition of letting the game win! A prime example of this is one of the many possible ways to play *Hidden Strike: The American Revolution* (Worthington) with the classic Benedict Arnold character . . . or some very surprising other founding father actually cooperating with the British.

A somewhat more elaborate version of the cooperative dynamic is presented by the so-called "semi-cooperative" titles. In these games, players are still called to answer the challenges offered by the game system itself, threatening to inflict a collective defeat to all the human participants, but are also playing for themselves since victory is adjudicated only to one faction. *Churchill* (GMT) aptly recreates the tension between the three major allied countries of World War Two (USA, United Kingdoms, USSR), fighting against Germany and Japan on highly stylized operational theatre tracks, but also contending each other the priority of issues regarding the conflict, as well as feverishly building a network of spies and puppet government to prevail in the immediate afterwar (Figure 4.5). On the same direction goes *Pericles* (GMT), with a team-based semi-cooperative dynamic set in the Peloponnesian War (two rival Athenian players against two rival Spartan players), or the venerable *Republic of Rome* (Avalon Hill), primary source of inspiration for colonialist game *John Company* (Wehrlegig Games), in which players contend the more prestigious positions while dealing with powerful external threats.

These games see players collaborating towards a success (*Repubblica Ribelle*, Aleph Studio Games, about partisan-controlled territories in German-occupied Italy, after the 1943 Armistice) or mere survival (*Land and Freedom*, Blue Panther, dedicated to the defense of the Spanish Republic against Franco's military insurrection in 1936), but at the same time striving to obtain the maximum prestige during the final parades, or obtain a final semi-victory that will still satisfy their factional objectives.

Even more elaborate interactions are provided by titles that could be defined as "semi-competitive". In these systems, oftentimes characterized by very tight balances, a single player against the system (*Peloponnesian War*, Victory Games/GMT) or more players against common enemies (*Geronimo*, Avalon Hill, and *Kings of Rome*, Acies) compete to obtain a better position, but with a very important twist: at

FIGURE 4.5 Mark Herman's *Churchill* (GMT) is a textbook example of the interaction between a semi-cooperative game design and a careful calibration of victory conditions aimed at giving a very recognizable historical rendition of the events object of the simulation.

Source: Photograph by the author.

predetermined moments of the game they actually switch sides or become the prominent leader of the faction and so on one side they have to deal with the scarce cooperation of all other players, and on the other have to contend with the effects of their own tactical decisions made while controlling "the other side" or with the results of the same scarce cooperation offered to the previous player occupying that leading role. The oscillating "pendulum" effect, while quite complicated to obtain with a mixed-experience player group, is truly phenomenal when it works and ensures memorable gaming sessions, with deep historical content.

Finally, even dear old competitive games can have more sophisticated dynamics than simple "win/lose" direct situations. Sometimes victory conditions are deeply asymmetrical and yet closely bound together (*COIN* series, GMT), other times negotiation and dealing is so relevant that in order to make a certain move you have to gain the explicit support of another player at the due price (*Coalitions*, Phalanx), other times still the entire scenario is so interconnected that in order to reach an objective you have to allow another player to obtain one of his (*The Barracks Emperors*, GMT, with its closely tied trick-taking situations on a very limited and constantly changing gameboard). There also times in which your own faction is not so unanimous in the support towards your final goal even when controlled just by you: examples include the confrontation between Haganah and Irgun militant groups in the struggle for the creation of Israel in the Palestinian scenario of *The British Way* (GMT), internal political party struggle between moderate and more radical sub-factions in *Prime Minister* (GMT) and *Prelude to Revolution* (Compass Games), or Cuban insurrectional movement and the somewhat "unsuitable" involvement of US military forces in their clash struggle against the Spanish colonialist forces in *Cuba, The Splendid Little War* (VPG).

Countless other variations are possible, to simulate more elaborate confrontational situations in many original and at the same time effective ways.[25]

So, in the end, what are games when seen from a subjective point of view, that is not from their cold material functions made by mathematical operations and logic functions, but from the actual personal experience of all people involved: game designers, publishers and finally players? In other words, from another point of view: *your own* point of view?

Redmond A. Simonsen, graphic designer and co-founder of SPI together with Jim Dunnigan, and as such one of the true authoritative voices of classic wargaming, had very few doubts about this. In the opening article for *Moves* issue 32,[26] he summarized not just the game design process but its entire final product as "an art product", and a commercial art product at that, considering all the financial and production assets involved in their realization, as well as the inevitable "shortcuts" to be taken in order to allow a game to be a publishable and justly profitable editorial object.[27]

By comparing simulation games to works of art, Simonsen declaredly refuses the idea that there can be a "definitive" title on any subject. This because, whatever the penchant for scientific jargon many wargamers might have when speaking of their beloved hobby (including the author of this very study . . .), game design, game production and finally gaming itself by the players are not at all purely scientific operations.

As such, there is no succession of designs completing or even totally surpassing previous ones, but only a series of different approaches, some more effective than others, but all very capable of capturing a specific portion of the historical reference material for the simulation, creating many different cognitive focuses.

> It is unlikely that one would ever be able to legitimately declare a game the *definitive* design on a given subject for much the same reason that there is no such thing as a definitive piece of music for the violin: each work of art (high or low) is an individual approach to a subject.[28]

But won't this vague, inconclusive and seemingly unscientific approach lead to an elusive and not so useful concept of simulation games? Will it not betray all the previous pretences of being a valid method for historical research, pre-emptive experimentation and intellectual insights and gatherings about specific situations taken out of the past, as well as hypothetical scenarios for the future?

On the contrary, still Simonsen declares:

> Why does it matter what we think of games as a product of art rather than of science? Doing so is a better approximation of reality (i.e., more scientific). It defuses the interminable debates over the possibilities of perfect games and disputes the mentality of the one-true answer to simulating a given type of conflict.[29]

Of course, this further passage—refusing to be limited by purely practical concerns coming from rigidly linear statistics as well as too specialized and compartmented historiographical approaches—requires an additional effort both from designers and from players, as well. The former will have to find new sources of inspirations than just mere readings of orders of battle, maps and existing historical studies in order to create the premises for believable as well as plausible narratives in their titles; the latter will need something more than just rules-consulting and factor-counting in order to go that crucial step "beyond" CRTs, modifiers and terrain effects . . . that last distance towards actually seeing what lies *under* and *behind* those column shifts, those morale procedures, those command and control issues.

This is what Dunnigan used to call the "dynamic potential" of simulations, a series of mental projections of the actual scenario obtained by a mere preliminary observation of unit factors, map positions and general conditions of a given situation even before materially starting the game.

This approach will free players from their very peculiar obsession with direct detail representation, sometimes more an obstacle to creative imagination based on scientific premises which is typical of the simulation experience:

> Notwithstanding all its numbers and probabilistic tables, a wargame is closer to a work of art than a work of technology—it is an abstraction of an aspect or aspects of the object. Just as in art, the level of abstraction is not directly related to the level of realism (strictly defined) found in a given game. The higher one goes into the levels of abstraction, the less obviously realistic the game will seem; the lower the level, the more apparently realistic the simulation will seem.[30]

So, what is "true" realism and what is not, the doubt about what is a truly "accurate" representation of reality and what is just a useless chase to only apparent "detail", is transformed into a theoretical declaration on the very concept of simulation gaming as an artistic, creative and highly imaginative activity based on all kinds of intellectual resources, numerical and human at the same time.

Only such a comprehensive take on the simulation game phenomenon manages to explain many of its effects on those who design, produce and practice this peculiar application of human intellect.

Breaking away from the "game tribalism" so rightly denounced by game designer Volko Ruhnke when he created the seminal *COIN* series which made extensive use of hybridization in its rules, material components and game mechanics, we can finally adopt a comparative method in our observations and see how generic boardgaming, as based on purely combinatorial and mathematical elements, can give you better resistance against practical cognitive biases, but also how historical simulation games in which game mechanics are actually representative of real historical dynamics and not just based on mere numerical relations, can give you better resistance against behavioural and psychological biases.

In so doing, our Flow finally runs complete and uninterrupted from the first moments of the creation of game in the designer's mind, to its material production steps, to the final fruition by its players thanks to the dedicated application both of its mathematical operations and of its creative dynamics. A reciprocal magic binds together creator, creation and final audience, out of and transcending any material element on the joined wings of numbers and images, logic and imagination, in a constantly active and unending dialectic movement.

And playing goes on. And on. And on.

NOTES

1   Modern information technology has played a significant role in this, considering shared platforms like the *Levy & Campaign* series *Discord* server, routinely used for creation and testing of new titles in the series. An unsurprising reality, remembering the fact that already in the 1970s publishers like SPI and Avalon Hill extensively advertised the use of the very first forms of home computers in their game design processes.

2   For a relevant example of the impact of later archeological discoveries and game design, see Miller, B., Alexander's weaponry: Recent research and its relevance to wargaming, in *Moves*, n. 47 (1979).

3   In that regard, see Jack Radey's interview in *Origins of People's War Games*, *Homo Ludens* YouTube channel, 2020. Radey remembers how he started from his personal views in order to obtain a better interpretation of war on the Eastern Front during World War Two, creating more balanced games dispensing with *Wehrmacht* mythology and negative stereotypes on Soviet Red Army's tactical and operational performance, then prevailing in the 1970s and 1980s.

4   The tradition of "Easter eggs" included in the game components is quite long and recognized. Many cases can be mentioned, in "serious" wargames like *Advanced Squad Leader* or *Combat Commander*. A good case is represented by the Thibaud and Blanchot counters present in *Ager Sanguinis* (Historic-One), directly inspired by the protagonists of a successful French TV series set during the Crusades era, complete with scenarios taken from some of the episodes.

5   Costikyan, G., *I have no words & I must design: Toward a critical vocabulary for games*, Tampere University Press, http://www.costik.com/nowords2002.pdf (2002).

6   Some of them date back to the very first stages of the hobby: see Kosnett, P., What is
     a wargamer? in *Moves*, n. 19 (1975) and Simonds, M. J., Wargamer and historian, in
     Moves, n. 36 (1977) for some cataloguing of typical archetypes present in the wargaming
     community. More analytical and structured studies have been recently conducted, as in
     Buchanan, H., Why do we play what we play, in *C3i*, n. 34 (2020).

7   For a broader and more anthropology-oriented approach to the relation between conflict-
     ual instincts and gaming, a reference text is Van Creveld, M., *Wargames: From gladiators
     to gigabytes*, Cambridge University Press (Cambridge, 2013), even if some of his final
     assumptions remain hotly debated in the community.

8   A critical study questioning some of the "true" motives behind wargaming (so critical
     that it met with a varied reception by the wargaming community, in spite of the value of
     its thought-provoking reflections) can be found in Buckley, J., Wargames: Simulation or
     stimulation? in *C3i*, n. 36 (2022).

9   This mirage is as old as modern wargaming (and even older): see Game design: A debate
     on the "Rommel syndrome", in *Moves*, n. 1 (1972).

10   Another instrument to maximize the self-relation dynamics in simulation games is the use
     of maps with period-inspired graphical styles and contemporary names for locations, up
     to the point reached by *Bayonets & Tomahawks* with the highly immersive (and appreci-
     ated) choice of using original native toponomy for villages and natural points of interests
     in the North American wilderness during the French and Indian War. On the opposite side
     of the spectrum, one might find the extensively frustrating (if not outright irritating) spell-
     ing mistakes that non-English speaking players regularly find on their maps and counters:
     speaking as an Italian wargamer here, how many wrong ways to spell "Forte Capuzzo" or
     "Forte Maddalena" have I found in most of the wargames dedicated to the North African
     campaign during World War Two?

11   So ever-present is uncertainty in simulation games, that even more deterministic war-
     games such as *Triomphe à Marengo* or *Fighters of the Pacific* still have to include it,
     respectively through fog of war and an exponential multiplication of possible choices by
     the opponent.

12   The relationship between modern wargaming, both professional and civilian, was already
     at the centre of very early elaborations such as Cleaver, T., Game theory: An introduction,
     in *Moves*, n. 10 (1973). The piece uses the basic principle of the theory to create a possible
     application to wargames and streamlined decision processes.

13   For an exhaustive study of this peculiar aspect, see Herman, M., Frost, M., Kurz, R.,
     Wargaming for leaders: Strategic decision making from the battlefield to the boardroom,
     McGraw Hill (New York, 2008).

14   It could be said that the vibrant "modding" community of digital games provides count-
     less variations to existing programs from among which a player can choose, in order to
     deeply modify the game. But also these additional options come from other designers
     and form other "closed groups" of possibilities: very rarely the average player has the
     possibility and knowledge needed to re-write entire pieces of a game code, let alone to
     change the graphics of a computer game. On the subject, see also Goodfellow, T., A new
     kind of history: The culture of wargame scenario design communities, in Harrigan, P.,
     Kirschenbaum, M. (curated by), *Zones of control: Perspectives on wargaming*, The MIT
     Press (Cambridge, 2016).

15   For a correct explanation of both positions, see Buchanan, H., Rules as written, in *C3i*, n.
     36 (2022).

16   The YouTube aggregation channel and its weekly video bulletins, *No Enemies Here*,
     https://www.youtube.com/@NoEnemiesHere, is a perfect starting point for those who
     want to explore the world of simulation gaming and its many evolutions.

17   Recently, this system has been coupled with another communication software, *Discord*, in order to create "virtual" conventions accessible by gamers all around the world and usually presented with a much greater offer in terms of game designer interviews, demonstrations, previews and other types of direct communication contents.

18   On the subject also see Masini, R., *Wargaming 2.0: Playing with history in the digital age*, panel held during the SDHistCon Winter Quarters 2024 virtual convention, https://youtu. be/HmXrt0TirEM (2024).

19   On the contrary, more and more rules handbooks include "virtualized" elements such as QR codes pointing to playthrough videos, additional assets such as errata and variations, and also specifically designed evocative music compilations to be play during your gaming session, in order to create a more immersive "atmosphere".

20   Arnaudo, M., *Storytelling in the modern board game: Narrative trends from the late 1960s to today*, McFarland Publishing (Jefferson, 2018).

21   See on this: Suckling, M., Storytelling and wargame design, in *Georgetown University Wargaming Society YouTube Channel*, https://youtu.be/wHf0LDvik2U?si=3229fG-W5Rkt2oGNk (2020). Many elements following in the next few passages are deeply in debt to Suckling's work, to which the reader is referred for a more comprehensive explanation of this particular topic.

22   Interestingly, a famous slogan printed on many Avalon Hill game boxes read: "Now, YOU are in command!". While not true from a purely narrative and strictly historiographic perspective, that phrase makes perfect sense if understood in the non-linear fashion defined theoretically by Dunnigan and practically by Suckling.

23   In *Moves*, n. 49 (1980).

24   In *Moves*, n. 54 (1981).

25   Also indirect confrontations about totally regular forces can be represented in many interesting ways. A highly peculiar solution is the one adopted by Dunnigan's masterpiece *Battle for Germany* (SPI): here, the Western Allied player controls also German forces deployed on the Eastern Front against the Soviet player, who in turn controls German forces deployed on the Western Front. This mechanic, also adapted to the Eastern and Western front of the American Civil War by Joe Miranda in *1863* (Decision Games) and by Chad Jensen and John Butterfield in *Downfall: Conquest of the Third Reich* (GMT), could be described as "cross-competitive".

26   Simonsen, R. A., Conflict simulation: Art or science, in *Moves*, n. 32 (1977).

27   In doing this, Simonsen started a line of thought and research brought forward in later years by other simulation experts like Peter Perla (*The art of wargaming*, 1990) and Greg Costikyan (*I have no words & I must design: Toward a critical vocabulary for games*, 2002).

28   Simonsen, R. A., Conflict simulation: Art or science.

29   Simonsen, R. A., Conflict simulation: Art or science.

30   Simonsen, R. A., Naturalism vs realism in simulation games, in *Moves*, n. 31 (1977).

5 Not All That Glitters
Issues and Pathologies of Simulation Games

"People take the longest possible paths,
digress to numerous dead ends,
and make all kinds of mistakes.
Then historians come along and write summaries
of this messy, nonlinear process and make it appear
like a simple, straight line."

Dean Kamen

Maybe some readers will have guessed or suspected it, but there still remains one core truth to be said about the object of this study, simulation. Most if not all of the elements exposed so far find their foundations about an unsolvable paradox: the idea of using an inherently finite object (aka, "games") and its firmly present-time related experience it generates (aka, "gaming") in order to recreate past events in all their infinite complexities (aka, "game subjects").

So, is simulation just a very elaborate illusion leading not to precious insight, but to useless cogitations upon pre-conceived historical interpretations, if not to dangerous false visions of what has happened centuries ago? Not at all, if we remain conscious of the difference between the two seemingly close, but in some regards quite opposite, terms of "illusion" and "game".

While the former is a pretence of truth proposed with the clear purpose of making the observer believe its validity, the latter is instead a pretence of truth made to people who remain perfectly aware of its disconnection to the actual events, even when that pretence is based on very accurate grounds.

Once again, Huizinga and his "magic circle" theory come to our rescue: if you always remember that everything happening when pushing counters on a map and rolling dice on piles of tables is and remain "just a game", whatever their degree of representation or historical research may be, no one (and no ruleset) gets seriously hurt.

This is the purpose of our last chapter to be spent together, a critical and honest study of where simulation games fail, when those failings can be remedied and even when they are unavoidable (or have to be "traded" for other, less undesirable failings).

A very strong temptation now would be to give the reader a long and exhaustive list of all possible issues of simulation games . . . but even that would be a failure, since this list would probably be too long and will never be exhaustive, considering that this kind of cultural product is constantly evolving, is divided in a multitude of categories and sub-categories, and its infinite facets will never be covered by just a single study.

 DOI: 10.1201/9781003429098-6

There are, in fact, extensive sources that, even when declaring themselves to be not totally complete, can be very good starting points in this research. One of the most systematic and easily readable is *Wargame Pathologies*, a study by the US Naval War College, available for free download and constituting something of a reference text in professional wargaming circles, as well as one of the primary sources of inspiration for the next few pages. In a much more relaxed civilian context, in fact, the value of the simulation remains fixed in the overall experience and not in the immediate utility of all its more minute details. The relative "futility" of game is a very good shield in that regard, allowing a much greater "margin of error" to civilian simulations in respect to their professional counterparts.

A greater margin, however, does not correspond to a general inaccuracy of commercial wargames, transforming them in uselessly approximate models: the many instances of professional military institutions using readily available "off the shelf" wargames in their programs are a testament to the fact that sometimes, even in those much more "serious" environments the value of the entire activity is much more worthwhile than all the unavoidable small inaccuracies present in the process.

As in many other fields of human existence, knowing the recurrent issues of simulation is the first step towards accepting them, and accepting them is a precious lesson in humility: what follows is then just a set of possible tools to use in order to recognize these individual symptoms of a simulation "pathology" to avoid it and contain its effects, whatever its peculiar nature and origin.

And also an exhortation to remember that, after all, this is still just a game.

5.1 ALL EVIL COMES FROM THE TOP: DESIGN-RELATED ISSUES

How do you design a game? And even more, how do you design a game whose purpose is not just to work as a mechanism contained in itself, but to represent an object outside the game and its trappings: the real world?

Having reached this point in our study, you might think that we have dealt with this subject with enough depth, highlighting all the different approaches to such a delicate and at the same time not strictly regulated "art" aimed at creating rules capable of delineating a new reality on your living room table every time you open a box full of cardboard chits, a couple of dice and a map.

Yet, there remains one single question to be answered in our quest for understanding this peculiar object called a "simulation game": how *not* to design it.

The very first step in our trip to the "dark side of simulation", that is the failures of its actual historical and representational value, starts with the very beginning: the creation of such a game.

It has to be said, even if Eurogames are based on much stricter and more numerous combinatorial mechanics, simulation games endure an even harder relationship with each single rule composing their "system". This happens because such rules cannot enjoy the luxury of having only other rules as reference points, but need to deal with the highly elusive, contradictory and multifaceted thing we call "reality". In so doing, those poor rules, as we have extensively seen in the previous chapters, have to insert into purely mathematical and linear equations some very irrational and non-linear elements such as Friction, personal attitudes, unforeseen events, weather conditions, political disturbances, cultural biases and other calamities.

This leads to the extensive set of interactions at the basis of the complex simulationist models upon which wargames, political games and even economic titles (set in past times, present situations or even future hypothetical scenarios) are constructed. Those interactions are clearly recognized by the followers of such games and even get a name: "moving parts". The term is very often seen in reviews and other forms of critical contents of such games, indicating all the different elements that seem to be moving independently from our another, but that are mutually related, reciprocally influenced and in a constant state of functional communication.

This (not so) hidden network of relations between counters, maps, cards, tables, tracks, victory conditions, player perception and inter-communication is not just some "background noise" under an extensive set of mathematic equations, but the very essence of the rendition of historical events and their almost infinite intricacy by something operating by such simple operations as an analog game, built on open algorithms and working by a human "engine".

The entire model, however, operates as we have seen both on the objective as well as on the subjective dimension, using numerical devices such as force ratios, statistical tables, arithmetic situational modifiers for terrain and other peculiar "states", as well as exploiting the human sensibility of the players themselves and its impact on their decisional processes. When considered under such premises, a game becomes not just a bunch of materially "moving parts", but an oscillating pendulum between permanently fixed objective elements (the "game functions", established by the designer) and highly mobile subjective factors (the "game choices", made by the players).

This oscillation can assume many faces, but at the core of its nature lies the fundamental relation between the game and its players: their perception of what is happening on the table at any given time or turn, at any given space or point on the map. Such perception is founded upon a cognitive activity and, as such, must obey the general laws of cognitive economy to keep up the essential "movement" which is at the very core of what we call a "game".[1] The maintenance of such a difficult balance lies partly in the good disposition of players in letting themselves be drawn in the depicted scenarios, but much more sits on the shoulders of game designers which are the first human beings with which the abstract concept of a game first comes into contact.

So, once again, it's all in the hands of the authors, also considering the fact that the mere term "cognitive economy" might seem a bit elaborate and difficult to understand for the average player. In its simpler and totally-applicable-to-games form, however, it means the possibility for someone participating in a game (or even casually looking from outside) to easily grasp, compute and lastly manipulate the sequential flow of information given by the game model itself in form of counter positions, success probabilities, conditional modifiers, final objective pursuit and so on. It is essential for a player to be able to manage such a flow with the minimum possible expense of energy, since the object of a simulation game is not to satisfy abstract victory conditions, but to immerse the players in the reference realities (be they historical or fictional) in order to give them something more than a simple points gathering competition: a true existential experience of "feeling to be there", in the shoes of a military commander or a prime minister taking epochal decisions when faced with difficult, breath-taking challenges. And, by the way, as Philip Sabin and many other supporters of simpler and more "cognitive-conscious" rulesets regularly point out, also learn some history in the process.

A good way to represent this in an intuitive fashion is what we could call the "shutter theory", borrowed from basic photography technique.

Every camera, no matter if elementary or technically elaborate, works on the very same principle of physics applied to the structure of its lens array. To take a picture, you have to make a fine balance between three great values regulating the amount of light allowed to hit the main image sensor: ISO "film" sensibility, diaphragm opening and shutter time. While the first is somewhat independent from the others and operates as a general parameter for their balance points, the latter two have a much more difficult relationship.

The more you keep a diaphragm open, the greater the detachment of the central elements in the picture from the background will be, while more closed values will give you a much deeper in-focus zone. The more you keep the shutter closed the more definite and "frozen in time" the final photo will be, while greater time intervals will keep the image movement more flowing and more adept for artistic purposes.

Those two elements, diaphragm opening and shutter times (as tempered by ISO values) have to be carefully considered and properly balanced: blurry pictures, excessively distracting details, wrong movement depiction or less impactful images are all the consequences of bad choices in this regard.

By understanding this we can now apply basic photographic theory to game design. ISO values are the scale of simulation chosen, diaphragm opening is the broader or narrower field of historical elements to be considered, shutter time is how you want to represent those events and their singular "states of motion". Bad choices will give you excessively light, banal and luck-driven shallow titles, or on the other hand titles chock full of useless details unbalancing the general cognitive economy of the experience. Or even plain wrong depictions when all these forces are not adequately researched, thought-of and calibrated, leading to overexposed or underexposed pictures: both ineffective cognitive economies, based on too few or too much info fed to the players in their experience of the game.

Of course, as every photographer knows, there is no set rule for taking a good picture and many of these ISO/diaphragm/shutter triangular points of balance are actually equivalent in their conceptual "correctness": they just give different depictions of the same object, be it in a light or detail-heavy mode, in an indirect representation or in a much more direct depiction. This also explains why individual sensibility of every single simulation follower will lead to very different opinions about the same titles, all of which should be considered valid when based on the same amount of knowledge and also open-minded approach to the study of a particular title. To be even clearer, this is why deeply diverse tactical systems like *Undaunted* and *Advanced Squad Leader* depict the very same situations in totally different ways.

Finding such particular points of balance is no easy task, as can be said for being a good photographer, and yet the cruel world outside an author's promising reasonings will almost assuredly be able to distinguish between a good picture and a bad picture, a good game and a bad game (Figure 5.1). And it is not by chance that the old SPI logo so closely resembles a photographic lens with its diaphragm and shutter . . .

If this sounds hard enough, also consider that after the designer, the players will also be called to create their own mental "shaping" of the situation, hoping to have the smaller quantity of distortions infiltrating in the entire process.

Such distortions do exist, however, and in many cases are unavoidable, even when (sometimes, *especially* when) they start inside the designer's mind.

Problems come when such author's vision is not just influenced by legitimate personal opinions, critical interpretations of studies results, comprehensive views of all the results gathered from a research or even individual choice of elements on which to focus the simulation[2] . . . but when such factors are included in the design process as partial, biased or even outright wrong information sources.

The worst part is that the game designer may be totally unaware of these issues and sincerely convinced of the validity of its data basis. Outside sources such as commonly held opinions in his time, political situation, cultural preconceptions and the like can exert a very strong and pervasive influence over anyone trying to translate all that information into a plausible interactive model, also known as "simulation game". Some of those deviations may be easily recognizable by a clever and careful observer, others may be much more hidden and difficult to catch.

Historical simulation games, for all their scientific ambitions, still remain popular culture products, and so when historical authors that are considered as highly authoritative in their time all concur over a certain interpretation of past events, it

FIGURE 5.1   It is probably pointless to look for a highly detailed rendition of medieval warfare in a light wargame such as *Saladin* (Nuts!), whose main purpose is instead the depiction of command issues and troop attrition during a battle.

Source: Photograph by the author.

is not at all trivial to go beyond their academic status and design a "simple" game going against their work. Nor it is so easy to propose an entirely groundbreaking and even controversial historical view to a general public composed of players that may not be so informed over the latest doctrinal debates to have a specific opinion on the facts, contenting themselves to play games that actually *confirm* widely acknowledged interpretations, also brought forward by other popular culture products such as movies or TV series.

Even primary sources can be deceiving in their influence over game design, because even they may be biased in their origins: government administrators may lie about their management of state resources, field commanders may hide their mistake and construct partial views of the events in which they were involved in order to justify their decisions,[3] even material primary sources such as archaeological findings and subsequent speculations may be surpassed by later findings.[4] Sometimes information is simply not available at the time and in the countries where some games are designed, as happened with certain Soviet armoured vehicles during the heights of the Cold War (that's why there are no T-64s in *Red Star/White Star*, published in 1972: no one on this side of the Iron Curtain knew that such a tank even existed!).

Even more, this is a recursive problem for so-called "instant games", simulations recreating conflicts and historical events designed just as those events are taking place: this includes games about war in Ukraine currently being developed or just published (*Ukraine 2022*, CLS, or *Defiance*, GMT), or in previous years *Sinai* (SPI), famously including a Yom Kippur War scenario developed by Jim Dunnigan just in the very same days in which those battles were taking place, using newspapers as immediate sources.[5]

In other instances, biases may not come from partial or outright distorted sources available to the designers, but from another often-overlooked element in their composition: their native language. Very often, entire games have not been developed over seldom covered battles or conflicts just because there are not enough sources about them available in English or French (and not all have the luxury of having access to local Afghan historiography as Cole Wehrle did for *Pax Pamir. . .*). Those language barriers keep information away from willing designers' grasp or sometimes, which is even worse, push them towards external sources too detached from the involved cultures and, as such, unavoidably plagued by biases and missing pieces of information.

All the pros and cons of simulation design and conventional historiography are thus comparable, operate under similar processes and exert different yet analog consequences on the final products, be they historical essays or historical games.[6]

The main point is that, aware or not, game designers follow the same precise methodological reference points guiding academic historians, right or wrong as they are. The game designer's individual choices about simulation focus, game mechanics, victory conditions, sources selection et cetera reverberate over the entire title, also contaminating the player's own experience. In fact, the author's biases resonate with the player's biases, so much that every single one of the game participants can obtain a very different, sometimes even contradictory, vision of the situation. Some players may get a greater quantity and quality of historical insights, others may grasp much less and stay focused more on the game itself than on its historical contents . . . others may obtain totally false and inaccurate information from the simulation, or even unexpected reflections, sometimes confirming their preconceptions, other times defying them.

The dilemma is regretfully unsolvable: since gaming is an inherently free activity, even the most accurate and effective game designer in the world will not be able to force people into accepting the insights contained in his or her title . . . which might not even be so bad, since even that author made some mistakes or had to accept some compromises in the design process. The only real solution would be to play more games dedicated to the same events, possibly with different or even opposite points of view and approaches, in order to obtain a broader and more comprehensive vision of the episode: luckily for us, modern day game production is so intense that even for more exotic topics outside the usual Waterloo or Bulge actions there are many choices . . . think about the Afghan 1800s scenario depicted in various and (very positively) contradictory ways by titles like *Pax Pamir* (seen from the Afghan clans) and *The Great Game* (seen from the great European powers).

Of course, the more a title is tied to a specific and highly recognizable historical vision, like Phil Eklund's socio-political reflections or the counter-insurgency models proposed in the *COIN* series or titles dedicated to controversial issues, the more they may be prone to biases and distortions not just on the game designer's side but also on the player's approach. The same can be said for games based on distinct historiographical views. *Victory & Glory: Napoleon* (Electric Games) proposes a bipolar hybrid military-cultural-economic challenge between Napoleon's First Empire and all the different coalitions held together by Great Britain: is it a genius historical intuition or an excessive simplification? *Wings for the Baron* (VPG) ties the progress of World War One to the efficiency of German military-industrial complex: was this single element so influential in determining the conflict outcome?

Individual conscience aside, some design-related distortions appear to be much more structural than subjective.

In a sense, historical simulation games and wargames in particular seem to have suffered a case of "victims of their own success". The constant advancement of traditional hex and counter and later CDG systems over decades of production and public appreciation have somewhat consolidated some notions in their design perceived as classic and almost for granted. Some of them, which in the simpler systems of the first generations of titles were re-absorbed in the general mobility of the overall representation, became later much more influential and distortive in the more elaborate systems of recent times. Once again, the Essig Paradox, that is the multiplication of errors in more complex systems rather than what happens in more essential rulesets and procedures, reared its ugly head.

Essential building blocks of what we usually define a wargame can hide very deviating elements.[7]

For example, movement over "clear" terrain in open country is not so clear at all, since even in the most recent conflicts armed forces need to move exclusively over established road networks not only just to "travel faster" but also to maintain a properly efficient logistics network (which explains much of the Napoleonic Hundred Days operations, with the importance of vital communication hubs such as Charleroi and Quatre-Bras, forming the functional basis for the entire maneuver segment in *Waterloo Campaign 1815*, C3i, by Mark Herman).

Often also the treatment of losses in just two steps—full power and reduced—or the scarce necessity for troop rotations to maintain their actual combat capability does not properly represent the constant and progressive degradation of combat effectiveness of units. This explains the advantages of systems like the many different values included in the Columbia Games block titles and the elaborate rotational procedures of frontline and second-line troops included in *Verdun 1916: Steel Inferno* (FoS).

Also, the much-vaunted fog of war solutions used by many wargames are often insufficient if not outright inadequate. In Clausewitz's own treaty, such uncertainty over the disposition and nature of troops regards not only the enemy forces but also the formations under our own command! Especially in pre-radio communication scenarios or in modern world-spanning conflicts it is not so easy to constantly have a clear picture of the deployment of an army's forces over a large area of terrain (and sometimes, not even in much more compact tactical engagements, by the way . . .), so systems like *Atlantic Chase* which leaves us in the dark about the true position of our naval task forces in the ocean are not just "eccentric": they are correct.

The worst fog of war about one's own forces might however pertain not just to the actual military forces but to the top brass will to fight, as well. Interfactional rivalries among bickering generals in the high command, or even worse in coalition armies are historically at the order of the day in most conflicts. Titles with reluctant or directly competing senior officers like *More Aggressive Attitudes* (Hollandspiele) or *The Other Side of the Hill* (MasQueOca) depict fairly well this phenomenon on the purely military level, while much more dangerous internal political quarrels among allies engaged in the conduit of a war form the core dynamic of WWII's *Churchill* (GMT) and *Betrayal!* (AtO), Spanish Civil War's *Land and Freedom* (Blue Panther), making those simulations so unique and interesting both from an historical and from a purely gaming point of view.

It has to be said that not all of these deviations have a determining effect only on professional simulations that need to combine actual playability for the highest number of personnel of varied game experience and utmost accuracy in their results to be truly effective in reaching their fundamental goals. In many cases, a civilian gaming experience does not need that precision in every single moment of the gaming session, and most of such distortions are "reabsorbed" during the entire play, indirectly represented or reciprocally exclusive, essentially self-eliminating each other turn after turn, move after move.

At the very least, conscious players should be aware of them, and thus take those games for what they are: simple representations of core historical dynamics meaning to give stimulating insight into their reciprocal interactions and thus show the inner causes of some events, not ideologically accepted "truths" over the past and its many contradictions.

Such players understand that in many cases game designers have to choose not between a "right" and a "wrong" way (and even less, between a more and a less "realistic" approach) to simulate a dynamic, but among different equivalent distortions, hoping to accept only the less offending ones and to include them in a generally plausible and acceptable depiction of history in game form. An interactive statistic and mathematical model aimed at representing reality, whose results cannot be considered an end in themselves, but only a first encouragement towards gaining a better understanding of what happened by completing the study with more traditional learning assets: also known as "history books".

5.2 ARE WE IN THE RIGHT PLACE? GAME-RELATED ISSUES

The next family of issues a simulation can incur is possibly the most difficult to classify: game-related issues.

In practice, these issues pertain to the very nature of a specific game or to simulation games in general. They represent the objective outer limits of what this kind of game and experience can do, so they can be contained, bypassed and made innocuous by clever game design techniques or also by the players' awareness . . . but they will always be there, ready to diminish the overall value of the entire thing. And most of them will be present in every simulation game ever designed, in the past as well as in the future.

Since it is so difficult to even take notice of their presence, this specific paragraph will directly mention some of the most frequent ones, being conscious however that the list will have no pretence of being exhaustive. Some of them have not been yet discovered, since formal simulation games studies are still a relatively young discipline and also because every new innovation in design and historiographic approaches brings with it the seeds of unheard-of structural deficits in those new solutions.

Maybe the best starting point in such a grievous numbering is, once again, the very top. In our case, that would be which historical vision a simulation game tries to convey to its players, remembering that even correct historical visions applied in the design process of a game are the result of conscious or unconscious choice by the authors regarding which historical aspect the game is focused on, how they are represented in the general balance of the rules, how they are presented to the players among all other elements.[8]

A simulation, we have seen, is an interactive, plausible and statistically sound form of representation. It also has very strong elements of narration operating at its core and in its reception by those who experience it; that is, the players. Every representation and narration, however, is formed by the positive or negative choices of what to "put on the stage" and of which "light" to use in order to present it to the audience.

When an author is creating a strictly kinetic tactical wargame, for example, some fundamental elements of the facts like political topics, cultural divides and economic factors will have to be excluded or represented in strong undertones. They will always be there, of course, since history does not work "by compartment" (much to the chagrin of some over-specialized historiographical approaches), but it would be impossible to represent all of these diverse factors with the same dedication and detail, for playability's and clarity of exposition's sake. Something will have to be consciously "dulled", kept in the background and downplayed in order to keep the cognitive focus on what is considered to be really important.

Most of the time, these issues exert only a theoretical effect on the actual simulative value of a title. It is true that direct battles *could* play a greater part on the *Levy & Campaign* series and be represented in much greater detail, but this does not mean that they actually *should*. After all, explaining these choices is exactly what designer's notes are written for.

The problem takes a much more practical (and dangerous) tone when such distortions are the consequence of incorrect or incomplete historiographical approaches excessively downplaying the importance of some factors, or even worse when they are consciously made to give an instrumentally partial historical depiction of the facts.

The word "propaganda" immediately springs to mind, and for good reasons. Games are very powerful, engaging and effective communication assets for all kinds of content, even more when they give a specific representation of some past or contemporary episodes. Andrea Angiolino repeatedly mentions a *Snakes and Ladders* version created during the Fascist regime to depict in a positive light the violent Italian colonial expansion in East Africa, with International Red Cross cases pushing back the player with their clandestine supply shipments to the local resistance fighters (a very common and obviously untrue accusation, brought forward by the very effective regime's propaganda machine).

There are, however, much subtler and even less aware distortions in simulation treatments, happening much more frequently and in many cases beyond the understanding of the designers and the players themselves.

Many kinetic tactical games, such as the hypothetical case we have encountered before, nowadays tend to include non-linear elements in their rules: morale, command and control, doctrinal differences and the like. Many similar games designed in less recent years (but also some highly appraised "modern" design as well . . .) gave much less importance to these factors, simply because there was not a great sensibility over these elements in professional literature of the times.

A good case study in this sense is the Vietnam War.

Just by comparing the evolution of wargames regarding this violent conflict over the decades, one can easily find traces of the evolution in historical perception of the war itself both by specialist authors as well as by the greater public.

Sure, it was seen as a "complicated" and different confrontation since the very beginning, and we can realize this by studying some special scenario and system rules of the great *opus* on the subject, *Vietnam 1965–1975* (Victory Games), published in 1984, creating negative consequences in certain sectors for the American player too eager to apply all US military might on the field. Those local and global political effects, however, still operated mainly on the kinetical dimension as well, so we had to expect 2010 and *Hearts and Minds* (Worthington, Compass Games) to see from the title itself a focus shift on less kinetic victory condition, a much more influential political track, the inclusion of cards with non-military events dictating the conduit of operations and other elusive, but no less consequential elements. The trip towards a truly non-kinetic depiction of the conflict would be completed only in 2014 by the *COIN* title *Fire in the Lake* (GMT): four players divided in two uneasy alliances (ARVN and US, North Vietnamese government and Southern Viet Cong), totally asymmetric victory conditions (the Americans win not by conquering or defending stuff on the ground, but by physically *leaving* the country!), event cards with prevalent political elements, military coups in Saigon, ineffective strategic bombardment campaigns, global public opinion backlash, rampant corruption, inconclusive field actions . . . you know, Vietnam War as we know it. Or not, since in 2023 we got *Saigon 75* (Nuts!) which follows the current approach looking for unexplained or seldom treated historical moments and shows us what happened *after* the end of a *Fire in the Lake* session, with the South Vietnamese government desperately trying to avoid its final collapse under the combined pressure of Northern troops and internal Viet Cong formations.

The funniest part of the whole story? All those titles can and should be considered at least "good" if not "excellent" simulations by any historical and gaming standards: they are just focused on different features, with different cognitive and experiential balances. Choose your own and have fun with it, or even better do not make a choice and enjoy them all to have a more complete vision of the conflict.

Obviously, we cannot trace a day-by-day picture of all historiographies on the subject just by looking at the games published over a specific episode in a certain year . . . but the trend is there, evident and clear to all.[9]

Sometimes this view is not so clear, of course. In *Twilight Struggle* (GMT) the Cold War is represented through one of the game's dominating dynamics, the so-called "Domino effect": when a country is conquered by one of the players (US or USSR), all neighbour nations are more easily swayed towards that side as well, either through card play or direct-action modifiers. This sounds correct since that geopolitical interpretation was at the foundation of, among others, the US involvement in the Vietnam War itself, decided to contain the diffusion of "pro-Communist regimes" in the crucial Southeast Asia sector.

Except that later analysis showed how partial and erroneous such vision was, how the change in alignment of a nation had no or limited impact on its neighbours, how resorting to direct military action in a country to protect adjacent strategic areas was even worse than a crime against humanity: it was a serious political mistake. *Labyrinth* (GMT) was based on just that premise and proposed a much more asymmetrical and non-linear depiction of the later confrontation with international terrorist groups and constant regional instabilities.

Anyway, should we consider *Twilight Struggle* a mistaken model, a failed simulation of the Cold War? Once again, not at all, because the inclusion of Domino effect as a dominating dynamic accurately portrays what *contemporary* decision-makers really thought about geopolitical developments and so it has to be present in the game, even if it is *now* considered a contentious historical representation!

Such a prevalence of the Domino effect talks much about what we thought of the Cold War in 2005, when the game was designed and published, and when we considered such an interaction between the Great Powers a key part in the historical narration of the events. As well as the current interest over social issues and their impact in past and present times portrayed by games like *Votes for Women* (Fort Circle Games) dedicated to the struggle for women's suffrage, or *Doubt Is Our Product* (Hollandspiele) about the influence of tobacco industry, it is a sign of today's more popular interests, as interpreted by the game designers and expected by the players' public. For sure, it will be the subject of studies on our current society by some future historical researcher, a few decades from now.

Let's get more practical, however, since not all game-related issues are so tied to the core concepts of simulation. Rather, many of them are due to much more mundane yet

FIGURE 5.2 *Twilight Struggle* (GMT) and its depiction of the influence of the Domino theory in Cold War geopolitical thinking transcends the actual strategic value of a now-contested vision of the world, commonly held as true during those events.

Source: Photograph by the author.

no less pressing needs: first of all, to get if not great financial returns from such small-scale productions, at the very least to get even on the final accounts. Or so is the point of view of those who put the real money behind the many games we take into our houses and celebrate as great historical and cultural products: the publishers, just to be clear.

Here the attention must shift from the high-minded rules elements to the material components of a simulation, that is all those pieces of paper, plastic and wood which physically compose a game (or virtually do, if we take also print-and-play titles into consideration). Contrary to what many players might believe, the composition, quantity and even quality of those pieces are not at all neutral factors in the final design. There is more than the final pricing at play, since even adding just a handful of counters might mean too steep production costs and might entail the difference between being able to actually create the game or keep it in the closet as a great but unfeasible idea, especially for small niche publishers operating in a niche editorial environment such as professional wargame distribution.

We are not just talking about the paper quality of game cards or having too few status markers on a counter sheet. There have been several cases in which maps, orders of battle, scenarios, entire pieces of rules had to be left out in order to be able to produce the game, with just the mere hope of recovering those components in future expansions if the base module sold well enough. Good designers and developers find satisfactory ways to compensate those "edits" in the general balance of the game, similarly to what movie directors sometimes have to do with their creations . . . or at least, to properly justify them to an ever more critical public. But sometimes even highly competent and creative authors made "one compromise too many", leaving to their players incomplete or distorted renditions of the events: missing important subordinate commanders forcedly joining their superiors into collective "HQ" markers, entire units absorbed in large comprehensive "formations" of dubious plausibility, events left out of exponentially growing card decks and so on.

To be honest, properly balancing all this stuff with the ever-pressing demands and constraints coming from the publisher (once again, the one struggling to make ends meet and maintain enough margin to be able to produce more games in the future) is not an easy mission for any designer. On the top of that, the author often begins his or her work with a pre-determined complexity rating and game duration time in mind, so even when the historical research brings many unexpected elements into the design process, those original objectives push the author towards more focused representations, at the expense of completeness and extension of the simulation itself. That is one of the main reasons why in game magazines you can often find additional scenarios, optional counters, variant rules referred to a title and proposed by its author in person: many of those are the pieces left "on the cutting room floor", belonging to the original design.[10]

"Games are never finished, at one point they are just published", as veteran author Mark Herman is fond of saying. The long history of "Designer's Editions", second or third printing and successive revisions in wargame chronicles is a testament of the validity of such a statement.

There are times in which those modifications are due to a completely legitimate change of heart by the game designer, possibly due to extensive player feedback or even later artistic decisions. The much-acclaimed *Twilight Struggle* (Figure 5.2) has been joined by an expansion, *Turn Zero*, expressly dedicated to creating different initial setups on the world map, with the declared intent of defeating the trend towards pre-set openings criticized by certain groups of players; designer Mark Simonitch has recently released a second edition of his CDG *Caesar: Rome vs. Gaul* (GMT), modifying the overall balance of the game after having decided that it did not suit his original vision well enough.

There are other times, regretfully, in which mistakes are made during the actual production of the game, either by missing key issues or practical errors in the graphical creation or printing of the maps, counters, cards and so on, or by poor editing of the rules and scenario layouts. This is the ambiguous world of "errata", almost unavoidable small mistakes often with great consequences on the final playability of a game, leading to the diffusion of a cornucopia of later documents, full of corrections, revisions, substitute counters and other elements.

It is something simulation players learned to live with ever since the first days of wargame history and will inevitably have to tolerate for the future. Nowadays the situation is much better than before thanks to social media and the Web diffusing such emendations instantly and efficiently all around the globe, compared to what happened even just a few years ago when the precious corrections could be found only in paper magazines or subsequent titles, or by word of mouth. This does not mean that such problems do not create disappointment for players having to accept sometimes pages and pages of corrections for their not-so-cheap new titles in their collection.

For however irritating errata can be as practical issues in game learning (and re-learning in the correct version of the systems . . .) and experience, they at least are undesired problems, leaving the publishers and designers intellectually innocent for the misfit. A totally different thing is when the systems themselves bring crucial issues inside their structures, due to a conscious decision made in their creation process.

It can sound like a weird form of paradox, but there are instances in which games can fail being a simulation . . . by being "too much" of a simulation. This happens when game designers, overly eager to include as much of the real situation as possible, somehow break the internal balance between game mechanics and player experience by introducing an excessive quantity of contents in the general equation of the system. This would seriously impair not only the practical management of the game systems (remember, we are speaking of analog games: there is no computer and the human participants are the actual "game engine"), but also the cognitive results provided by the session.

To fully understand the phenomenon, it could be helpful to call on a literary quotation: "On Exactitude of Science", a short story by Argentinian writer Jorge Luis Borges. In the few allegorical paragraphs of the story, Borges tells us the tale of an ancient realm where a group of mapmakers were tasked with providing the most exact charting of all the known lands under the dominion of the emperor. So precise they decided to make that map, that it was as great as the empire itself, covering all its regions, inch by inch, and in so doing they covered all crops and farmlands, transforming them into lifeless deserts . . . where now some tattered remains of the ancient and forgotten map remain, as a testimony of the final consequences of a truly exact scientific approach.

Symbology and existential messages aside, a not so improbable risk hangs over the head of simulation as well. Even if we discard all the unavoidable distortions due to uncertain historiography and the vagaries of statistical systems (and we know by now that they are *many*), what use do we have for a system recreating reality in such exactitude to be practically undistinguishable from reality itself?[11]

In many cases, this can represent a hindrance towards that elusive goal. An excessive *quantity* of detail, as we have seen, introduces more distortions into the mathematical model upon which the game is based, damages the cognitive economy of the entire experience by forcing players to be more focused on rules and exceptions rather than on the actual situation and the reference subjects, introduces circular mechanics in the perception of events by creating "illusions" of historical detail enclosed in the game environment itself but totally independent of actual historical reconstruction.

These are the cases of overly abundant "chrome" rules, endless exceptions, proliferation of conditional phases and subphases in the turn sequence, counter overcrowded with different values and symbols, proliferation of game components and the like.

That fault can also be expressed in a *qualitative* sense. Here is where games somehow fall in love with themselves and their own mechanics, introducing superfluous or ineffective rules in lieu of much simpler procedures capable of obtaining the same simulative results.

A good example is represented by the reproduction of order transmission along the chain of command of pre-radio era armies. Many older highly detailed games, and even some of the more recent ones, resort to an age-old tradition of miniature wargaming: written orders, with slips of paper reporting phrases like "Division X shall march up to Hill 92, and then engage any enemy force present there or in its area of operation". This is perfectly fine when you are running a multiplayer *Kriegsspiel* session, complete with senior officers acting as referees, helping you to understand how to plot an invasion of France through Belgium, but not so much when you want to spend a nice evening with your friends at home or in a public game convention. There, if you really want to get so accurate in your historical reconstruction over this specific aspect, a simple system with generic orders like Advance, Hold or Withdraw and the relative modifiers will be more than enough: varied complexity versions of this approach can be found in Enrico Acerbi's Napoleonic wargames, Rob Markham's 3W titles or even in Amabel's Holland order chits used in the *Shields and Swords* series.

Because perception of reality is a profoundly individual experience, to everyone his or her simulation.

Yet, some boundaries remain regarding how far a simulation could and probably should go. A common mistake is, for example, give too much information to players, granting them an excessively accurate bird's eye view of the events, complete control over the single elements of the mathematical equations working under the hood of a simulation, an immediate understanding of all the probabilities of success and failure pertaining to a specific decision.

Such an excessive knowledge introduces sterile min-maxing calculations to the experience, which real decision-makers did not have: this alone creates a distance between the actual situations, their protagonists, the players and the simulation itself, a cognitive gap so great that no bridge could ever cross it.

Dynamics like factor counting (the endless hunt for that small unit granting you the magic 3:1 force ratio), card counting (the unrealistic wait for a certain event card that you know will come up in your hand, sooner or later), or enemy army's exact locations are a dangerous detriment to the value of game models as simulations since the earliest years of the hobby. This is why so much energy has been used by game designers over the decades to introduce perturbative elements like diversified conditional modifiers, fog of war systems (block games), variable deck composition (*COIN* titles deliberately not using all cards even in a full play). Some systems like Mike Nagel's *Dawn of Battle* (Worthington, Blue Panther) have even come to the point of using multiple combat results tables reported on different cards, drawing a different one for every single engagement (Figure 5.3).

On the opposite side of the quantity of information spectrum lies the fact that the underlying model of an analog simulation must remain constantly and totally open to its players, well known and (relatively) understandable.[12] If the model becomes more "opaque", though, players will no longer be able on one side to critically appreciate the historical vision of the author (nor to modify it if they feel the need . . .), on the other to be fully engaged in the gaming narration since many of its fundamental segments will remain hidden or ambiguous.

Once again, the gaming Flow must be preserved at all costs, and every situation that disrupts it in any way will be a serious detriment to every game, regardless of the accuracy of its historical research or the theorical efficiency of its mechanics.

FIGURE 5.3 The apparently simple combat resolution system of *Dawn of Battle* (Worthington, Blue Panther) is based on a set of different effects tables contained on randomly drawn cards, with the declared purpose of avoiding endless pre-calculations by the players.

Source: Photograph by the author.

Intuitively and following what has been said about complexity as a knowledge obstacle for the Simulation Flow, we could be brought to think that this lack in clarity is an exclusive trademark of more elaborate systems, in which the overabundance or rules and exceptions and sub-procedures keep the players away from entirely perceiving the actual situation on the table. However, gaming catalogues are full of legitimately "complex" wargames remaining fluid enough to avoid this problem, as well as much simpler rulesets with key aspects managed in unclear fashion or outright excluded from the simulation. Excessive detail as well as excessive abstractions can hinder a system's validity and its immediate comprehension by the players in equal measure, representing a serious design challenge. However, when a game has to fill a peculiar role in the market or is conceived to satisfy the needs of a specific public niche, be it "fully detailed" or "fast playing", sometimes these issues become structural and simply cannot be avoided in full.

There are, however, issues that could have been avoided, or better, that *should have been* avoided . . . but were not. Because games can be hard or easy, detailed or abstracted, historically sound or mostly narrative experiences, but they can also become "broken": some faults may lie hidden among the pages of a rulebook for years until someone, somewhere comes out and shows a fundamental bug in the system or, even worse, un unbeatable sure-win strategy.

These things are the equivalent of a death stroke to the very essence of gaming, that is looking for ways to overcome your opponent (or the system, for solitaire titles), challenge after challenge, turn after turn. The free exploration of the system and its many elements in order to obtain a final success is a prerequisite of any gaming experience, and not being aware from the start of the winning strategy is a key portion of the entire thing.

Admittedly, tried and true principles of hex and counter, area impulse, card-driven and other families of historical titles have been tested and refined so much over the several decades of their existence that can now be considered quite reliable and rarely pose many problems, even in the balance of an entire game.

It is those peculiar features that make the bulk a of a new title, or the fundamental data portion (combat values, setup positions, victory conditions . . .) of its core that are more prone to fail, for the simple fact that being so innovative or mixed among smaller details they can have obscure contradictions or be brought up only after repeated plays when the specific case arises. Which generally makes their overall effect even more devastating, since it can be really difficult to correct them through add-on modifications or house rules.

In many instances it becomes necessary to rewrite entire portions of the system or vary its initial conditions. This is exactly what happened to the most famous example, *A Few Acres of Snow* (Treefrog) by Martin Wallace.

A few months after the publication of the highly successful game, which used deckbuilding mechanics for a proper simulation of the French and Indian War, gamer Michael Fitz shared what he thought was an unbeatable strategy for the British player base on a series of expansions and attacks along the Halifax-Louisbourg-Quebec route, calling it the "Halifax Hammer". Regretfully for Wallace and the game, Fitz was right: the strategy was effectively unstoppable.

This threatened to drastically reduce the impact of such an innovative and interesting title, so Wallace had to quickly respond first with some modifications (which were found to be not so effective) and later with a rule for a random initial setup that rendered that tactic much more difficult or even impossible to achieve. Once the "secret route" to victory had been found, the challenge of the game shifted from looking for it to looking for the ways to implement it, or for equally valid alternative paths.[13]

Wallace, however, was brought to some important reflections by the event, both as a designer and as a historian. In essence, he suggested that no game can be exempt from the risk of someone discovering a way to "break" it, especially in today's scenario dominated by constant global communication between players and for what regards two-player games in which the human interactions tend to be much more linear, and thus an optimal strategy can be much more easily found and applied. Sadly, the fact that such a route was actually the one that was historically followed to gain the final victory in the conflict is of no particular significance in a competitive gaming environment (even if, it has to be said, it took the British quite a few years and battles to find it!), nor the high efficacy and engagement value of all the other game systems, since this fundamental imbalance spoiled the entire experience in one stroke.

It is hard to oppose Wallace's view on the matter. Even other games like *Twilight Struggle*, as we have seen, had to provide for specific expansions generating random setups for a title that is played in tournaments or even casual games so frequently and with such deep studies about its internal factors and their interactions. There will always be people coming out of nowhere, with a much more efficiency-oriented mindset, that will min-max the whole thing to the extreme and finally find the right combination of actions capable of derailing the system.

Once this happens, the entire (and literal) house of cards comes down. A good solution might be to extend the playtesting procedures or even encourage a cooperative attitude among designers, players and reviewers in order to immediately suggest the necessary correction and modifications.

Surely, in many titles those imbalances are so evident that they cannot be anything but a deliberate choice of the designer, especially those that are necessary to respect the actual imbalances of the historical situation object of the game. In those instances, they are effectively expected by the players who, as wargamers, are much more interested in a correct representation of the simulated events rather than in competitive equality among the different factions.

There are times however when these "delicately balanced imbalances" are too hard to obtain and so games can become not just harder for a player with respect to others, but structurally almost impossible to win. Even in this case, the gaming Flow is threatened by a fatal interruption, since there seems to be no enjoyment possible in dealing with an unavoidably losing situation in which you are not just fighting against all odds, but also against reality as well.

But we have so many games about essentially forlorn situations like Thermopylae, Caporetto, the Alamo, Pearl Harbor (and some might say the Battle of the Bulge, too) to understand why and how imbalanced titles are still not just designed and published, but deeply appreciated by players, too.

Some of them are graced with the necessary remedies to that issue in the form of flexible victory conditions based on the principle that you win by losing "a bit better" than your historical counterpart (like in *Durchbruch*, Acies), others leave the final outcome unchangeable stopping the clock just one minute before the end and asking you to face the inevitable defeat in an acceptable final state (*Lanzerath Ridge*, DVG), others carefully balance the difficulty level or even leave that to you in order to maintain a glimpse of possible success against all expectations (*In Magnificent Style*, VPG and Worthington).

There are however examples of games which could be defined just "experiential", in which the outcome is almost always assured when played by same-level or just competent players. This is the case of many scenarios of systems like SPI's *PRESTAGS* or Richard Borg's *Commands & Colors* system, suggesting to the players to play a specific battle twice by switching sides and counting the final score of the two sessions to determine a winner.

The important element of all this remains, however, in the premise about the awareness of the situation by both the designers and the players. Strategic imbalance can still be an acceptable element of a simulation game without turning into a critical issue, but it must be carefully managed in a well-calibrated fashion. This does not happen in games in which that imbalance is not previously known to all but rather produced during the game session itself by the very dangerous and irritating dynamic called "snowballing", causing one player to progressively ease up his or her path to victory, exploiting some sort of inertial movement whereby a small initial success on one side increases the potential for later gains, and on the other decreases the possibility for the opponent to turn the tide and regain the upper hand.

To avoid this problem, once detected (no easy task, as we have seen), several solutions can be found. For example, random events unexpectedly changing the situation may be introduced, or fixed "rhythm-changes" in the overall situation can be predetermined along the way, or one-time powerful assets may be given in the hands of the players to be used in the direst of times, like double-turns or pivotal events to be acted at will.

All of these remedies are good and effective but pose the final structural problem of all: they must not be *too* effective, in excess of the simulated historical situation. Because, once again, this kind of game exists not to work by itself but for the exclusive purpose of recreating the real-life events that inspired their creation.

This is what distinguishes this highly peculiar family of titles from all other forms of boardgaming. It is much harder to obtain as a designer and even sometimes to understand as a player . . . but, partly borrowing words pronounced by an American president several years ago, people accept the challenge posed by simulation gaming not because it is easy, but because it is hard.

5.3 THE EYE OF THE BEHOLDER: PLAYER-RELATED ISSUES

After having seen how critical issues in game experience can start at the very origin of system design or even before (design-related issues), and when they pertain instead the structure itself of a simulation (game-related issues), there is still a third group of possible detriments to the final value of a game to consider. This is the most elusive and difficult to track family of critical elements, centred on an element that no game designer or publisher will ever be able to study in advance: players themselves.

Such player-related issues are even more potentially damaging than all the others combined, because being tied to the actual behaviour and situational perception of the participants can deeply influence the final outcome of a session. Also, since we are dealing with analog games, players are the ultimate "game engine" of a paper-based simulation, and so any distortion working on their level will inevitably permeate every single aspect of the entire game Flow, from rules interpretation and enforcing to strategic decision making and instant reactions. In other words, if game pathologies related to design struck at the roots of the "game tree", and game-related issues affected the structural cohesion of its trunk, player-related critical elements can spoil the very life essence of the entire plant.

Many are the ways through which players can make even the best simulation derail from its course, especially when speaking of multiplayer games, in which the greater multitude of players and direct or indirect relations between them creates an exponentially greater quantity of possible issues.

Just to start, one might mention some *mechanical* issues, thus tied to practical player relations inside the game, chief among which is the dreaded "kingmaking" effect of some negotiation or hybrid warfare/diplomatic titles. With the term we can identify all those instances in which, after a good portion of a game session, a single player might find himself or herself excluded from any real possibility of winning the game but in a position to actually decide who the final winner is, by applying all the influence and resources gathered during the previous turns. Such a fundamental decision would bear no particular fruits to the player, who will always remain behind in terms of victory points or conditions, and so the final outcome of the game will be decided just on a personal whim.

Kingmaking deprives the game of most of its internal attraction elements, such as fair competition and the tie between decision-making and useful (in game terms) decisions: you just decide who wins, but for you everything stays the same . . . you lost—choose the winner, close the box and go home. Hooray . . .

Such a problem is so common, in effect, that most game designers are able to introduce satisfactory elements to contain or even prevent it. Random events, point gathering correctives and variable victory conditions are just some of the possible solutions used, if not to avoid kingmaking, to at least include it as a possible game success option by itself. It is not always easy to avoid it, however, and even today kingmaking represents one of the most common critiques brought forward against strategic multiplayer titles, together with mid-session player elimination or excessively random game durations and sudden winner identification.

The ideal opposite to kingmaking can be found in "bash the leader" situations. In this case, instead of giving their victory away, players coalesce against the first player concentrating all their efforts against him or her. Even if those sessions in which that player manages to resist such concentric assaults become epic experiences for all involved, much more frequently everything devolves in a constant and mechanical attack against whoever is in the lead in victory points.

The fun is thus spoiled not by the futility of strategic decisions, but by their absolute obviousness: choosing to attack the second or third most successful player is almost useless if not damaging to one's prospects of victory, and only a collective attack of everyone against the same player is a profitable game choice. This deprives contending players of meaningful decisions, relegating them to being mere executors of a self-evident optimal strategy and thus nullifying their quest for finding an effective approach, while also creating much irritation in the first player which will always find himself or herself faced with a hopeless fight against insurmountable odds . . . with the sole prospect of becoming in turn a contending player once again. Even worse, some players seem to be unable to shift their opposition from a fellow participant to another, and carry on their unidirectional attacks against a formerly first player even when the general situation is changed and someone else has taken the lead: the "bandwagon effect", and once again a very unpleasant cause for resentment, outside the normal boundaries of a healthily competitive game experience.

It is very difficult to correct leader-bashing dynamics in games which are built around the notion of having only a single player clearly in command. Of course, one could always find ways to hide the identity of the leading player, possibly by keeping victory points tracking hidden, or even by splitting several players in two teams, like in Academy Games' *Conquest of America* series or in the various *Quartermaster General* titles. Some authors even get to the point of accepting its existence and actively exploit it as a valid game mechanic: Richard Berg in *Successors* does just that with the "Pretender" title automatically putting everyone against the temporarily most successful contender to Alexander the Great's throne, as Wray Ferrell does in *Time of Crisis* in which conquering Italy and the Roman Imperial Throne immediately paints a great target ring in front of you for all other players. In those cases, kingmaking is in a sense the purpose of the game itself, and stands in support of the historical interpretation of the events, instead of distorting it into excessively "gamey" behaviours.

A very original solution is used in Mark Herman's "semi-competitive" title *Churchill* (GMT), in which being too far ahead in victory points is actually detrimental to the final success of a player: an excessively detached first player will discover that the second and third player's nations will get together in the post-WWII scenario created during the game, which will then be considered a defeat. In this situation, bashing the leader and containing the points gap might lead to his or her final victory!

Surely, it is not easy for a designer to "trust" players, fearing that they might misuse their freedom to introduce distortions of their own into such a complex system such as a simulation game. Many authors resort to progressively more intrusive solutions in order to avoid this, introducing more extensive limitations or even influencing the progression of the game so that it follows along the historical narration and also the intended development of game sessions: in other words, using a technique called "scripting".

The encouragements mentioned earlier might take the form of simple behavioural "nudges", with great freedom of choice left to the players but with the system rewarding only plausible decisions and punishing evident tactical mistakes, like the importance for maintaining line formation in the streamlined ancient wargame *With It Or On It*, Hollandspiele. For CDGs like *Twilight Struggle* or *Paths of Glory*, specific era decks might also give a distinct narration to a game, dividing it into clearly distinguishable "segments" with differing balances due to the chronological evolution of historical events or because of certain game decisions.[14] In other cases, much tighter cause-effect chains might be introduced in the possible play sequences of some multiple event cards, like in Michael Rinella's *Shifting Sands* (MMP) and *Festung Europa* (Compass Games), or the possible opening of certain "combinations" of action and reaction, as in the *Table Battles* series (Hollandspiele).[15] Not to mention the greatest and most evident nudge of all: victory conditions, pushing players towards certain game behaviours, through rewarding victory points or even promising instant success with the occupation of a certain hex or the exhaustion of the opponent's card hand (Figure 5.4).

So, even scripting might have a very positive value, especially in giving precious advice to newcomers to a certain system on how to avoid evident mistakes and guiding them in those terrible first moments in which there are far too many consequential choices to make at the same time. As a counterpoint, however, an excess of scripting deprives games of their actual interest and takes simulation many steps too close to a simple pre-set reproduction of events.

What game designers and players alike need to be aware of is that mechanical player-related issues are possible in all kinds of games.

Among cooperative titles, the most common is the recurrence of "alpha" players, which are participants already familiar with the game systems or boardgaming in general that tend to organize not only their own decisional process but also to micro-manage that of other less experienced players, all too happy to leave all the most important

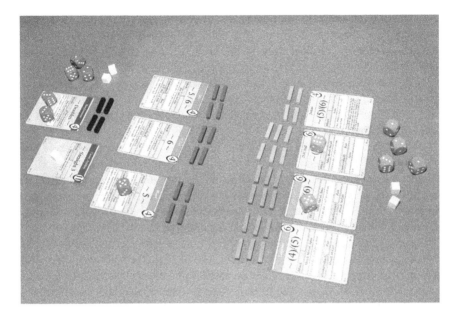

FIGURE 5.4 Some players consider the strict combinations of cause and effect provided by the cards of *Table Battles* (Hollandspiele) to be too constraining. The almost "straight jacket" is instead an integral part of designer Amabel Holland's vision of fixed battle plans and action-reaction dynamics on the battlefield.

Source: Photograph by the author.

decisions to someone else. In so doing, they avoid the strategic challenges posed by the game, but also their thrilling and engaging factors, and consequently will very soon lose interest in the game session itself. Experience gaps can be fateful elements also for purely competitive two-player games, whatever their level of complexity is: simpler games will be utterly dominated from their very start to the end, and more elaborate titles will make hours-long gaming sessions just a very refined form of intellectual torture for the beginning player struggling against an objectively unwinnable veteran.

Then there are "beta" players whose scarce competence might lead to erratic decisions disrupting the entire system or stripping the fun even of the more capable participants, faced not with engaging challenges to solve together but with unavoidable collective failures due to evident strategic mistakes or rules misinterpretation by other players, or with tactical successes dependent exclusively on illogical choices made by an inept opponent.

Finally, one cannot exclude the possibility of having "omega" players at the table, which are individuals that are not at all interested in what is happening in the simulation or even in gaming altogether. They will not be immersed in the game Flow, representing a deeply dangerous "external" element that will take decisions outside any logical thinking, just by chance or even out of spite for having been involved in an uninteresting and boring activity, totally detrimental to what the game designer and the game itself would consider a proper strategic behaviour to be applied inside the structural framework of the simulation.

All these mechanical player-related distortions damage the game Flow and all connected experiences by depriving it of elements of fundamental value, like competence, engagement, rational strategic thinking, balanced competition and effective cooperation.

There are other player-related issues, however, that in some sense do the exact opposite, including external elements into the equation even before and beyond its functional dynamics: they can be defined as *conceptual* issues, and are no less dangerous in their nature.

The fact is that sometimes we tend to consider simulation games like a series of purely mathematical equations and procedures composing elaborate algorithms. After so many pages of this very study one might find the following statement a bit odd, but at the opening of every wargame box, one should always remember they are much more than that: they are at least equally composed of numbers and statistics, as they are of human perception and derivative behaviours.

The first of these highly subjective factors, how we consider the events and what interpretation we as players have of them as well as of the author's own vision translated into the simulation, is dependent on sources and causes that are totally external to the game itself. Have we seen films dedicated to those historical events recently? Do we have any personal relation as individuals or in our family to those facts? What is the dominant interpretation of the subject in our cultural environment? And what do we think of the designer's historical approach? And of his or her peculiar idea of what wargaming is and should do?

Questions upon questions, in a long series of pre-judgements (which we have to carefully avoid becoming prejudices) which greatly influence the value and the very nature of our experience with a simulation game.

As game designer and expert Maurice Suckling wrote:

> By doing, players are feeling, and so therefore most memorably learning. . . . Games are machines for making us feel. So lessons learnt by way of feeling them, through having done them, sounds not so much like a theoretically viable alternative means of learning, as a theoretically evidently superior (and tangibly testable) means of learning.[16]

This undoubtedly grants them a much higher learning value than just passive reading of endless paragraphs of historical essays, yet at the same time exposes them to much higher risks due to their much higher psychological engagement.

That perception, equally made of ideal premises as of direct "on the paper field" experience, is of paramount significance in ascertaining the final intellectual result of a simulation, always remembering that this peculiar kind of game does not only content itself with generating excitement in the players, but also aims at increasing their knowledge and awareness about its reference realities. A truly ambitious objective, for sure, but a fundamental one, being at the very foundation of why simulation games are created, even before being played.

The issue here is that *feeling* is a much more personal concept than just *learning* or even *recreating*. This should be clear by now: a simulation game is not just a reproduction, but an interactive representation of an event through a scientifically rigorous description of how that event *might have occurred* . . . but did not actually occur. In a sense, it is the most elaborate and convincing form of lie ever created, except that in order for it to work no one should ever believe it.

That is the nature of the game, and when we lose that we make a fateful step outside Huizinga's closed circle, effectively breaking the spell and making the entire experience totally distorted.

This can happen in many ways in the practice of simulation games. By "feeling" too much what is happening on the table we might be shocked at the consequences of our decisions and introduce improper behaviours dictated by our own contemporary sensibility . . . and that is a distortion, since in order to remain "inside" a simulation we have to dissociate a bit from our modern self and try to reason like contemporary decision-makers. At the same time, we must avoid getting too engaged with contemporary thinking, remember that we live in a different time and a different reality, and for example avoid putting our prejudices or even our inclinations towards this or this other faction, expecting our games to justify them.

Even just assumed player's expectations can exert a negative influence on a game, oftentimes long before it is published. Market-based decisions, like adopting a more rigorous stance on the game mechanics in order to appease traditional wargames, or on the other part try to find at all costs original solutions thinking that a game can obtain more visibility just for appearing "more innovative" than others, are equally despicable sins from the viewpoint of ludic historiography.

In fact, as Suckling affirmed, simulation games truly are a form of historiography, even if more "applied" than theoretical. But as such, they can partially or even totally fail both for their own innate faults as well as for the reception had of them by their players at the time of their publishing or after, or for how much their perceived reception by the players would distort the design process making it closer to what players would like to play, than what they should play.

In short, this is just another of the many fine threads upon which simulation games have to walk in their path. They have to be engaging, but also historically sound and statistically plausible. They need to be innovative, but only in order to better represent the reference realities and never just for innovation's sake. They should encourage players to detach themselves from their current way of thinking and adopt a contemporary's mindset, and yet stay on the same page of the most recent historiography and keep from refraining old popular clichés. They have to present immediately recognizable reference points to their public . . . without trying to please the very same public too much. Et cetera, et cetera.

It is no wonder that there is no such thing as a "perfect" simulation game about a specific historical event. About *any* specific historical events.

The most grievous facet of this issue is that players are not always collaborative not just in identifying a solution to these specific conceptual issues, but also in correcting them after they have been brought out in the open.

Effectively, it is not so easy to renounce your own preconceptions and expectations, especially when you are supposedly engaged in a leisurable and free activity as gaming is. Yet, this is not just "generic boardgaming", this is simulation gaming— thus trying to be *both* engaging and informative at the same time for it to have any real value—and so at least a tiny bit of methodological rigor is more than necessary, it is intellectually mandatory.

But there is also something deeper than that, something that is not so easily recognizable or redeemable.

There are in fact some deeply rooted attitudes in wargaming which still make their presence felt, even after so many decades of hobby history. These are preconceptions not just about history, but about historical gaming itself.

Many are the ways in which players can "impose" some of their consolidated convictions upon games as designed or even just as played, and we have already seen quite a lot of their number.

Most of them, however, trace their most fundamental roots into a "control mania" over every single aspect of the simulation, leading to excessive micromanagement, total information knowledge and even obsessive reliance upon mathematical factoring of every single element of the simulation model. Seen under this light, even disruptive habits like factor or card counting, lack of fog of war, tables and modifiers proliferation, linear probability calculation and so on can find a common point of origin.

In short, some players expect a wargame to give them all the right answers to their game decisions, instead of posing to them all the right questions related to a certain historical event, taking all information for granted and expecting the designer to have created a totally perfect model that allows them to relive the past "as it was". On the contrary, every game expert knows that simulation can, at best, recreate the past "as it was intended by the designer" and that there is no such thing as a perfect historical model, since there is no such thing as a perfect historical knowledge upon which that ideal all-encompassing simulation should be based.

Nonetheless, players frequently tend to appreciate games that involve them in far too many roles than reality would allow, for example issuing orders at very different steps of the chain of command, enjoying far too much tactical or operational freedom, making strategic choices free of key factors and preconditions. This freedom of action surely is part of the allure of traditional as well as modern wargaming (who doesn't want show everyone that he could fight better than Hannibal, or even win at Waterloo in the shoes of Napoleon himself?), but it is in direct contrast with every historical and even practical consideration regarding conflict and historical events of any form.

Even here, a fine balance must be found to avoid two distinct but almost symmetrical excesses: the transformation of wargames into "multi-solitaire" experiences only based on constant min-maxing of one's resources punctuated by single moments of intense (but historically distorted) competition or, on the other side, a total loss of perspective upon the general situation as simulated by the game itself.

Failure to obtain those two goals, correct representation and meaningful perspective, means losing the only centre focus around which the entire gaming experience should revolve: a sufficiently faithful but justly interactive reconstruction not only of the single historical facts, but also of their deepest dynamics, both as they happened and as they might have happened.

In order to do so, a game has to simultaneously keep its players aware of its ludic nature and also strictly focused not on the rules but on the situation. It should then reach its first innate objectives while avoiding its last and most dangerous hurdle, provide insights and stay away from hindsight.

Management of the information base is one of the key elements of simulation, and surely one of the toughest to uphold at the design stage as well as during the actual practice of wargaming. "Hindsight" is the collective name that can be given to all violations of this cardinal rule, encompassing all those forms of knowledge (real or assumed) that go beyond the information base originally foreseen by the system, which instead players obtain from other sources external to the simulation itself.

The different types of hindsight are many and hard to categorize. However, for the sake of this discussion, two main groups can be identified based on the nature of the external knowledge origin.

The first is "experiential hindsight", which is all that information coming not from the simulated events but from a prior familiarity with the system itself. Veteran players have a distinct advantage over novice ones due to their general wargaming practice, of course, and that can even be considered a positive factor, since it encourages them to teach general strategic principles and game management techniques to the new recruits, who will be eager to get to the same level of their masters and possibly even surpass them. When this greater competence derives just from familiarity with the single material rules and not the underlying historical dynamics, a very dangerous distortion occurs, since that superiority will depend not on a better interpretation and manipulation of the game situation but just on "learning the tricks" or the convenient "gamey" loopholes unavoidably present in every game system.

Luckily, this is also the most curable of the two types. Solutions like random card elimination during the game setup avoids card counting and limits the importance of prior deck knowledge, chit pull systems make unit activation a much more flexible phase and leave room to unexpected turns of events, fog of war rules make factor counting almost impossible and encourage more creative tactics to deceive your opponent regardless of his or her knowledge of the map and the orders of battle.

The second hindsight family is, regretfully, much more difficult to recognize for game designers and, even after being aware of it, much more resistant to possible countermeasures: situational hindsight.

These are instances in which an excess of actual historical knowledge might come to the detriment of the game itself, with players already knowing the most convenient historical paths and focusing only on them, or expecting some events to occur in later turns of the game and basing their strategies in consequence. The already mentioned "Grouchy Paradox" is a perfect example of this: we all know that you should not divide your army as Napoleon did after Ligny, so we avoid even considering that mistake upon which the fate of the entire campaign possibly depended. Why attack over such a large front with diverging advance paths as the Germans did during Barbarossa? Shouldn't we wait before committing our entire formation into going after the retreating Carthaginian first line at Cannae?[17]

This particular bias might operate even in weirder, more indirect ways, since that prior historical knowledge might not depend on actual recognition of the historical situation, but on its dominant historiography whose accuracy might not be as good as expected: in other words, your hindsight might be totally wrong, and still affect your decision process altering its outcome (Figure 5.5). For example, you might be tempted to play overly defensive as the Anglo-Allied commander at Waterloo because "everybody knows" that this is what British troops did best.[18] You might avoid even profitable

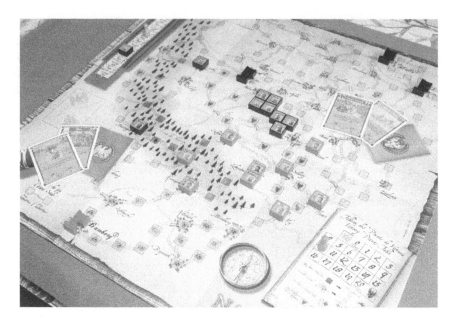

FIGURE 5.5   Historically lopsided episodes such as the Jena-Auerstadt campaign depicted in *Napoléon 1806* (Shakos) are usually the hardest to represent in simulation games, due to the difficulty of recreating the evidently mistaken decisions which led to the actual outcome.

Source: Photograph by the author.

advances on the Russian steppes because "everybody knows" that German armoured spearheads suffered from constant logistical issues. You could be overly prudent as the Roman commander and not profit from a simple mistake made by your Hannibalic counterpart.[19]

The solution, here, must be found mainly on the players' side, since no rule or exception can avoid this peculiar issue alone. The final recipients of all the game design process should operate two different kinds of psychological detachments: from their previously assumed vision of historical events which may or may not prove correct and, even harder, from their own personal vision of what wargaming is or "should" be.[20]

Once again, the innate freedom of gaming activities and the critical independence needed when approaching historical interpretations cannot but impose a drive towards experimentation, innovation and constant revision in simulation game practice. Historical research cannot stop itself from exploring new methods of study, reevaluate previously obtained results, try to find new ways to understand past events and dynamics the same has to be done by simulation games, if they want to propose themselves as a valid counterfactual version of that same scientific research . . . and not just a closed-community hobby which finds its sense and purpose not in the representation of reality, but only in the consolidation of past practices and limited stereotypical visions. As far challenges go, this is quite an important one to win, in order to truly preserve a definite scientific value of simulation.

In this scenario, some behavioural elements can be very helpful, even when they appear to be a detriment to some single elements of the relationship between games and reality.

As an example, the lack of direct consequences for one's actions and decisions made during a game has often been considered a great limitation to the simulation. No one ever felt the risk of being exiled to a remote island in the middle of the Atlantic Ocean after losing a game of *Napoleon at Waterloo*, nor even to lose his or her job if the D-Day invasion didn't go as planned . . . and many observers (including myself, I have to be honest) have traditionally considered this to be a distortion, since it breaks the feeling of direct player immersion which should be at the centre of any simulative experience.

Regardless, after some more careful consideration, one has to admit that detaching the player's personal destinies from those of their simulated counterparts on one side preserves the "closed circle" principle which makes a game what it truly should be, and on the other allows a more objective and neutral stance over the represented facts and characters which cannot be anything but helpful to maintain a lucid and adequately rational approach so vital to any historical study.

The ultimate bias that we as players can have when approaching a game is to consider the entire experience as something different than its true nature, considering simulation as some sort of mathematical oracle capable of giving us perfect and unquestionable models of all reality, down to its most hidden facet. In other words, going far beyond the intended sense of Dunnigan's famous comparison of wargames as "paper time machines", adopting a truly literal interpretation of the words.

This is after all the most important lesson that we should obtain from studying all the possible pathologies of simulation games: becoming aware that with all their applied mathematics, statistics, topography and historiography they are just constructs of the human mind and as such are inherently fallible, based on "educated guesses" as many designers rightly affirm in their notes. Those games can give us only vague insights into our past and never a truly complete knowledge of what actually happened, nor of how it felt to be in the middle of a battle with the burden of command on our shoulders. And mercifully so, one should add.[21]

In the end, we all come back to the very heart of analog simulation, its core human "engine" both in function as ultimate rule enforcers and in the recipient of the game "message". As the Greek philosopher Plato famously said, one can learn so much more about another person's character in an hour of play rather than during an entire lifetime, and even modern psychology would confirm how much of the inner nature of an individual appears during a challenging activity such as gaming. And we can learn so much more from the study of our mistakes than from that of our successes, since it is in our errors in perception and decision that our true nature really shines.[22]

We are often so focused on what we get out of a historical simulation in terms of insights and knowledge, that we sometimes fail to evaluate what we bring into that experience and how we change it starting from our own previous personal attitude towards the represented facts . . . and even gaming in general. And if sometimes designers have to choose which distortion to accept, and game structures can sometimes fail as simulations (especially when their structures are actually too solid in relation with the historical situations they are supposed to represent), it is also true that many of these distortions can be made right or wrong, becoming issues or features only based on how they are perceived by the beginning and the end of simulation: its own players.

NOTES

1 Such an elaborate concept is probably much easier to understand for Italian-speaking readers (and writers). In Italian language, "game" or "gioco" has also a secondary meaning of "free movement". "Il gioco (game) degli ingranaggi fa muovere l'orologio" is Italian for "The movement of gears keeps the clock moving on".

2 Sometimes those personal and even ideological views are openly declared by game designers, willing to captivate their players' attention and guide them towards the study of specific historical dynamics as seen by a chosen point of view. For a specific view on this aspect, see Wargames and politics: Interview of Jack Radey, in *Homo Ludens YouTube Channel,* https://youtu.be/LuhhG8mHb2c?si=WgI0NNnIEufa6jsm (2023).

3 A vivid example of this can be found in the interviews to German senior officers held in captivity during World War Two gathered in Liddell Hart, B. H., *The other side of the hill,* Papermac (London, 1951).

4 A perfect case of this can be found in Miller, B., Alexander's weaponry, in *Moves,* n. 47 (1979), mentioning the results of then-recent diggings in the Mediterranean area to suggest important modifications to unit counter values and special rules of the venerable *PRESTAGS* series, published by SPI.

5 A somewhat different—but by no means less significant—case is represented by *AFU: Armed Forces of Ukraine* (Kilogames), in which a Ukrainian designer created a game about that struggle as seen by one of its contenders. This is a rare example of games becoming a primary historical source, just as if we had a game about the Second Punic Wars designed by a Roman citizen just after the battle of Cannae or an Austerlitz simulation conceived by a *grognard* of the Grande Armée just before the successive battle of Jena.

6 Several scholars have highlighted this proximity, but few have produced a more telling study than what can be found in Suckling, M., Board with meaning: Reflections on game design and historiography, in *CEA Critic,* vol. 79, no. 1, The Johns Hopkins University Press (2017). The next paragraphs are much in debt to that comprehensive synthesis.

7 Some of these structural distortions in simulation are eloquently exposed in Todorov, S., The tyranny of binaries: How wargame rules build narratives, in *Georgetown University Wargaming Society YouTube Channel,* https://youtu.be/pZz6l6u275o?si=ngN2QccuNdU-JXu_v (2023).

8 An extreme form of this pathology can be found in those designs whose historical narration has been consciously altered to make the system run better and actually work as a game in the most mechanical sense, rather than a simulation.

9 See on the subject Bucholtz, A., *History is political: Games are propaganda,* https://sdhist.com/history-is-pooitical-games-are-propaganda/ (2023). Different games can give very different visions of key elements in a simulation as the nature of war, geographical features, political systems, economic processes and so on. Once again, the more detailed a game is, the more distortions can appear in it.

10 A very peculiar issue is the one brought by materially missing, insufficient or inadequate components. Even if out of the control of the designers, there have been cases of games in which hidden unit mechanics did not work since most of the counters were physically distinguishable due to bad graphics and production, or when there were not enough components to physically track the necessary victory conditions. These issues are usually quite easily recovered, but remain a source of irritation and concern for players, nonetheless.

11 On the subject, see also Baudrillard, J., *Simulacres et simulation*, Éditions Galilée (1981). The relationship between Borges's allegories and historical simulation has been explicitly stated, among other sources, in urban unrest game *Corteo*'s rulebook introduction and by Italian ludologist Giampaolo Dossena in his studies on wargames' excesses.

12 A point could be made regarding app-enhanced analog simulation games, such as *UBOOT: The Board Game* (Phalanx), combining both openly readable rules and significant portions of the game itself based on digital calculations beyond the players' knowledge. Their reception by the public has been somewhat mixed, though, and mostly for the very reason that a good part of the experience happened "behind the players' backs".

13 This did not placate the debate on the event, as proved by the strongly critical post of another *BGG* user, Dean, J., *A few acres of snow and the critical silence on the biggest flawed game of 2011*, https://boardgamegeek.com/blogpost/9073/few-acres-snow-and-critical-silence-biggest-flawed (2012).

14 Not all game designers agree on this specific solution, and also the balance between the alternative Operation Points and the importance of an event on a single card is open to much debate: should obvious decisions be highlighted, or should the players be faced with difficult choices every single turn? See Herman, M., To script or not to script, in *C3i*, n. 25 (2011) and Sam I am: who you are tells the story! in *C3i*, n. 28 (2014).

15 On the *Shifting Sands* page on *BoardGameGeek*, you may find a specific flux diagram showing all the distinct alternative narrative lines that the campaign in North Africa might take, depending on the "paths" you follow with the different combination of cards becoming available turn after turn.

16 Suckling, M., Board with meaning: Reflections on game design and historiography, in *CEA Critic*, vol. 79, no. 1, The Johns Hopkins University Press (2017).

17 In order to avoid hindsight, you could also accept simulations based on commonly held opinions at the time of the events that have later been proven as fallacious. And, all of a sudden, *Twilight Struggle*'s dependency on (erroneous) Cold War Domino theory or the feared (and non-existent) "rogue nukes" in *Labyrinth* can become important instruments in avoiding this peculiar distortion due to our later knowledge of the facts.

18 On this, Simonsen, R. A., The bias that nobody knows . . ., in *Moves*, n. 3 (1972).

19 The distortive effect is then multiplied when those two issues are combined: that is when one expert player has a deeper knowledge of what is about to happen in a game and how to better exploit it, while his or her greener opponent does not possess the same historical competence and will be at a total loss in how to control the unforeseen events just about to happen in the simulation.

20 In order not to be too harsh in our judgement of these biased behaviors, one should include also very peculiar psychological attachments to the *status quo* both in upholding single historical interpretations (for example, when they are referred to closely-relatable events for familiar or national heritage reasons) or specific game mechanics (to which we can find ourselves attached for the simple fact that they were our very first wargaming experiences). As a personal note, since part of my family comes from Cassino and was present in the town until just a few days before the devastating Allied bombing in 1944, I still find very hard to accept even the existence and moral value of wargames focused on strategic and tactical bombing operations. No one said that obtaining rational and emotional detachment from certain historical events is an easy task.

21 A fine recollection of many aspects of the complex relationship between situational analysis, game mechanics and player behaviour when faced with diverse historical situations and their related play balances can be found in Smith, D. A., In the game: Real and unreal aspects of simulation gaming and play, in *Moves*, n. 49 (1980).

22 To get a bit more practical, this is especially true regarding professional simulation games and their committers. On this, read Schneider, J., What war games really reveal, in *Foreign Affairs*, https://www.foreignaffairs.com/united-states/what-war-games-really-reveal (2023).

Conclusions
All Good Games Must Come to an End Turn

*"We create history by our observation,
rather than history creating us."*

Stephen Hawking

Recurrently, a vignette pops up on some *Facebook* groups dedicated to wargaming. It is a strip, actually, drawn by comic artist Stan Mack for his *Real Life Funnies* series, representing various evenings spent by him and other friends in the kaleidoscope that had to be the social life in New York City at the end of the 1970s and into the early 1980s.

What is exceptional about that group of drawings is that the story takes place in a very familiar location for all the first-generation historical gamers and almost like a legendary place for all the younger enthusiasts of the hobby: the SPI headquarters. There, every week on every Friday night, James Dunnigan, Redmond A. Simonsen and all the company staff held a regular free playtesting evening with lots of games put on the many tables and asking everyone to just step in, play a few turns, and give their impression. Literally *anyone*—since the location was fully open to the public, every bystander could get in and get a glimpse of these strange games which dealt with obscure topics of history. Of course, if you were a regular wargamer, a trip to one of those nights could be considered something akin to a pilgrimage to a place out of time and space, where everything was possible if you put together the right force ratio on your preferred CRT.

The strip shows our protagonist led in a semi-Dantesque way by another more expert character in this veritable dungeon of historical and even fantasy simulation, all mixed together. Arcane lines like "Do I get divisional integrity on overruns?" immediately make sense, instigation to suicidal tactics against Klingon battle cruisers looks like very logical, assertions on Hapsburg royalty's ugly physical appearance and its impact on European seventeenth- and eighteenth-century politics appear to be valid and even quite acute, as warnings about a not-too-well specified "Belgian ferocity rule".

All these phrases, especially when pronounced by SPI staff members and regular attendants, caricaturized but easily recognizable, prompt an immediate, instinctual response from any wargamer who reads them: they are home.

This is because this sense of absolute freedom in playing with history by recreating its inner dynamics through arithmetic sequences, coupled with an almost excessively detailed knowledge of the tiniest bit of historical information (including some not-so-important fragments which would go on creating the delicious "chrome"

 DOI: 10.1201/9781003429098-7

wargamers are so fond of!), is a trademark of the hobby since its earliest, weirdest days. In effect, exactly this idea of being able to reproduce past events with just a few modifiers and die rolls was what led Charles S. Roberts to devise an entirely effective statistical combat table in total independence and just during his spare time, much to the chagrin of the more bureaucratized and rigid RAND Corporation's elaborate research programs.

This was the spirit of that amazing first generation of wargamers (made of brave publishers, genius designers and dedicated open-minded players): get together, research, throw some dice, experiment, change the rules, create new models and find new pathways in time and space. Something that lives on still today and which truly represents the "strange result of over education", as summed up in the final line of the strip by the Virgil-like guide of our protagonist, in direct reference to Dunnigan's definition of wargaming as "a hobby of the over educated".

What can we make out of that funny vignette about the nature of historical gaming and, even more, about the psychology of those who practice it regularly?

If we look at the objective side of the phenomenon, we can find traces of the deepest obsession of any simulation games fan: transforming his or her knowledge into elements of a great mathematical algorithm capable of generating a model potent enough to transport those who use it to other time and space locations. Those "paper time machines" are then powered by numeric equations, operations and procedures, whose definition is based on previous historical research on direct and indirect sources, as well as on free interpretation of the results of such research by the game designer.

While all this might sound a bit complicated and high-minded (in many respects, it is . . .), one should not lose a truly fundamental notion of the entire process: that this mathematic is not your average completely rational process, but is deeply influenced in its nature by the final purpose of the entire endeavour. Here, the outcome is not just a number or a geometric figure nor an algebraic curve, at least not in its most apparent form. Here, the result is another graphical and immediately relatable projection on a map or gaming table of a totally recognizable historical situation, which could be drawn on alternative history books in which Carthage won the Punic Wars and hegemony over the Mediterranean or Napoleon didn't lose as badly at Waterloo and maybe managed to remain at the head of a constitutional monarchy in France.

To put it more simply, this mathematics is made of numbers, of course, but those numbers are generated by distinct human choices and direct manipulation of physical objects like counters and cards, generating not just a series of numeric operations but a true narration. Even if based on numerical elements and linear procedures, this very peculiar kind of mathematics tells us stories, becoming something closer to a fictional literature piece than to an arithmetic problem. It is exactly this that leads generations of people to wargames and simulation games in general, their incredible storytelling value which finds its deepest roots in the intellectual projection capabilities of human beings, the same capabilities that prompted Johan Huizinga to consider gaming (and in particular all forms of gaming aimed at representing the outside world in alternative visions) as the primary point of origin of everything we call "culture".

Closely tied to this is also the more subjective aspect, the fact that those who practice and love simulation games almost live by the unshakable conviction that past history is something that you can freely play with it, in order to explore its infinite and fascinating facets not just by "pretending" it through simple words, but with the scientific and absolutely rational tools made available by advanced statistics applied to rigorous historiography.

This is a somewhat "scandalous" idea, the concept that by adopting a counterfactual approach one can live not just a simply personal idea of history, such as the one provided by novels or movies or TV series, but a plausible vision of the past, which did not happen but really *could have* happened; because by playing even the simplest wargame on that crucial battle, we are not just pretending that Napoleon won at Waterloo like in mere child's play . . . we are instead *assuming* that Napoleon *could have* won, had he made some very distinctive tactical choices and maybe had a bit more luck.

All of a sudden, history loses its character of being an immutable monument, a closed region whose totality we don't know. Instead, through simulation gaming, history reacquires the status of an open world, of which we still have to explore all the possible outcomes, both those that actually happened and the others that did not but still could have. In this multiverse orgy of rational speculation, even our relationship with the past suffers a deep and dramatic change: from a unilateral search in an isolated room left in the dark, we pass on a truly bidirectional interaction between the events succeeding one another in the past and creative imagination processes conducted in the present (and, possibly, even a third direction: the future, where we will take the expertise and awareness gathered during our simulations).

Of course, this is all nice and true, but one always has to keep eyes open and avoid falling for the illusion of gaining an absolute knowledge about the past and a perfect awareness for the future simply through a repeated practice of simulation games. Dunnigan's assertion might be captivating and even valid in some respects, but wargames will never be true "paper time machines", only mirrors of our own conscience that use mathematics and historiography to keep our individual mental projections as close to reality as possible, with all the issues and vagaries we have found in our journey: the destination of our simulated "time travels" is at least as much history itself as the game designer's and our own historical *visions* of those same events. We must never be mistaken into believing that the universe of human history is actually contained inside the telescope of simulation games we devised in order to get a closer look at its mysteries. But that distorted and partial vision is one of the best views we will get of those objects, anyway.

Still, the potential of simulation is so great that, even when we make all possible efforts to highlight its innate limitations, especially in comparison to more traditional research methods, we cannot help but be fascinated by the extent of its capabilities. As game designer Jeremy White eloquently put it while speaking of the goals he set up for his creation, *Atlantic Chase*, "[A] wargame is no substitute for an exhaustively researched text, it is also not merely frivolous entertainment. It lies somewhere between."

The exploration of this "somewhere between" has been the subject of this entire work, and now, at its conclusion, it is finally time to put the results of our study together and find some reference points, especially regarding one basic question: why did we invent such a strange thing as simulation and why are we so attracted to the games that use it as their primary mechanic?

One could easily answer, "To obtain a better knowledge of history and a deeper understanding of its dynamics, of course".

Following that approach to the letter, we might conclude that simulation games are the perfect tool for both representing and illustrating to a learning auditorium all the conflicts of human history, with all their diverse features and unique dynamics. Which is true . . . up to a certain measure.

Sure, starting from historical data and accurate statistics you can (if your sources are reliable enough) build a sufficiently valid mathematical model capable of recreating those events, especially if your objective is to just visualize them on the map as they happened, moment after moment. What else could be better suited for the purpose than a map with a grid superimposed on it and used to regulate the movements of so many counter chits to accurately portray all the maneuvers, the battles and the logistical challenges met or enforced by the involved armies? A rare opportunity, especially if you content yourself with recreating just the kinetic element of a confrontation, but thanks to more modern design techniques you can also portray even more abstruse and elusive non-linear and non-kinetic aspects like politics, economy, public support, diplomacy and the like.

There is just one single issue with this actually effective method of using simulation as a precise re-enactment asset: in doing so you unavoidably take the game element out of the entire equation, since that crucial factor always depends on players' decisional choice (even if regulated by the parameters deriving from the previous historical research). As proof of that, even if several rules manuals and playbooks included in game boxes have a specific chapter dedicated to reproducing the historical events as they happened through the assets and mechanics composing the title itself, game designers are all too happy to tell players that this is just a possibility and that they retain all the freedom of changing that very sequence through their decisions.[1]

In so doing, simulation games and all the subjects involved in their existence (designers, publishers, players and even critics . . .) appear to be quite jealous of the margins granted by such a flexible tool.

This intimate pulsion is so strong as to capture also all the efforts by affirmed historians that decide to create new systems or even modify existing ones, to provide more accurate models of historical events. A recent demonstration has been the veritable debate between two such historians, Philip Sabin and Charles J. Esdaile over the most mythicized battle of all time: Waterloo—as seen through the lens of the quintessential introductory wargame, so simple to be used for decades by SPI and other publishers to introduce people to the hobby, and thus particularly suited for an applied historiographical use: *Napoleon at Waterloo*.

Sabin fired the metaphorical first shot with his revision of the system which, while maintaining the original simplicity in showing the main principle of classic simulation in full on-the-field action, effectively corrected some evident mistakes in setup locations and order of battle composition, as well as some conscious distortions introduced by Dunnigan in order to make the game more balanced and interesting for novice wargamers, finally coupled with some issues typical of first-generation wargames like unrealistically drastic combat tables and the lack of some special rules capable of reproducing key historical aspects of the battle.

With all these changes, the old basic *NaW* ruleset took on a new life, proposing itself as, if not faithful, at least a very functional historical rendition of the actual events, a powerful tool both for research and teaching purposes, combining the three main elements of the wargaming experience: engagement in playing the game, better knowledge of the simulated facts, awareness of the basic principles of Napoleonic tactics and general battlefield management gained by their direct manipulation.

Then came Charles J. Esdaile, starting from Sabin's endeavour and further expanding on it by another set of suggested modifications.[2] Those variations effectively increased the level of complexity of the game from basic to medium but added even more historical detail to the representation, consequently providing an even clearer demonstration of the potential of simulation games in historical representation.

But it was not over yet, since Sabin, after having expressed great appreciation for Esdaile's study, formulated a declared answer to that with a second edition of his revision, expressly aimed at obtaining the same or a superior level of historical accuracy but still retaining the original simplicity of the system as well as deliberately avoiding the introduction of additional counters or components of any sort.[3]

What came out of this debate was firstly an ideal demonstration of the value and design process of house rules in analog simulation games, one of their greatest assets and the source of their peculiar versatility especially when confronted with their more extensive but inherently rigid digital counterparts. After that, and possibly even more meaningful for our purposes, also a very interesting discussion over the merits of historical research and the use of historical simulation games as a powerful tool for its conduit.[4]

This might sound like something of an anathema to the main body of historians, as both Sabin and Esdaile pointed out in their respective works, *Simulating Wars* and *Wargaming Waterloo*. In those texts the two confronting historians mutually agreed on two points: firstly, that simulation games, with all their critical issues extensively identified and studied (and also, by now familiar also to readers of this very study), truly represent one of the most powerful and functional tools in historical research thanks to their great analytical capabilities, versatility and extension of applicable contents; secondly, that in order to do so they need to stay free and avoid being restricted to mere static reproductions of the studied events, an exercise whose utility is more than questionable and that mortifies the real potential of the asset.

The recognition of the variability in decision processes and their related plausible outcomes remains at the very core of what a simulation game is, constituting at the same time its final objective as well as its original precondition of existence.

This has been quite masterfully exploited both by designers and players alike in order to push the instrument up to its limits, creating from scratch or modifying titles with the aim of recreating hypothetical situations in the past, present and future. Historical "what ifs" like the strategic consequences of a Confederate victory at Antietam or Gettysburg, the actual enforcement of Operation Sealion against Great Britain, the dreadful prospect of an Axis victory in World War Two with the consequent confrontation over the domination in North America, or also the ever-present NATO/Warsaw Pact direct conflict in Europe with the endless variations of the

"Cold War gone hot" scenario are not just the subject of countless science-fiction and alternative history novels, but also of equally numerous wargames produced since the earliest years of the hobby.

In fact, one could argue that the first incarnation of modern wargaming, the Prussian *Kriegsspiel*, was actually focused on the representation of such hypothetical scenarios, from fantasy "Red on Blue" engagements up to the evaluation of possible military operations on real terrain and between existing and explicitly identified nations, for example with the famous series of German "Cases" as well as American "Plans" formulated during the inter-war period in the 1920s and 1930s. Or, if considering the topic from a more conceptual point of view, with the famous observation repeated by many authors and designers that all wargames, even the most detailed and "realistic" ones, become purely hypothetical exercises after the first move of the first turn.

There are even authors who specialized themselves in these "counterfactual" exercises, regularly creating games and writing articles based on such an interesting and thought-provoking method.[5] Significantly, with all their wildest speculations and creative scenarios, all those designers are especially careful in including extensive bibliographies and complete studies regarding the nature and possible development of those same hypothesis and validating their work through a scientific, even if quite "creative", historiography.

It is not a surprise, actually. Since the beginning of historical studies, comparative analysis of real events with possible alternative situations has been a mainstay of research methods. Counterfactual approaches have always provided useful results and suggested new paths for enquiry to all those authors that are capable of taking them for what they are: simple tools for their work, with all their related benefits and limitations. In such a family of instruments, simulation games can and do represent very viable applications, showing not just possible past routes of events that could have happened, but also why they didn't happen and most of all which were the deep forces that led things to go as they actually did.

In fact, even when not taken to such counterfactual and hypothetical extremes, we should always keep in mind that simulation games do not tell us what should have really happened, but only what *could* have reasonably happened if different conditions were verified. The fact that they put us in the concrete possibility of creating those different conditions makes the games truly engaging, but does not detract in any way from the scientific value of their processes and foundational statistics.

In such a context, to a historian those conclusions are if not equally at least comparably important as factual analysis to understand what actually happened, even when taking into account the many biases and distortions getting in the way before reaching such an ambitious goal—biases and distortions which, it should be said, are quite present even in more conventional historiography and even in the vast majority of direct sources.

So, the observation of unit values, map positions, possible choices, tables and modifiers composition, victory conditions, special rules and the whole host of tiny bits that compose the average simulation game becomes a precious exercise for all those who want to know or just be a little more aware of the past of humankind. In this sense, the "dynamic potential" postulated by Dunnigan, that is the deeper and closer look at a specific historical situation obtained just by looking at the components of a game during setup, is as useful to game designers and players as it is to historical researchers and students.[6]

This is a value confirmed and regularly used also by analysts and strategic experts every single day of our modern life, shaping both the understanding and the consequential shaping of geopolitical and military scenarios all over the world. On this aspect, the importance of simulation gaming in the comprehension and successive manipulation of the present scenarios does not even need to be demonstrated but should be taken for granted. Just like their potential as powerful tools for developing a better general awareness of "how things go in the outside world", with a double vision focused on gathering that knowledge from the simulation of the past and reprojecting that same amount of cognitive experience in our vision for the future, through comparison with how and why things have happened in previous centuries and how and why those very same dynamics will be verified in the coming years.

In this regard, you might have noticed that very few mentions were given to professional wargaming in this book. This was intentional and was done certainly not to diminish its importance, but to highlight the independent dignity and peculiar features of commercial recreational wargaming.

Yet, there is one common thing that needs to be more clearly stated: just as in professional wargaming there are no discussions about good or bad mechanics per se but only about whether a certain design solution is useful or not towards obtaining the intended results of the experience, in recreational wargaming, mechanics should only be judged for their effective portraying of specific historical dynamics and not to satisfy perceived landmarks of so-called "traditional wargaming".

Furthermore, if we want to step away from the gaming table and enter a more "academic" environment, it is only by accepting this functional approach that we can truly exploit wargaming as a valid instrument for gaining better historical awareness and even conducting innovative and highly historical studies with all their exciting results just waiting to be discovered, in an interesting parallel with the use of professional simulation to obtain better insights in strategic analysis. It is my hope that this book managed to stress this particular point, whose importance cannot be ignored.

Even with all that, as in all good simulations, the last portion of this study must go beyond the mere practical components of the game and be oriented towards something more elevated, situated behind all the rules, and mechanics, and numbers, and even discussions about historical sources and the possible fallacies of their use.

Why? Because there are even deeper and more compelling reasons for the enduring success of all these incredibly elaborated, hardly accessible, almost intimidating editorial products that are simulations games and that, with all their moments of crisis, are still walking among us, almost a century after their first incarnation in their modern and more recognizable boardgame form, and more than two centuries after their first appearances as pastimes for a bored royalty and their resenting officers in the exiled Prussian court.

In this study, in fact, we have tried to understand and describe what it is that pushes people to be the sole "engine" of such complex games which could be much more efficiently managed by a computer, and yet still today fascinate many enthusiasts with their openly readable and modifiable algorithms, allowing everyone to project himself into a different time and location (real or assumed, it is a detail of little importance for all those concerned) with just a few pieces of cardboard, a handful of dice and some tables. Games and practices, even long preliminary sessions of study and preparation, that require so much time, so much energy, so much attention, so many compromises with the "real" life . . .

And the answer simply is this: because, for all their undeniable intellectual value, for many curious and possibly "overeducated" people they are just incredibly fun to play, discuss and even just look at. Fun is such an essential element of the very core nature and material practicing of the hobby, a proof that the two terms—"simulation" and "game"—are so mutually related that taking one of them out means destroying the entire thing, transforming it into a mere leisurely occupation or a sterile reproduction of events of no real value. Only by taking us to the very helm of the situation, making us the possible points of origin of those amazing and still plausible perturbations of history, does the entire experience acquire any significance.

In this sense, it is correct to say (and has actually been said many times over the decades) that wargame design and simulation game practice are both forms of scientific exercise as well as very peculiar art forms.

However, a final question awaits an answer. Coming back to our poor infantryman on the Somme battlefield and looking at his representation on a game counter possibly with different eyes, how can we "play" with his life in a way that is not diminutive and truly makes justice of his sacrifice on the battlefield? How can we avoid just playing with the bones of our own dead, and give a value even higher than the engagement, knowledge and awareness benefits that are granted by a conscious historical simulation practice?

It is quite hard to find the right words to solve such a dilemma. Personal emotions, family recollections, national heritages all conspire to obfuscate our rationality and prevent us from having a serene judgement on the matter. And maybe it is even good that they do so, because for all our objectivity and declared neutrality in our study of the past, we still remain human beings observing the acts made by fellow human beings, all living in the same small and closed world, distant only in years and miles, some bit in cultural context, but not so much in basic physiology and psychology.

In this context, gaming can become way to both honour the men and women who endured terrible sufferings during the endless conflicts of human history and to truly condemn war as the great "blundering thing" of Wellsian memory. It could truly be considered our only way of defeating the very concept of war, not by pretending it doesn't exist, but by becoming more aware of its nature and confining it to a gaming table, armed just with a handful of dice and a rulebook.

Yet, what would happen if, in thinking of our collective human past, we embraced those very same forces threatening to undermine our cold rationality? If we accepted the challenge posed by games, with all their freedom and flexibility and struggle towards just "plausible" alternative results? If we finally understood that history surely happened just in one way, one that we will never be able to fully know and even less understand it, while being also aware that under certain circumstances it could have gone entirely another way?

Maybe, only then we will be able to just approach those games and even the greater historical studies at their foundation with more humility and honesty. We could consider them for what they are, projections of ourselves, our desires, our fears, our limitations as well as our ambitions, capabilities and incredible perspicacity.

As we have repeatedly shown, if simulation games are a lens through which we consider history and the world, their study becomes the observation of the evolution of our own perception of history and the world. All those elements are so super-imposed and inter-related to one another to defy the very concept of "distinction" among them, and so, consequently, the more we play simulation games, the more we know (or presume to know) about the rules of the world they attempt to represent . . . and the more we know (or presume to know) about the world and its history as seen through this equally powerful and distorted lens of simulation games, the more we know (or presume to know) about the rules of the greatest game of all: ourselves.

NOTES

1 This happens even when game designers write articles aimed at demonstrating the same punctual representation capability provided by their titles, quickly followed by paragraphs reasserting the fact that following the historical cause-effect sequence is only one of the many paths available to players. On the subject, see Collins, G., Madison's war: The game as history, in *C3i*, n. 30 (2016).

2 Esdaile's house rules are included in Esdaile, C. J., Napoleon at Waterloo: The events of June 1815 analyzed via historical simulation, in *Journal of Advanced Military Studies* 2, no. 2, https://muse.jhu.edu/article/805917 (2021).

3 This second set of variations can be found at the *BGG Napoleon at Waterloo* page, under Sabin's post *Simple rules tweaks for greater realism*, hosted in the Files section: https://boardgamegeek.com/filepage/199517/simple-rules-tweaks-greater-realism. The file also includes Sabin's very informative notes about every single rule change and the general study approach to the project, in explicit relation to Esdaile's work.

4 For a more extensive treatment of the mentioned Sabin's house rules and even of the his-torical debate with Esdaile, see Masini, R., Napoleon at Waterloo: Sabin's house rules–part two, in *WLOG*, https://youtu.be/Clzqe7_F9Hw?si=LLG9h0qX8oRBDsnk (2024). Part One of this miniseries had been dedicated to Sabin's first revision, while Part Three (still unrecorded at the moment of writing this book) will deal with Esdaile's variations. In the meantime, the revision process and the debate are still going on *BGG* in the thread *Much improved 2nd edition of my popular tweaks, with game video*, https://boardgamegeek.com/thread/3201688/much-improved-2nd-edition-my-popular-tweaks-game-v (2023).

5 Many are the possible mentions of designers that indulged in this fascinating sub-field of simulation games, but two names come clearly out in front of the rest: Ty Bomba and Tre-vor Bender. For the former, it suffices to remember here *Dagger Thrusts* (Decision Games) with two operational possibilities on the 1944 Western theatre alternative to Market Gar-den, as well as *Three D-Days* (Compass Games) comparing the historical 1944 Operation Overlord in Normandy with two other landing options in 1942 (Operation Sledgehammer) and 1943 (Operation Bolero). The latter is the author of the articles and related game sce-narios Disaster at D-day, in *C3i*, n. 31 (2017) and Disaster on the Dnieper, in *C3i*, n. 32 (2018); the experience gained in these two existing game variations led Bender to design a new series of games (*Kursk: The Tigers Are Burning* and *Desert Victory*), in which coun-terfactual options represent both key simulation points and relevant topics for discussion among players during and after the gaming sessions.

6 For a good example of this application through a scientific approach, see the very detailed and honestly critical article Teehan, M. F., Kursk in parallel: An analysis of 1943 Eastfront operations with the aid of conflict simulations, in *Moves*, n. 22 (1975).

Bibliography

Masini, R., *Historical simulation and wargames: The hexagon and the sword*, https://orcid. org/0009-0007-2109-8763.

BOOKS

Allen, T., Curry, J., *War games: Professional wargaming 1945–1985*, lulu.com (2015).
Alphonse, X., "The Wise", *Libro de los juegos*, curated by Canettieri, P., Cosmopoli (Bologna, 1996).
Angiolino, A., *Che cos'è un gioco da tavolo (What is a boardgame?)*, Carocci Editore (Rome, 2022).
Angiolino, A., Alegi, G., *Il gobbo maledetto*, Novecento GeC (Milan, 2002).
Angiolino, A., Sidoti, B., *Dizionario dei giochi*, Zanichelli (Bologna, 2010).
Arnaudo, M., *Storytelling in the modern board game: Narrative trends from the late 1960s to today*, McFarland Publishing (Jefferson, 2018).
Asti, C. (curated by), *Mettere in gioco il passato: La storia contemporanea nell'esperienza ludica*, Unicopli (Milan, 2019).
Baudrillard, J., *Simulacres et simulation*, Éditions Galilée (Paris, 1981).
Berg, R., Dunnigan, J., Isby, D., Patrick, S., Simonsen, R., *Wargame design: The history, production, and use of conflict simulation games*, Simulations Publications Incorporated (New York, 1977).
Besinque, C., Role simulation, in *Fire & Movement*, n. 55 (1987).
Bolaño, R., *Third Reich*, Adelphi (Milan, 2010).
Caillois, R., L'univers de l'animal et celui de l'homme [The universe of animals and the universe of men], *International Conference Le robot, la bête et l'homme [robots, animals and men]* (Genève, 1965).
Caillois, R. (dir.), *Jeux et sports*, Gallimard (Paris, 1967).
Caillois, R., *Les jeux et les hommes*, notes by G. Dossena, Bompiani (Milan, 1981).
Ceccoli, G., *La simulazione storica*, AIEP Editore (San Marino, 2006).
Chiavini, R., *Guida al gioco da tavolo moderno. Dalle origini agli anni Ottanta*, Odoya (Città di Castello, 2019).
Costikyan, G., *Uncertainty in games*, MIT Press (Cambridge, 2013).
Csíkszentmihályi, M., *Flow: The psychology of optimal experience*, Harper Perennial Modern Classic (New York, 2011).
Curry, J., *Innovations in wargaming, vol. 1: Developments in professional and hobby wargames*, lulu.com (2012).
Curry, J., Matrix games for modern wargaming developments in professional and educational wargames innovations, in *Wargaming*, vol. 2, lulu.com (2014).
Curry, J., Price, T., *Modern crises scenarios for matrix wargames*, lulu.com (2017).
Delbrück, H., *History of the art of war*, University of Nebraska Press (Lincoln, 1990).
Dossena, G., *Giochi da tavolo. Dalla Tàbula ai War Games i 45 giochi più belli e importanti degli ultimi 4000 anni*, Mondadori (Milan, 1984).
Dossena, G., *Enciclopedia dei giochi*, curated by De Toffoli, D., Mondadori (Milan, 2009).
Dunnigan, J., Designer's notes: The game is a game, in *Strategy & Tactics*, n. 22 (1970).
Dunnigan, J., *The complete wargames handbook*, Morrow (New York, 1980).
Eco, U., *Lettera a mio figlio, from Diario minimo*, Mondadori (Milan, 1963).
Errigo, M. B., *La mia vita con un geek*, Unicopli (Milan, 2020).

Evans, R., *Altered pasts: Counterfactuals in history*, Little, Brown and Company (London, 2014).

Faina, M., *Storia del mondo in 100 wargame*, vol. 1, Edizioni Chillemi (Rome, 2023).

Featherstone, D. F., *War games*, Stanley Paul (London, 1962).

Featherstone, D. F., *Advanced war games*, Stanley Paul (London, 1965).

Featherstone, D. F., *Featherstone's complete wargaming*, David & Charles (Exeter, 1989).

FitzGerald, F., *Fire in the Lake: The Vietnamese and the Americans in Vietnam*, Little, Brown (1972).

Freeman, J. et al., *The complete book of wargames*, Fireside (Simon & Schuster) (New York, 1980).

Gigerenzer, G., *Quando i numeri ingannano. Imparare a vivere con l'incertezza [Reckoning with risk: Learning to live with uncertainty]*, Cortina Raffaello (Milan, 2003).

Gigerenzer, G., *Imparare a rischiare. Come prendere decisioni giuste [risk savvy: How to make good decisions]*, Cortina Raffaello (Milan, 2013).

Giuliano, L., *In principio era il drago*, Proxima (Rome, 1991).

Harrigan, P., Kirschenbaum, M. (curated by), *Zones of control: Perspectives on wargaming*, The MIT Press (Cambridge, 2016).

Henninger, L., La nouvelle histoire-bataille, in *Espace Temps* (1999).

Herman, M., Frost, D., *Wargaming for leaders: Strategic decision making from the battlefield to the boardroom*, McGraw-Hill Education (New York, 2008).

Hofer, M., *The games we played: The golden age of board and table games*, Princeton Architectural Press (China, 2004).

Huizinga, J., *Homo Ludens*, Einaudi (Turin, 2002).

Jackson, S., Schluesser, N., *Game design, vol. 1: Theory and practice*, Steve Jackson Games (Austin, 1981).

Kahneman, D., *Pensieri lenti e veloci [Thinking, fast and slow]*, Mondadori (Milan, 2017).

Keegan, J., *Il volto della battaglia [The face of battle]*, Mondadori (Milan, 1978).

Keegan, J., *La maschera del comando [The mask of command]*, Il Saggiatore (Milan, 2003).

Keene, R., *Chess: An illustrated history*, Simon & Schuster (New York, 1990).

Kolb, D. A., *Experiential learning*, Prentice Hall (Upper Saddle River, 1984).

Krohn, J., *Band of brothers battle manual*, CreateSpace Independent Publishing Platform (Scotts Valley, 2016).

Lewin, C., *War games and their history*, Fonthill Media (Stroud, 2012).

Liddel Hart, B., *Scipione l'africano [A greater than Napoleon: Scipio Africanus]*, Le Monnier (Florence, 1929).

Liddell Hart, B. H., *The other side of the hill*, Papermac (London, 1951).

Martin, R. A., *Cardboard warriors: The rise and fall of an American wargaming subculture 1958–1998*, UMI (Ann Arbor, 2001).

Masini, R., *Il gioco di Arianna: Guerra, politica ed economia nel labirinto della simulazione non lineare*, Acies Edizioni (Milan, 2020).

Masini, R., Masini, S., *Le guerre di carta 2.0. Giocare con la Storia nel Terzo Millennio*, Unicopli (Milan, 2018).

Masini, S., *Le guerre di carta. Premessa ai giochi di simulazione*, Guida Editori (Naples, 1979).

Masini, S., Masini, R., *Le battaglie che cambiarono il mondo*, Rusconi (Santarcangelo di Romagna, 2019).

McHugh, J., *The fundamentals of war gaming*, U.S. Naval College Press (Annapolis, 2016).

Palmer, N., *The comprehensive guide to board wargaming*, McGraw-Hill (New York, 1979).

Perla, P., *The art of wargaming: A guide for professionals and hobbyists*, Naval Institute Press (Annapolis, 1990).

Peterson, J., *Playing at the world: A history of simulating wars, people and fantastic adventures, from chess to Role-Playing games*, Unreason Press (San Diego, 2012).

Prados, J., *Pentagon games: Wargames and the American military*, HarperCollins (New York, 1987).

Preti, I., *Wargame, la guerra sul tavolo*, Il Castello (Milan, 1970).

Ruhnke, V., COIN series variety: Familiar not samey, in *C3i*, n. 30 (2016).

Sabin, P., *Lost battles: Reconstructing the great clashes of the ancient world*, Bloomsbury Academic (New York, 2008).

Sabin, P., *Simulating war: Studying conflict through simulation games*, Bloomsbury Academic (New York, 2012).

Saladino, G., *Introduzione ai giochi di guerra (wargames)*, Mursia (Milan, 1979).

Sciarra, E., *Il simbolismo dei giochi*, Unicopli (Milan, 2017).

Sciarra, E., *L'autore di giochi*, Unicopli (Milan, 2018).

Setear, J., *Simulating the fog of war*, RAND Library Collection (Santa Monica, 1989).

Simonsen, R., Image and system: Graphics and physical systems design, in *Wargame design: The history, production and use of conflict simulation games*, Hippocrene Books (New York, 1977).

Stanton, N., Baber, C., Harris, D., *Modelling command and control: Event analysis of systemic teamwork*, Ashgate Publishing Ltd. (Farnham, 2008).

Thaler, R., *Nudge. La spinta gentile [Nudge. The final edition]*, Feltrinelli (Milan, 2014).

Thaler, R., *Misbehaving: La nascita dell'economia comportamentale [Misbehaving: The making of behavioral economics]*, Einaudi (Turin, 2018).

Tosi, U., *I giochi di guerra*, Sansoni (Florence, 1979).

Vadalà, R., I giochi card driven, in *ioGioco*, n. 9 (2019).

Valzania, S., *Strategia e tattica nel Risiko*, Sansoni (Florence, 1985).

Valzania, S., *L'arte marziale del poker*, Solfanelli Editore (Chieti, 1989).

Van Creveld, M., *Wargames: From gladiators to giga-bytes*, Cambridge University Press (Cambridge, 2013).

Von Clausewitz, C., *Della guerra [On war]*, curated by Cardona, G., BUR (Milan, 2009).

Von Hilger, P., *War games: A history of war on paper*, The MIT Press (Cambridge, 2016).

VV. AA., *Introduction to war gaming*, SPI (New York, 1977).

VV. AA., *Wargame design*, SPI-Hippocrene Books (New York, 1977).

VV. AA., *War films. Quaderno 2015 della Società Italiana di Storia Militare*, Acies Edizioni (Milan, 2015).

VV. AA., *Future wars. Quaderno 2016 della Società Italiana di Storia Militare*, Acies Edizioni (Milan, 2016).

VV. AA., *Economic warfare. Quaderno 2017 della Società Italiana di Storia Militare*, Acies Edizioni (Milan, 2017).

Wayne Thomas, D., *Small wars: New perspectives on wargaming counter insurgency on the tabletop*, Independent Publishing (2018).

Wells, H. G., *Piccole guerre [Little wars]*, Sellerio (Palermo, 1990).

Wells, H. G., *Gioco da pavimento [Floor games]*, Sellerio (Palermo, 2000).

Wojtowicz, N., *Wargaming experiences: Soldiers, scientists and civilians*, Independent Publishing (2022).

Woods, S., *Eurogames: The design, culture and play of modern European board games*, McFarland Publishing (Jefferson, 2012).

ARTICLES

Angiolino, A., Chi ha paura del dado cattivo? in *ioGioco*, n. 30 (2023).

Buchanan, H., Why do we play what we play, in *C3i*, n. 34 (2020).

Buchanan, H., That's not a wargame! and Ruhnke, V., What is a wargame? in *C3i*, n. 35 (2021).

Buchanan, H., Rules as written, in *C3i*, n. 36 (2022).

Buckley, J., Wargames: Simulation or stimulation? in *C3i*, n. 36 (2022).

Chapman, A., Linderoth, J., Exploring the limits of play: A case study of representations of Nazism in games, in Mortensen, T. E., Linderoth, J., Brown, A. M. L. (curated by), *The dark side of game play: Controversial issues in playful environments*, Routledge (New York, 2015).

Cleaver, T., Game theory: An introduction, in *Moves*, n. 10 (1973).

Collins, G., Madison's war: The game as history, in *C3i*, n. 30 (2016).

Essig, D., In brief: The simulation of what? in *Operations*, n. 2 (1991).

Essig, D., Out Brief: History, the wargame, and the wargamer, in *Operations*, n. 5 (1992).

Essig, D., Game resolution, in *Operations*, n. 9 (1993).

Greenwood, D., Hill, J., Hock, H., Game design: Art or science, in *The General*, n. 14 (1978).

Haggart, B., What is a simulation? (I-III), in *Fire & Movement*, n. 139–141 (2005–2006).

Herman, M., To script or not to script, in *C3i*, n. 25 (2011).

Herman, M., Sam I am; who are you tells the story! in *C3i*, n. 28 (2014).

Herman, M., Pentecontetia: Strategy in Pericles during the first Peloponnesian war, in *C3i*, n. 32 (2018).

Herman, M., Take me to your leader or "where's the bot?", in *C3i*, n. 32 (2018).

Hill, J., Designing for playability, in *Moves*, n. 14 (1974).

Kosnett, P., What is a wargamer? in *Moves*, n. 19 (1975).

MacGowan, R., History of tactical games, in *Fire & Movement*, n. 53 (1987).

MacGowan, R., Interview: John Hill, all American, in *Fire & Movement*, n. 23 (1980).

MacGowan, R., Portrait: James F. Dunnigan, in *Fire & Movement*, n. 30 (1982).

Miller, B., Alexander's weaponry: Recent research and its relevance to wargaming, in *Moves*, n. 47 (1979).

Nakamura, J., Csikszentmihalyi, M., Flow theory and research, in Snyder, C. R., Lopez, S. J. (Eds.), *Handbook of positive psychology*, Oxford University Press (Oxford, 2009).

Nonaka, I., Toyama, R., Byosiere, P., A theory of organizational knowledge creation: Understanding the dynamic process of creating knowledge, in Dierkes, M., Berthoin, A., Child, J., Nonaka, I., *Handbook of organizational learning and knowledge*, Oxford University Press (Oxford, 2003).

Sayre, C. L. Jr., Simulation of morale, in *Moves*, n. 9 (1973).

Sheikh, S., C3i interview—Mark Herman, in *C3i*, n. 31 (2017).

Sheikh, S., C3i interview—Volko Ruhnke, in *C3i*, n. 32 (2018).

Simonds, M. J., Wargamer and historian, in *Moves*, n. 36 (1977).

Simonsen, R. A., The bias that nobody knows . . ., in *Moves*, n. 3 (1972).

Simonsen, R. A., Physical systems design in conflict simulations, in *Moves*, n. 7 (1973).

Simonsen, R. A., Conflict simulation: Art or science, in *Moves*, n. 32 (1977).

Simonsen, R. A., Naturalism vs realism in simulation games, in *Moves*, n. 31 (1977).

Smith, D. A., In the game: Real and unreal aspects of simulation gaming and play, in *Moves*, n. 49 (1980).

Southhard, J., By chance . . . or by design? The problems of solitaire, in *The Grenadier*, n. 31 (1987).

Starkweather, A., On to victory—victory condition considerations in bravery in the sand, in *Operations Special Issue*, n. 2 (2009).

Suckling, M., Board with meaning: Reflections on game design and historiography, in *CEA Critic*, vol. 79, no. 1, The Johns Hopkins University Press (Baltimore, 2017).

Teehan, M. F., Kursk in parallel: An analysis of 1943 Eastfront operations with the aid of conflict simulations, in *Moves*, n. 22 (1975).

Vasey, C., Chaos gaming, in *Battles Magazine*, n. 4 (2010).

VV. AA., Game design: A debate on the "Rommel syndrome", in *Moves*, n. 1 (1972).

White, J., Moonshine in Atlantic chase, in *C3i Magazine*, n. 35 (2021).

Zucker, K., The image of battle, in *Fire & Movement*, n. 9 (1978).
Zucker, K., Accuracy vs playability, in *Fire & Movement*, n. 136 (2005).

ONLINE RESOURCES

@jrg262, A subversive dice chucker and welcome addition to the ACW genre, in *Board-GameGeek*, https://boardgamegeek.com/thread/3166201/subversive-dice-chucker-and-welcome-addition-acw-g (2023).

Alonge, J., Playing the Nazis: Political implications in analog wargames, in *Analog Game Studies*, http://analoggamestudies.org/2019/09/playing-the-nazis-political-implications-in-analog-wargames/ (2019).

Angiolino, A., Il gioco in scatola più complesso del mondo, in *Gioconomicon*, http://www.gioconomicon.net/modules.php?name=News&file=article&sid=6108&title=il-gioco-in-scatola-pi-complesso-del-mondo (2012).

Antomarini, B., Il gioco nella filosofia, in *Gamification Lab Magazine*, http://www.gamificationlab.net.

Ardwulf's Lair, *The chit show, designing across many eras with Joseph Miranda*, https://www.youtube.com/live/qgZmxcvt3aE?si=Z49tIDwJPu2LWGWo (2023).

Ardwulf's Lair, *The wargames that changed wargames: Transformative wargames*, https://www.youtube.com/live/IywQWKSfRTI?si=yjKIDF4wKp2MUVzw (2023).

Bae, S. (Ed.), *Forging wargamers*, https://www.usmcu.edu/Portals/218/Forging%20Wargamers_web_1.pdf (2022).

Banks, D. E., The methodological machinery of wargaming: A path toward discovering war-gaming's epistemological foundations, in *International Studies Review* 26, no. 1, https://academic.oup.com/isr/article/26/1/viae002/7595765 (2024).

Barzashka, I., Wargaming: How to turn vogue into science, in *Bulletin of the Atomic Scientists*, https://thebulletin.org/2019/03/wargaming-how-to-turn-vogue-into-science/ (2019).

Bender, T., Comparing labyrinth II with twilight struggle, in *Inside GMT*, http://www.insidegmt.com/2015/03/comparing-labyrinth-ii-with-twilight-struggle/ (2015).

Bender, T., Labyrinth: The forever war—challenges in designing a simulation game based on current events, in *Inside GMT*, http://www.insidegmt.com/2019/06/labyrinth-the-forever-war-challenges-in-designing-a-simulation-game-based-on-current-events/ (2019).

Beyerchen, A. D., *Clausewitz, nonlinearity and the unpredictability of war*, https://clausewitzstudies.org/item/Beyerchen-ClausewitzNonlinearityAndTheUnpredictabilityOfWar.htm.

Bierbach, M., Kaminski, K., Germany's confusing rules on swastikas and Nazi symbols, in *DW*, https://www.dw.com/en/germanys-confusing-rules-on-swastikas-and-nazi-symbols/a-45063547 (2018).

Brynen, R., *Gaming the non-kinetic*, https://youtu.be/Lv4cWw7kMM8?si=KKsuKMxleBmwCYeY (2020).

Bucholtz, A., *History is political: Games are propaganda*, https://sdhist.com/history-is-pooitical-games-are-propaganda/ (2023).

Burden, D. J. H., The battles of Hue: Understanding urban conflicts through wargaming, in *Journal of Strategic Security* 16, no. 3, https://digitalcommons.usf.edu/jss/vol16/iss3/9/ (2023).

Caffrey, M., *Toward a history based doctrine for wargaming*, https://www.airuniversity.af.edu/Portals/10/ASPJ/journals/Chronicles/caffrey.pdf (2000).

Caffrey, M., *On wargaming*, U.S Naval College, https://digital-commons.usnwc.edu/newport-papers/43/ (Newport, 2019).

Carr, J., The Arjuna chronicles, in *Inside GMT*, http://www.insidegmt.com/2019/04/the-arjuna-chronicles-1-an-intro-to-gandhis-arjuna-system/ (2019).

Comben, P., June 17th ... and all that jazz, in *Wargame Design* III, no. 10, https://www. napoleongames.com/wargame-design (2017).

Costikyan, G., *SPI died for your sins*, http://www.costik.com/spisins.html (1996).

Costikyan, G., *I have no words & I must design: Toward a critical vocabulary for games*, Tampere University Press, http://www.costik.com/nowords2002.pdf (2002).

Costikyan, G., Davidson, D. (Ed.), *Tabletop—analog game design*, http://repository.cmu.edu/cgi/viewcontent.cgi?article=1051&context=etcpress, ETC Press (2011).

Davidson, L., *What is a wargame? A case study*, https://www.beyondsolitaire.net/blog/what-is-a-wargame-a-case-study (2023).

Dean, J., A few acres of snow and the critical silence on the biggest flawed game of 2011, in *Boardgamegeek*, https://boardgamegeek.com/blogpost/9073/few-acres-snow-and-critical-silence-biggest-flawed (2012).

Delwood, R., *Writing war gaming rules correctly*, Medium, https://robertdelwood.medium.com/writing-war-gaming-rules-correctly-43e0428fd966 (2019).

Draper, K., Should boardgamers play the roles of racists, slavers and Nazis? in *New York Times*, https://www.nytimes.com/2019/08/01/style/board-games-cancel-culture.html (2019).

Dunnigan, J., *Simulation Games Design*, https://dl.acm.org/doi/10.5555/2031882.2031885 (2011).

Ellis-Gorman, S., But why Pickett's charge? Or, how I liked the game but not the slaver, in *BoardGameGeek*, https://boardgamegeek.com/thread/3154585/why-picketts-charge-or-how-i-liked-game-not-slaver (2023).

Engelstein, G., *Who are you?* https://katiesgamecorner.com/2018/01/25/who-are-you-by-geoff-engelstein/ (2018).

Esdaile, C. J., Napoleon at Waterloo: The events of June 1815 analyzed via historical simulation, in *Journal of Advanced Military Studies* 2, no. 2, https://muse.jhu.edu/article/805917 (2021).

Foasberg, N., The problematic pleasures of productivity and efficiency in Goa and Navegador, in *Analog Game Studies*, http://analoggamestudies.org/2016/01/the-problematic-pleasures-of-productivity-and-efficiency-in-goa-and-navegador/ (2016).

Germany lifts ban on swastika, Hitler mustache in Wolfenstein video game, in *DW*, https://www.dw.com/en/germany-lifts-ban-on-swastika-hitler-mustache-in-wolfenstein-video-game/a-45024101 (2018).

Goeree, J. K., Holt, C. A., *Ten little treasures of game theory and ten intuitive contradictions*, University of Virginia, https://www.stat.berkeley.edu/~aldous/157/Papers/goeree.pdf (2001).

Herman, M., Wargame CRTs or how to resolve Chaos, in *C3i Magazine*, n. 36 (2022).

Holland, A., *Do board games need victory conditions?* https://youtu.be/QxZcDZ1MUjk (2023).

Holland, A., Russell, T., *Time distortion in wargames*, Hollandspiele, https://hollandspiele.com/blogs/hollandazed-thoughts-ideas-and-miscellany/time-distortion-in-wargames-by-tom-russell (2017).

Holland, A., Russell, T., *Distance in this guilty land*, Hollandspiele, https://hollandspiele.com/blogs/hollandazed-thoughts-ideas-and-miscellany/distance-in-this-guilty-land (2018).

Kirschenbaum, M., Granular worlds: Situating the sand table in media history, in *The University of Chicago Press Journals* 20, no. 1, https://www.journals.uchicago.edu/doi/abs/10.1086/726299 (2023).

Kleinhenz, G., Interview with John Poniske designer of bleeding Kansas from decision games, in *The Players' Aid*, https://theplayersaid.com/2019/07/08/interview-with-john-poniske-designer-of-bleeding-kansas-from-decision-games/ (2019).

Masini, R., *Gli scacchi e l'arte della guerra: mito e realtà*, https://www.goblins.net/articoli/scacchi-e-arte-della-guerra-mito-e-realta (2020).

Masini, R., From chessboard to mapboard, in *Conflicts of Interest Magazine*, n. 1, https://sdhist.com/conflicts-of-interest-zine/ (2023).

Masini, R., *Napoleon at Waterloo: Sabin's house rules–part two*, https://youtu.be/Clzqe7_F9Hw?si=LLG9h0qX8oRBDsnk (2024).

Matthews, J., *Politics in wargaming and wargaming politics*, https://youtu.be/ub2Nj6iKBbM?si=RitL2osZ5ToXC-nq (2021).

Molotov Cockatiel, *Hexes part 1: A brief history*, https://molotovcockatiel.com/hexes-part1-a-brief-history/ (2021).

Nash, J., Thrall, R. M., *Some war games*, Project RAND, https://www.rand.org/pubs/documents/D1379.html (1952).

NATO, *NATO wargaming handbook*, https://paxsims.files.wordpress.com/2023/09/nato-wargaming-handbook-202309.pdf (2023).

OCSE, *The BASIC toolkit—tools and ethics for applied behavioural insights*, https://www.oecd.org/gov/regulatory-policy/BASIC-Toolkit-web.pdf (2019).

Paletta, A., War games: On Roberto Bolaño's the third Reich, in *The Millions*, https://themillions.com/2012/02/war-games-on-roberto-bolanos-the-third-reich.html (2012).

Pasic, J., This war of mine—review by survivor of the siege of Sarajevo, in *Boardgamegeek*, https://www.boardgamegeek.com/thread/1816826/war-mine-review-survivor-siege-sarajevo (2017).

Perla, P., Wargaming and the cycle of research and learning, in *Scandinavian Journal of Military Studies*, https://www.researchgate.net/publication/363686757_Wargaming_and_The_Cycle_of_Research_and_Learning (2022).

Rael, P., On Freedom: The underground railroad, in *Boardgamegeek*, https://boardgamegeek.com/blogpost/64567/freedom-underground-railroad (2017).

Rael, P., Playing slavery in the new edition of struggle of empires, in *Boardgamegeek*, https://boardgamegeek.com/blogpost/93147/playing-slavery-new-edition-struggle-empires (2019).

Rangazas, S., *Guerrilla generation: COIN beyond COIN*, https://www.youtube.com/watch?v=keUR15gYwSM&t (2023).

Ruhnke, V., Stock & flow in wargames, in *C3i Magazine*, n. 33 (2019).

Ruhnke, V., *Cards in wargames*, https://www.youtu.be/WIBpCJ09KhA (2021).

Ruiz, J., CDG solo method, in *Boardgamegeek*, https://www.boardgamegeek.com/filepage/128764/cdg-solo-method-display-and-materials (2018).

Sabin, P., *Simple rules tweaks for greater realism*, https://boardgamegeek.com/filepage/199517/simple-rules-tweaks-greater-realism (2020).

Sabin, P., *Much improved 2nd edition of my popular tweaks, with game video*, https://boardgamegeek.com/thread/3201688/much-improved-2nd-edition-my-popular-tweaks-game-v (2024).

Saenz, M. J., Cano, J. L., *Experiential learning through simulation games: An empirical study*, https://www.researchgate.net/publication/257614743_Experiential_learning_through_simulation_games_An_empirical_study (2009).

Saunders, M., *A few acres of snow—interview with Martin Wallace*, Yellow Parable, https://yellowparable.com/a-few-acres-of-snow-interview-with-martin-wallace/ (2017).

Schneider, J., What war games really reveal, in *Foreign Affairs*, https://www.foreignaffairs.com/united-states/what-war-games-really-reveal (2023).

Suckling, M., *The postcolonial turn in commercial historical board wargames*, https://youtu.be/RxETwdPNYCo?si=ylgHqYsTjY_iqWXp (2023).

Szepessy, J., A historical review by a person who witnessed some of the events that 1989: Dawn of freedom portrays, in *Boardgamegeek*, https://boardgamegeek.com/thread/809681/historical-review-person-who-witnessed-some-events (2012).

Thomas, J., Ancient and medieval armies, in *Moves*, issue not identified, http://www.spigames.net/MovesScans/Prestags_Article.pdf.

Train, B., Spielenexperiment: Turning 4 into 2, in *Brtrain Ludic Futurism*, https://brtrain. wordpress.com/2016/05/13/spielenexperiment-turning-4-into-2/ (2016).

UK Ministry of Defence, *Wargaming handbook*, https://assets.publishing.service.gov.uk/ media/5a82e90d40f0b6230269d575/doctrine_uk_wargaming_handbook.pdf (2017).

Upton, K., *An interview with Andrea Angiolino*, https://www.wingsofwar.org/forums/showthread. php?284-An-Interview-with-Andrea-Angiolino (2009).

VV. AA., *Developments in business simulation and experiential learning: Proceedings of the annual ABSEL conference—simulation games and experiential learning in action*, vol. 2, https://journals.tdl.org/absel/index.php/absel/issue/view/2 (1975).

VV. AA., *Pergioco magazine*, https://www.ludostoria.it/rivista-pergioco/ (Milan, 1980–1984).

Wake, P., Token gestures: Towards a theory of immersion in analog games, in *Analog Game Studies*, http://analoggamestudies.org/2019/09/token-gestures-towards-a-theory-of-immersion-in-analog-games/ (2019).

Weuve, C. A. et al., *Wargame pathologies*, CNA Corporation, https://www.cna.org/CNA_files/ PDF/D0010866.A1.pdf (2004).

Zucker, K., The fourth phase, in *Wargame Design* III, no. 10, https://www.napoleongames. com/wargame-design (2017).

VIDEO SOURCES

Bucholz, A., *Clio's Boardgames on historical game content*, https://www.youtube.com/live/ TCJvj63QE7o?si=IPhb4xpw3wTZ125E (2024).

Georgetown University Wargaming Society, https://www.youtube.com/@georgetownuniversity wargam6881.

King's Wargaming Network, Wong, Y., *Developing an academic discipline of wargaming*, https://youtu.be/nwa02IMRZ_k (2020).

LudoStoria, https://www.youtube.com/@ludostoria.

Masini, R., *Crossing the line: The hidden realm of non-linear simulation*, https://youtu.be/ IqWMMggTGMY (2022).

Masini, R., *Wargaming 2.0: Playing with history in the digital age*, https://youtu.be/ HmXrt0TirEM?si=e0v-ad5Gj8pMhc6T (2024).

Masini, R., *WLOG*, https://www.youtube.com/@RiccardoMasiniWLOG.

Pancaldi, D., *No enemies here*, https://www.youtube.com/channel/UCx2aMyAIPSwp7yOp UdygKWA.

Seek Out and Play, *Wargaming: The reverse engineering of history*, https://youtu.be/ Sjy7YlWgXfM?si=i-zzNYknPiF4tANX (2023).

Serval, F., *Wargamology—what is a wargame—part 2 (game design, families of wargames)*, https://youtu.be/OnD24unVVCc (2020).

Serval, F., *The future of wargaming with Brian Train*, https://youtu.be/vyyxGy_xF7I?si= wXjClVl9InZDzs2q (2023).

Serval, F., *Wargames and politics: Interview to Jack Radey*, https://youtu.be/LuhhG8mHb2c?si= WgI0NNnIEufa6jsm (2023).

Serval, F., *Homo Ludens*, https://www.youtube.com/@HomoLudens1871.

Shut Up & Sit Down, *The psychology of why we play*, https://youtu.be/wFtw9D_OjMw (2019).

Shut Up & Sit Down, *Making asymmetric games*, https://youtu.be/duAsXAOqLhQ.

Suckling, M., *Storytelling and wargame design*, https://youtu.be/wHf0LDvik2U?si= 3229fGW5Rkt2oGNk (2020).

Todorov, S., *The tyranny of bynaries: How wargames build narratives*, https://youtu.be/ pZz6l6u275o?si=ngN2QccuNdUJXu_v (2023).

Train, B., *The future of wargaming*, https://www.youtube.com/watch?v=vyyxGy_xF7I (2023).

PODCAST

Buchanan, H., *Harold on games*, https://soundcloud.com/harold-buchanan.
Davidson, L., *Beyond solitaire*, https://www.beyondsolitaire.net/.
Masini, R., *Checkpoint Charlie*, https://checkpointcharlie.podbean.com/.
Schiavi, S., *Mappe di Guerra*, https://www.dsimula.com/podcast.
Serval, F., *Homo Ludens*, https://podcasts.apple.com/us/podcast/homo-ludens-podcast/.
VV. AA., *Armchair Dragoons*, www.armchairdragoons.com.

Index

Page numbers in *italics* indicate a figure on the corresponding page.

For Product Safety Concerns and Information please contact our EU
representative GPSR@taylorandfrancis.com
Taylor & Francis Verlag GmbH, Kaufingerstraße 24, 80331 München, Germany